OXFORD STUDIES IN PHILOSOPHY OF RELIGION

EDITORIAL BOARD

Oxford Studies in Philosophy of Religion

Volume 1

Edited by
JONATHAN L. KVANVIG

OXFORD
UNIVERSITY PRESS

OXFORD
UNIVERSITY PRESS

Great Clarendon Street, Oxford OX2 6DP

Oxford University Press is a department of the University of Oxford.
It furthers the University's objective of excellence in research, scholarship,
and education by publishing worldwide in

Oxford New York

Auckland Cape Town Dar es Salaam Hong Kong Karachi
Kuala Lumpur Madrid Melbourne Mexico City Nairobi
New Delhi Shanghai Taipei Toronto

With offices in

Argentina Austria Brazil Chile Czech Republic France Greece
Guatemala Hungary Italy Japan Poland Portugal Singapore
South Korea Switzerland Thailand Turkey Ukraine Vietnam

Oxford is a registered trade mark of Oxford University Press
in the UK and in certain other countries

Published in the United States
by Oxford University Press Inc., New York

British Library Cataloguing in Publication Data
Data available

Library of Congress Cataloging in Publication Data
Data available

Typeset by Laserwords Private Limited, Chennai, India
Printed in Great Britain
on acid-free paper by
Biddles Ltd., King's Lynn, Norfolk

ISBN 978–0–19–954265–9
978–0–19–954266–6 (Pbk.)

1 3 5 7 9 10 8 6 4 2

Contents

Editor's Introduction

It is with great pleasure that we present this inaugural volume of the Oxford Studies in Philosophy of Religion. The initiating of such a series is long overdue, given the explosion of work and interest in recent history. Instead of being a collection of topics that individual philosophers occasionally addressed, the philosophy of religion has come to be another staple subfield in the discipline alongside other standard subfields such as metaphysics, epistemology, ethics, philosophy of language, and philosophy of science. To be sure, competent work in philosophy of religion requires expertise in these other subfields, though that point can be made about any subfield in philosophy. Just as philosophy of science did not become an identifiable subfield of philosophy until well into the twentieth century, so with philosophy of religion, though the emergence of the former pre-dates the latter.

The time is thus ripe for a non-sectarian and non-partisan series which aims to provide a snapshot of the subdiscipline on an annual basis. The intention for the series is that it attract the best work from the premier philosophers of religion and also that it include the work of top philosophers outside the field when their own work and interests lead them into this field. It is therefore presented with the explicit aim of providing an inclusive approach to the field, and it is an honour to be able to do so in the context of the outstanding group of Oxford Studies Series, the leading group of publications to provide such recurring collections of this sort.

With this introduction, we present the first volume in the series, a volume with work from some of the most impressive philosophers of our time and on topics of central importance to the philosophy of religion.

JONATHAN L. KVANVIG

List of Contributors

Alicia Finch is Assistant Professor of Philosophy at Northern Illinois University.

John Martin Fischer is Distinguished Professor of Philosophy at the University of California, Riverside.

Bryan Frances is Associate Professor of Philosophy at Fordham University.

Alan Hájek is Professor of Philosophy at the Research School of the Social Sciences, Australian National University.

Robert Koons is Professor of Philosophy at the University of Texas, Austin.

Timothy O'Connor is Professor of Philosophy and Chair of the Philosophy Department at Indiana University.

Alexander R. Pruss is Professor of Philosophy at Baylor University.

Michael Rea is Associate Professor of Philosophy at the University of Notre Dame.

Thomas D. Senor is Professor of Philosophy and Chair of the Philosophy Department at the University of Arkansas.

Eleonore Stump is the Robert J. Henle Professor of Philosophy at Saint Louis University.

Peter van Inwagen is the John Cardinal O'Hara Professor of Philosophy at the University of Notre Dame.

Linda Zagzebski is the Kingfisher College Chair of the Philosophy of Religion and Ethics at the University of Oklahoma.

1

Presentism and Ockham's Way Out

Alicia Finch and Michael Rea

Presentism is, roughly, the thesis that only present objects exist; *eternalism* is, roughly, the thesis that past, present, and future objects exist. *Ockham's way out* purports to be a way out of fatalist arguments for the impossibility of free action. Fatalist arguments come in two varieties: logical and theological. Arguments for logical fatalism run something like this:[1]

Let t_{-1B} = a time that obtained exactly 1 billion years ago.
Let p_S abbreviate: one billion years after t_{-1B}, S will perform A.
Let q_S abbreviate: p_S was true at t_{-1B}.
Let r_S abbreviate: S performs A now.
Let t_S abbreviate: it is now exactly one billion years after t_{-1B}.

1. (q_S & t_S) is true, and S does not have, and never had, any choice about (q_S & t_S).

2. $\Box$ [(q_S & t_S) $\supset$ r_S].

3. Therefore, r_S is true and S does not have, and never had, any choice about r_S.

We are grateful to Michael Bergmann, Alvin Plantinga and Dean Zimmerman for helpful comments on earlier versions of this paper, and we are especially grateful to Michael Bergmann for many helpful conversations and extended correspondence about the issues discussed herein. Alicia Finch's work on this paper was supported by the Notre Dame Center for Philosophy of Religion; Michael Rea's work on this paper was supported by an NEH Summer Stipend.

[1] Those familiar with the literature on fatalism will note that fatalist arguments more commonly open with a premise like this:

(1*) It is true at t_{-1B} that S performs A at t and S does not have, and never had, any choice about the proposition that it is true at t_{-1B} that S performs A at t.

And, of course, subsequent premises would then have to be modified accordingly. For present purposes, however, we have chosen to work with a 'presentist-friendly' version of the standard fatalist argument—that is, a version that takes tense seriously and that doesn't implicitly presuppose (as 1* does—for example, by employing the locution 'it is true at t_{-1B}') that non-present times exist.

Arguments for theological fatalism are similar, but they replace q_S with something like:

k_S: God knew at t_{-1B} that p_S was true.

They then go on to derive the same conclusion: that for any agent S and act A, S does not have, and never had, any choice about the proposition that S performs A. Of course, it is trivially true that if an agent does not have and never had a choice about the proposition that she performs a particular act, then the agent does not perform the act freely. So, the fatalist's conclusion is that no agent acts freely.

Ockham's way out of the problem of fatalism is of interest to *liber-tarians* with respect to the metaphysics of free will. A libertarian is one who accepts the theses that: (a) agents perform free acts in the actual world and (b) agents cannot perform free acts if determinism is true.[2] Non-libertarians who accept (a) accept *compatibilism*, where compatib-ilism is the thesis that (c) even if determinism is true, agents might perform free acts. Fatalist arguments present no special problem for com-patibilists. Whatever considerations can be marshalled in support of the position that:

(C) An agent S might act freely even if the combination of the state of the world in the distant past and the laws of nature is inconsistent with S's acting other than she does.

can also be marshalled in support of the position that:

(C*) An agent S might act freely even if the past truth of future contingents[3] is inconsistent with S's acting other than she does.

as well as the position that:

(C**) An agent S might act freely even if divine foreknowledge[4] of S's act is inconsistent with S's acting other than she does.

So, the proponent of free will who needs a way out of fatalism is the libertarian.

---

[2] Determinism is the thesis that the proposition P0 that expresses the complete state of the world at some time in the distant past (at, say, t_{-1B}) and the proposition L that expresses the entirety of the laws of nature entails every true proposition whatever—including, of course, every proposition about which acts agents perform at various times.

[3] The relevant 'future contingent' in our argument is p_S. The argument from logical fatalism is sometimes referred to as the argument from future contingents.

[4] k_S is a proposition about divine foreknowledge: God knows that S will perform A 1 billion years before she does so. The argument from theological fatalism is sometimes called the argument from, or problem of, divine foreknowledge.

What way out does Ockham offer? Ockham offers us a distinction between *hard facts* and *soft facts* about the past. While the distinction is somewhat difficult to characterize, the rough idea is that a hard fact about the past is *entirely* about the past whereas a soft fact is not: a hard fact about, say, t_{-1B} is a fact whose obtaining is entirely independent of whatever might happen after t_{-1B}, whereas a soft fact about t_{-1B} somehow depends on, involves, or includes events that take place at later times.[5] This distinction is supposed to help the libertarian respond to the fatalist by allowing her to insist that past facts about future contingents, as well as past facts about divine foreknowledge, are soft, and therefore dependent in some way upon events that lie in their future. Once this dependence is granted, there is no longer any clear obstacle to saying that present agents can have a choice about such facts.

Some will find Ockhamism incredible. And why not? At first blush, the view seems to imply that agents have the power to change the past. Ockhamists say that their view implies no such power. But even if they are right about this, their insistence that facts about the past can depend in some way upon the present acts of purportedly free agents might, all by itself, seem problematic enough. Our goal in this paper is to show that whether this claim is problematic depends crucially on whether presentism or eternalism is true.

We will proceed as follows. In the next section, we will lay out the fatalist's argument more clearly, making sure to clarify which dialectical moves are available to the libertarian. We will then offer a more robust presentation of Ockhamism, responding to obvious objections and teasing out the implications of the view. At this point, we will discuss presentism and eternalism in more detail. We will then present our argument for the claim that the libertarian cannot take Ockham's way out of the fatalism argument unless she rejects presentism. Finally, we will consider and dispense with objections to our argument. In the end, it ought to be clear that the libertarian must make a choice between Ockham's way out and presentism.

I. FATALISM

There is a great deal of debate about whether the two types of fatalist argument are logically equivalent: some say that they are, while others

---

[5] For a good start into the literature on Ockhamism and the hard-fact/soft-fact distinction, see John Martin Fischer (ed.), *God, Freedom, and Foreknowledge* (Stanford: Stanford University Press, 1989).

insist that the theological argument is stronger. Given that we are arguing that the presentist libertarian cannot use Ockham's way out of fatalism, and given that no one seems to think that the logical fatalist argument is more difficult to quash than its theological analogue, we will hereafter focus our attention on the logical fatalist version of the argument. Moreover, we will hereafter drop the 'logical' qualifier and use the terms 'fatalism' and 'fatalist argument' to refer to the logical versions of each.

The fatalist argument as we have presented it relies on two premises and a somewhat controversial rule of inference. We will first consider the rule of inference, then the premises, in order to see which avenues of response are available for the libertarian confronted with the fatalist argument.

We can present the rule of inference more elegantly if we employ the following abbreviation:

N_S p abbreviates: p and S does not have, and never had, any choice about whether p is true.

With this, it becomes clear that the fatalist relies on the following inference principle (substituting (q_S & t_S) and r_S for p and q, respectively):

$$[N_S \text{ p} \ \& \ \Box \ (\text{p} \supset \text{q})] \text{ entails } N_S \text{ q}.$$

This sort of principle will be familiar to participants in the debate over the compatibility of causal determinism and free action. In his famed 'Modal Version of the Consequence Argument' for the incompatibility of determinism and free action, Peter van Inwagen stipulates that:

N p abbreviates: p and no one has, or ever had, any choice about whether p is true.

He then introduces 'Principle β', the rule of inference according to which:

$$(\beta) \ [N \text{ p} \ \& \ N \ (\text{p} \supset \text{q})] \text{ entails } N \text{ q}.$$

Though van Inwagen's original β is demonstrably invalid, many 'β-style' inference principles are on offer and, at the very least, the following principle has remained immune to counter-example:

$$(\beta_\Box) \ [N \text{ p} \ \& \ \Box(\text{p} \supset \text{q})] \text{ entails } N \text{ q}.$$

Principle $\beta_\Box$ is relevantly similar to the inference principle we employed in presenting the fatalist's argument. Granted, our presentation of the fatalist's argument relies on a version of β that relativizes the N-operator to a particular agent S. However, the fatalist's rule of inference is clearly of the 'β-style'. We will christen it '$\beta_{S,\Box}$':

$$(\beta_{S,\square})\ [N_S\ p\ \&\ \square\ (p \supset q)]\ \text{entails}\ N_S\ q$$

Given that $\beta_\square$ is valid only if $\beta_{S,\square}$ is, libertarians-qua-incompatiblists who are inclined to accept $\beta_\square$ ought to be inclined to accept $\beta_{S,\square}$ as well. But it is a vexed question whether the libertarian-qua-incompatiblist must endorse the modal version of the Consequence Argument, let alone $\beta_\square$. For this reason, it is fortunate that the issue is irrelevant in the present context. Our purpose in this paper is to consider Ockham's way out of fatalism and Ockham's way out does not depend on a denial of the validity of β-style inference principles. It is worth noting, though, that $\beta_{S,\square}$ certainly *seems* to be valid and that, given its association with arguments for the incompatibilist component of libertarianism, it would seem to be in the libertarian's best interest to find a way out of fatalism that does not require a rejection of that principle.

Since Ockham's way out does not involve a rejection of Principle $\beta_{S,\square}$'s validity, it obviously involves a rejection of one of the fatalist's premises. Moreover, the Ockhamist qua Ockhamist has no objection to either the first conjunct of the fatalist's first premise:

1a. $(q_S\ \&\ t_S)$ is true (i.e., the conjunction of the proposition that it was true at t_{-1B} that one billion years after t_{-1B}, S will perform A and the proposition that it is exactly one billion years after t_{-1B} is true).

or to the second premise of the fatalist's argument:

2. $\square\ [(q_S\ \&\ t_S) \supset r_S]$

While some libertarians reject both 1a and 2 on the grounds that the locution 'true at t_{-1B}' is nonsensical, and other libertarians reject 1a on the grounds that q_S is false given that bivalence fails for future-tensed propositions, neither strategy is part of Ockham's way out. Ockham's way out of fatalism is to assert the falsity of the second conjunct of the fatalist's first premise:

1b. S does not have, and never had, any choice about $(q_S\ \&\ t_S)$.

Moreover, the Ockhamist thinks that S has, or had, a choice about the truth of the conjunction $(q_S\ \&\ t_S)$ in virtue of the fact that S has, or had, a choice about the truth of q_S: it is no part of the Ockhamist's position to assert that an agent has, had, or might have a choice about the passage of time.

In the next section, we will explain the Ockhamist's strategy in some detail, dispensing with the obvious objections along the way. But first we must offer a few words about the locution 'S has a choice about whether p is true' or, what is the same thing, 'S has a choice about whether it is true that p'. We take it as trivially true that S has a choice about whether it is true that p if and only if:

a. S is able to render p false.
b. S can render p false.
c. S has the power to render p false.

and:

d. S has power over the truth value of p.

This assumption is standard both in the free-will literature generally and in the literature on fatalism in particular. Given this, and given that it will be far easier to explain the Ockhamist's position if we talk in terms of the ability to render a proposition false rather than in terms of having a choice about a proposition, we will employ the former terminology from here on out. Thus, for example, instead of focusing on the Ockhamist's denial of:

1b. S does not have, and never had, any choice about (q_S & t_S).

we will instead focus our attention on the Ockhamist's denial of the equivalent proposition that:

1b*. S does not have, and never had, the power to render (q_S & t_S) false.

II. OCKHAM'S WAY OUT

As we have just seen, Ockham's way out of the fatalist argument is to reconcile the affirmation of:

1a. (q_S & t_S) is true.

with a denial of:

1b*. S does not have, and never had, the power to render (q_S & t_S) false.

Given that the Ockhamist does not attribute to S any power over the passage of time, it might seem that 1a and the denial of 1b* are reconcilable only if agents have the power to change the past; however, the Ockhamist emphatically denies that this is so. Indeed, the very heart of Ockhamism is the insistence that there is an analysis of 'power to render a proposition false' such that an agent might have this power over q_S without having the ability to change the past.

    When Ockhamists give an account of the power to render a contingent proposition false, they include a condition similar to this:

(P) S has the power to render p false only if there is an action X such that (i) S has the power to perform X and (ii) necessarily, if S performs X, then p is false.[6]

We can see how this partial account of 'S has the power to render P false' aids the Ockhamist's response to the fatalist if we recall our terminological stipulations:

p_S = the proposition that, one billion years after t_{-1B}, S will perform A.
q_S = the proposition that p_S was true at t_{-1B}.

Given this, it obviously follows that the affirmation of the following proposition entails the denial of the fatalist's (1b*):

(O) S has the power to render q_S false.

Moreover, if the Ockhamist cashes out (O) by applying the condition on 'power to render p false' given in (P), the Ockhamist denial of (1b*) implies:

(O*) There is an action X such that (i) S has the power to perform X and (ii) necessarily, if S performs X, then q_S is false.

Obviously enough, the relevant act X will be some act distinct from A—perhaps the very act of refraining from A—such that S's performance of X entails that S refrains from performing A one billion years after t_{-1B}. So, according to the Ockhamist, because S performs A now, it is and always has been the case that, at t_{-1B}, it was true that S will perform A exactly one billion years later. However, S has both the power to perform A and the power to refrain from performing A; and given the latter power, S therefore also has the power to render q_S false—*contra* 1b*. Thus, 1b* is false.

And now the distinction between hard and soft facts becomes relevant. Recall that hard facts about the past are, roughly, facts that obtain wholly independently of whatever events lie in their future; soft facts are facts that are not so independent. According to the Ockhamist, q_S expresses a soft fact about the past; for the truth of q_S depends partly on the way in which S exercises her power now, one billion years after t_{-1B}. But if the truth of q_S depends partly on what S does now, then there is no clear obstacle to saying that S has the power to render q_S false. To be sure, this is no argument for the conclusion that S *does* have this power; but offering such an argument is

---

[6] While there may be some Ockhamists who would prefer to tweak this condition a bit, a commitment to Ockhamism requires a commitment to an analysis of 'power to render P false' that includes a condition relevantly similar to it. We will thus proceed on the assumption that (P) is part of the Ockhamist's response to the fatalist: nothing of importance will hinge on the details of any particular analysis of 'power to render false'.

not the Ockhamist's goal. Ockhamism is entirely a defensive manoeuvre.[7] And, at this juncture in the dialectic, if the fatalist wants to carry on with her insistence that S lacks that power, she owes the Ockhamist further argument.

What more can the fatalist offer? The only way forward is to try to defend 1b*—or, more to the point, to defend the truth of the claim that the Ockhamist denies:

1b*$_{qs}$ S does not have, and never had the power to render q$_S$ false.

Towards doing so, the fatalist can begin by noting that all parties to the debate will admit that:

i. q$_S$ is a proposition that expresses a fact about the past—indeed, a fact about t$_{-1B}$, a time 1 billion years prior to the present time.

But (i) implies:

ii. q$_S$ was true before S came into existence.

Moreover, the Ockhamist herself will agree that:

iii. q$_S$ cannot change its truth value.

But, surely, the fatalist will say, nothing could be more obvious than that (ii) and (iii) imply:

1b*$_{qs}$ S does not have, and never had the power to render q$_S$ false.

This is the pith of the fatalist's support for 1b*$_{qs}$: S did not exist at t$_{-1B}$ and q$_S$ is (and has been, at least since t$_{-1B}$) unchangeably true.[8] But if an agent did not yet exist when a proposition was (already) unchangeably true, the agent cannot have (and can never have had) the power to render the proposition false. Thus, if q$_S$ was true a billion years before S ever existed, and if q$_S$ has been unchangeably true for as long as it has been true at all, then S does not have, and never has had, the power to render q$_S$ false. Hence, 1b*$_{qs}$ is true.

Given that the Ockhamist assents to (ii) and (iii), the dialectical standoff is this: the Ockhamist rejects the inference from (ii) and (iii) to (1b*$_{qs}$); the

[7] For this reason, there is nothing question-begging in the Ockhamist's strategy. She cannot be accused of assuming what she is trying to prove because she is not trying to prove anything. Rather, her strategy is simply to assume what the fatalist denies—that S has the power to perform some act other than A—and to expose the fact that the fatalist still has not offered any reason for thinking that S lacks precisely those powers that she must possess in order for that assumption to be true.

[8] Whether q$_S$ was true—and unchangeably so—prior to t$_{-1B}$ depends on how seriously one wants to take the tense of the verb in q$_S$. Out of respect for the presentist position, we are throughout taking tense as seriously as possible.

fatalist takes the opposite view. So, the issue, then, is which of the following two claims is more plausible:

I. (ii) and (iii) imply ($1b^*_{qs}$)

or

II. S has the power to perform an act other than A.

In the next section, we will argue that the Ockhamist can easily reject (I) in favour of (II) provided that she is an eternalist. We will further argue that if the Ockhamist commits to presentism, her position is untenable. Thus, we will conclude that if libertarians want to employ Ockham's way out as a way of responding to fatalist arguments, they must abandon presentism.

III. PRESENTISM, ETERNALISM, AND OCKHAM'S WAY OUT

As we have said, presentism is (roughly) the thesis that only present objects exist while eternalism is (again, roughly) the thesis that everything that ever did or ever will exist does exist. A more precise expression of presentism is: it has always been and always will be the case that there are no actual but non-present objects.[9] Eternalism can be more precisely characterized as the thesis that past, present, and future objects (and, by extension, events) exist; the phrase 'everything that exists' refers not only to things that occupy the present time, but also to objects that occupy past and future times. According to the eternalist, past, present, and future events bear relations of *earlier-than, simultaneous-with,* and *later-than* to one another, but each time has the same ontological status. So, on the presentist view, all of reality—all that exists *simpliciter*—is what exists now, whereas on the eternalist view, what exists *simpliciter* includes everything that exists at every time.

But what is a 'time'? The literature on presentism and eternalism includes at least two different ways of answering this question. On the one hand, times may be thought of as abstract states of affairs; on the other hand,

---

[9] The 'always' quantifier is added so that presentism does not turn out to be true at the beginning of time (if time had a beginning) and false thereafter. The actuality qualifier is added so that presentism does not imply the falsity of David Lewis's brand of possibilism, according to which there are objects that do not exist in the actual world and therefore do not exist in our present time by virtue of not existing in our space-time at all (David Lewis, *On the Plurality of Worlds,* Mass.: Blackwell, 1986). Given that we are assuming that every event involves an object, we take it that insofar as presentists and their rivals differ about the existence of past and future objects they also differ about the existence of past and future events. We also assume that every event with non-zero duration is composed of momentary events.

they may be thought of as concrete events. Abstract times are analogous to abstract possible worlds. Abstract times might fruitfully be thought of as *present-tense maximal* states of affairs. Intuitively, and very roughly, a present-tense maximal state of affairs is a total state of the world at an instant, *minus* all of the past- and future-tense truths. More rigorously: Say that a state of affairs S is *future directed* just in case either S's obtaining entails that some contingent thing will exist or S's obtaining entails that no contingent thing will exist; and then define a *past-directed* state of affairs in the obviously parallel way.[10] Then a state of affairs S is present-tense maximal if and only if, for every atomic state of affairs S* that is neither future-directed nor past-directed, either S includes S* or S precludes S*.[11] A concrete time might then be thought of as the event of some particular abstract state of affairs obtaining.

For convenience, we will assume that times are concrete events. On this assumption, the presentist denies that there are past or future times whereas the eternalist says that there are. And now let us begin to consider how the eternalist and the presentist each fare when confronted with the fatalist's argument.

Recall that the Ockhamist must explain why:

ii. q_S was true before S came into existence

and

iii. q_S cannot change its truth value

fail to imply

1b*$_{q_S}$ S does not have, and never had the power to render q_S false.

The eternalist Ockahmist blocks this inference by pointing out that it seems plausible only if one assumes the truth of the suppressed premise that:

ii*. q_S was true before S came into existence only if there was a time t* such that (a) q_S was true at t*, and (b) it was false at t* and at every time prior to t* that S exists.

The eternalist Ockhamist then points out that the truth of eternalism implies that, given that there is some time or other at which it is true that S exists, condition (b) in (ii*) cannot be satisfied.

---

[10] 'Contingent things' might be objects or events; and we assume that an event exists when and only when it occurs.

[11] We shall assume that states of affairs that include laws of nature will not be atomic. One state of affairs includes another just in case the obtaining of the first state of affairs entails the obtaining of the second. One state of affairs precludes another just in case the obtaining of the first entails that the second does not obtain.

Moreover, the eternalist Ockhamist can go on to point out that, just as it has always been true that S performs A one billion years later than t_{-1B}, so too it has always been true that S exists. To say that S did not exist at t_{-1B} is not to say that, at t_{-1B} it was false that S exists. Rather, it is just to say that none of the events of S's life are located at t_{-1B}. Thus, given that it was true at t_{-1B} that S exists, it is hard to see any obstacle to saying that the truth of q_S is ontologically dependent on S's actual performance of A at the present time. Indeed, from an eternalist point of view, q_S is quite plausibly viewed as just an alternative (if rather oblique) way of expressing the conjunction of r_S and t_S: i.e., S performs A now and it is now one billion years after than t_{-1B}. And since everyone will agree that it is plausible to say that the truth of this latter proposition depends on what S does (in particular, r_S clearly depends on S), rather than the other way around, so too everyone should agree that q_S depends on what S does.

Thus, the eternalist Ockhamist can tell the following story: since q_S depends for its truth value on what S actually does at the present time, it makes perfect sense to say that S performs A freely and that S has (or had) the power to render q_S false. S's performing A at t is, we might say, 'ontologically prior,' even if not temporally prior, to the truth (at t_{-1B}) of the proposition that S will perform A one billion years later than t_{-1B}. Thus, on this way of thinking about why the inference from (ii) and (iii) to ($1b^*_{qS}$) fails, the fatalist simply gets things the wrong way around: the fatalist assumes that since the truth (at t_{-1B}) of 'S will perform A one billion years later than t_{-1B}' is temporally prior to S's performance of A, its truth is ontologically prior as well; but this is precisely what the eternalist Ockhamist denies.[12]

Of course, it would be nice if the eternalist Ockhamist could give a thorough explication of the notions of 'ontological dependence' and 'ontological priority' that figure in her response to the fatalist. As it is, it is simply not clear whether such dependence or priority is best thought of in terms of explanation, or supervenience, or causation, or what. But it seems that, in the present case, the eternalist Ockhamist need not work this out completely. Indeed, it seems that she can point out that, ordinarily, we do not think that the truth of the proposition that S

---

[12] Of course, the eternalist Ockhamist need not deny that there are concrete events that are both temporally *and* ontologically prior to other events. For instance, the eternalist Ockhamist need not deny that there are causal events that are both temporally and ontologically prior to their effects. Indeed, the eternalist Ockhamist qua eternalist Ockhamist is not committed to any unusual claims about the relations between concrete events. What sets her apart is her conception of the relationship between the truth value of contingently true propositions and the concrete events on which their truth values depend.

performs A is ontologically prior to S's performance of A. Indeed, we are fully prepared, in the ordinary case, to think that the proposition that S performs A is ontologically dependent on S's performance of A and, moreover, that S's performance of A is ontologically prior to the truth of the proposition that S performs A. The eternalist Ockhamist's point is that, however we ordinarily understand the relationship between true propositions about agents' actions and the agents' actions themselves, this is how we should understand the relationship between true propositions like q_S and S's performance of A at t. The action comes first, in some ontologically significant sense of 'first', and the truth of the proposition succeeds it.

Note too that the eternalist Ockhamist can make her points about the ontological dependence of past truths like q_S on present acts of free agents in any number of ways. If she relies on the distinction between hard and soft facts, she can say that a fact F is soft (simpliciter) just in case (i) F is contingent and (ii) F is not included in any present-tense maximal state of affairs; and F is a hard fact about the past (from the point of view of a time t) just in case F is included in some present tense maximal state of affairs that obtains earlier than t. She can then add, as seems plausible, that soft facts about the past are ontologically posterior to and dependent on the hard facts about the past. Moreover, the eternalist Ockhamist might offer, as a heuristic device, the image of two 'levels' of reality: first, there's the level of hard facts, which includes the concrete events that bear relations of temporal simultaneity, priority and posteriority to one another; then there is the level of reality that includes soft facts, the temporal relations among concrete events.

Alternatively, the eternalist Ockahmist might think in terms of two distinct 'ontological moments': what's ontologically 'first' is the moment that includes all the concrete events and the relations of temporal simultaneity, priority, and posteriority that they bear to one another; what's ontologically 'second' is the moment at which all the contingent propositions about the course of concrete events are true. But we must not allow this notion of ontological moments to confuse us: on the eternalist scheme, every concrete event that ever takes place in the course of history exists *simpliciter* just as every true proposition that describes the concrete course of events has its truth value *simpliciter*. On this scheme, a principle of unrestricted bivalence holds at all times, and every true contingent proposition is ontologically dependent on the course concrete events that exists *simpliciter*.

At this point, we hope that it is obvious that the presentist Ockhamist cannot tell the same story as the eternalist about the failure of the inference from:

ii. q_S was true before S came into existence.

and

iii. q_S cannot change its truth value.

to

$1b^*{}_{qs}$ S does not have, and never had, the power to render q_S false.

The presentist, after all, insists that the only time that exists *simpliciter* is the present time. She believes that the only concrete events that exist *simpliciter* are the events that are currently taking place and the only concrete objects that exist *simpliciter* are those that exist now; she cannot abide an ontological distinction between what exists *simpliciter* and what exists at the present time. So, according to the presentist, S's performance of A exists only if S is performing A at the present time. Since the presentist denies that S's performing A exists when other times—times at which S is not performing A—are present, she obviously cannot say that the truth value of q_S depends on anything that S is doing or has done. For, again, q_S was true (and unchangeably so) nearly a billion years before S ever existed; so its truth value does not depend on S's existence. Moreover, it seems clear that if presentism is true, then temporal priority implies ontological priority. So, not only are earlier events ontologically prior to later events, but the truth of propositions true at earlier times is ontologically prior to later events.

The presentist, therefore, must affirm the suppressed premise that the eternalist denied:

ii*. q_S was true before S came into existence only if there was a time t^* such that (a) q_S was true at t^*, and (b) it was false at t^* and at every time prior to t^* that S exists.

But (ii), (ii*) and (iii) together seem to imply:

iv. The unchangeable truth of q_S is temporally prior to and therefore ontologically prior to S's existence.

Moreover, it obviously follows from (iv) that:

iv*. The unchangeable truth of q_S does not depend on S or any of S's actions.

And it is difficult to deny that:

v*. If the unchangeable truth value of q_S does not depend on S or anything that S does, S does not have the power to render q_S false.

But, of course, (iv*) and (v*) together imply $1b^*{}_{qs}$. Thus, in short, the truth of (iv) seems to lead ineluctably to the truth of $1b^*{}_{qs}$. Given that this is so, and given that Ockham's way out of fatalism depends crucially on S's having the power to render q_S false, the presentist Ockhamist must deny the truth of (iv).

But to deny the truth of (iv) is to affirm the truth of:

(M) Possibly: there is a time t, proposition p, and agent S such that at t, S has the power to render p false, and S does not exist at t.

Meinongians may not balk at M's clear implication that non-existent things can be quantified over and can have and even exercise powers; but the rest of us will. And if it turns out that presentists can ward off fatalist arguments only by becoming Meinongians, most of us will be inclined to say, 'So much the worse for presentism'. At any rate, so *we* say. Thus we conclude that presentists cannot, in the end, rely on the Ockhamist strategy as a way out of fatalism.

IV. AN OBJECTION

But is this really fair to the presentist? After all, presentists have developed various strategies for accommodating the truth of sentences that apparently make reference to merely past or merely future objects; and they have likewise developed strategies for making sense of apparent assertions of cross-time relations (such as causal relations). So a natural thought at this junction is that perhaps these same strategies might help presentists who are attracted to Ockhamism to avoid the sorts of objections that we have been lodging against the conjunction of those two positions.

Perhaps the most promising strategy for accommodating the sorts of sentences just mentioned is what might be called the 'essence strategy'. We will briefly consider what this strategy amounts to and how it might be adapted as a response to the fatalist. We will then argue that the essence strategy fails to provide the presentist Ockhamist with a satisfactory response to the fatalist's argument. Though we acknowledge that there are other strategies on offer for accommodating apparent reference to merely past and future objects and for making room for apparent assertions of cross-time relations, we omit consideration of these because they all strike us as being subject to the same sorts of objections that we will raise against the essence strategy.

The essence strategy is just an extension of a familiar strategy for handling apparently problematic modal claims like:

(L) Possibly, David Letterman does not exist.

On the standard semantics for modal claims, L implies:

(L*) There is a possible world in which it is true that David Letterman
does not exist.

The trouble, however, is that it looks as if the proposition that Letterman
does not exist *cannot* be true in any world because in worlds where
Letterman does not exist, he is not available to be a subject of predication.
In other words: the proposition that Letterman does not exist is true only
if it is about Letterman; but if it is about Letterman, then it cannot be true;
for only existing things can stand in relations (and 'aboutness' is a relation).
Thus, many philosophers are inclined to treat (L) as equivalent to not (L*)
but to:

(L**) There is a possible world in which nothing exemplifies an essence of
David Letterman.

An essence of David Letterman is a property that is essential to Letterman
and that cannot be exemplified by anything distinct from Letterman. The
attraction of understanding (L) as equivalent to (L**) should be obvious:
properties are abstract objects, so they exist necessarily; thus, they are
guaranteed to be available in every world to be subjects of predications.
Whereas it is deeply problematic to suppose that 'Letterman does not exist'
is about Letterman himself in worlds in which that proposition is true, it
is wholly unproblematic to suppose that it is instead a proposition about
Letterman's essence—equivalent to something like 'Letterman's essence is
not exemplified'.

So goes the essence strategy for modal claims. And, of course, the
presentist can adopt it to accommodate both sentences that seem to be
about merely past or future objects, as well as sentences that appear to imply
that there are objects that stand in diachronic relations to one another. The
trick is simple: treat the problematic sentences as equivalent to claims about
(necessarily existing) essences rather than as claims about concrete objects.
Thus, 'Abraham Lincoln was tall' will get treated as equivalent to something
like 'The property of being identical to Abraham Lincoln was exemplified
by a tall person.' Likewise, 'Many philosophers admire Aristotle,' will get
treated as equivalent to a claim about an essence of Aristotle, the causal
relations between the exemplifier of that essence, things that coexisted with
him, later things that coexisted with them, and, ultimately, various feelings
of admiration in contemporary philosophers. The details of this story do
not much matter in the context at hand. What matters for our purposes
is just the basic fact that, on the essence strategy, sentences that appear to
refer overtly or covertly to non-existent 'things' will get treated as expressing
propositions about necessarily existing properties rather than propositions
about concrete objects.

The question, however, is whether the essence strategy will be of any help to the presentist in rendering plausible the claim that:

(M) Possibly: there is a time t, proposition p, and agent S such that at t S has the power to render p false, and S does not exist at t.

Obviously the proponent of the essence strategy won't want to employ the strategy in so ham-fisted a way as to make (M) imply that S's *essence* has power over the truth value of p. For, after all, essences, being properties, can't have such powers. Rather, the most natural way of employing the strategy would be to begin by arguing that:

(R1) S has the power to render p false

is (in some contexts, anyway) equivalent to something like:

(R1$_E$) S's essence will be exemplified by something that has the power to render p false.

Likewise, then,

(E1) E does not exist

may be treated as equivalent to:

(E1$_E$) S's essence is not currently exemplified.

So, then, (M) becomes:

(M$_E$) Possibly: there is a time t, proposition p, and essence S$_E$ such that it is true at t that S$_E$ will be exemplified by something that has the power to render p false, and S$_E$ is not exemplified at t.

Unlike (M), (M$_E$) carries no commitment to the claim that non-existent 'things' can have or exercise powers, or stand in relations. Thus M$_E$ has the virtue of avoiding what was the primary objection to M.

The trouble, however, is that even if we grant that M$_E$ is on better footing than M, we still must acknowledge that the fatalist can offer against M$_E$ almost the exact same argument (with only minor alternations) that she offers against 1b*$_{qs}$. Thus:

v. q$_S$ was true at a time prior to S$_E$'s being exemplified.
vi. q$_S$ cannot change its truth value.

Therefore:

vii. S$_E$ cannot be exemplified by something that has the power to render q$_S$ false.

Eternalists could (if they wished) resist this argument in just the same way that they would resist the earlier argument from (ii) and (iii) to 1b*$_{qs}$. But the basic problem for the presentist remains: q_S is unchangeably true *before it is ever true that S exists*; thus, it is difficult to see how S could possibly have power over the truth value of q_S. Asserting M_E — presumably with an eye to saying that it was true one billion years ago that S's essence will be exemplified by someone who has the power to render q_S false — does not demonstrate how S could have power over the truth value of q_S. Rather, it simply asserts that it can. This is not argument; it is merely contradicting the fatalist's conclusion.

So, the essence strategy seems unpromising. Again, there are other strategies upon which a presentist might try to draw; but, as we said earlier, all of those strategies are subject to similar objections. This is because every extant strategy for accommodating sentences that appear either to refer to merely past or merely future things or to posit cross-time relations between objects will share one thing common with the essence strategy: they will imply that, for times at which S does not exist, a sentence like 'at t, S has the power to render p false' is to be understood as expressing a proposition that is either (a) false; (b) about a non-existent object; or (c) about something other than S. But — for exactly the reasons discussed in our treatment of the essence strategy — none of these alternatives will issue in a translation of M that will help us to see how S could have the power to render q_S false at those times prior to S's ever having existed.

And so we conclude that eternalists are able to adopt Ockham's way out of fatalism while presentists cannot. At this point, at least one of us wishes to leave open the possibility that the presentist can offer a successful response to the fatalist's argument. But we must conclude that the response that some consider the best response available — Ockham's way out — is unavailable to the presentist.

2

Molinism

John Martin Fischer

In the last few decades, much has been written about Luis De Molina's views about God's omniscience and also the relationship between God's omniscience and such ideas as God's providential powers and human freedom and moral responsibility. The literature is enormous, and the issues can be complex. In this paper I do not set myself the (daunting) task of fitting my views into an overall framework that captures the broad sweep of the discussions of the various components of Molinism. Rather, I shall focus on what I take to be the kernel set of ideas in Molina's theory of God's omniscience, and I intend to show that, although they can profitably be employed in seeking to understand God's providence over the world, they (contrary to what many philosophers apparently think) *cannot* be invoked to provide a solution to the problem posed by the relationship between God's omniscience and human freedom. In a nutshell, Molinism does not provide such an answer—it presupposes it.[1] I shall explain why this is so.

I. FREDDOSO'S MOLINISM

Alfred J. Freddoso's introductory essay to his impressive translation of Luis De Molina's *On Divine Foreknowledge (Part IV of the Concordia)* is an

I benefited from reading a previous version of this paper to the Department of Philosophy at St Louis University I am particularly grateful to comments on that occasion by Eleonore Stump, John Greco, and Scott Ragland. Additionally, I have been helped significantly by thoughtful comments on previous versions of this paper by Michael Rea, Thomas Crisp, Jonathan Kvanvig, Neal A. Tognazzini, and Robert Adams.

[1] I am not the first to note this point. For example, William Hasker says: 'The theory of middle knowledge, in all its historical forms, presupposes the compatibilism of divine foreknowledge and human freedom, so a successful argument for incompatibilism, if one can be mounted, would render superfluous a separate refutation of middle knowledge'

important presentation of (and commentary on) Molina's views, and it has been highly influential in the subsequent evaluation of those views (and their application to the traditional problem of the relationship between an omniscient God and human freedom).[2] It will be helpful initially to follow rather closely Freddoso's presentation of the argument that divine foreknowledge is incompatible with human freedom.[3]

The term 'accidental necessity' (which derives from William of Ockham) refers to a kind of contingent temporal necessity. Things (propositions, states of affairs, and so forth) said to be accidentally necessary at a time are at that time 'fixed' or out of one's control to affect; if a true proposition *p* is accidentally necessary at a time *t*, then it is out of one's power at *t* (and after) so to act that *p* would not have been true. Freddoso lays out four principles that pertain to accidental necessity, which he claims are presuppositions of the argument that divine foreknowledge rules out human freedom (in the sense that involves 'freedom to do otherwise'). The first principle is:

(A) *p* is accidentally necessary at *t* if and only if (i) *p* is metaphysically contingent and (ii) *p* is true at *t* and at every moment after *t* in every possible world that shares the same history with our world at *t*.[4]

Freddoso points out that (A) entails that accidental necessity is closed under entailment for metaphysically contingent propositions:

(B) If (i) *p* entails *q* and (ii) *q* is metaphysically contingent and (iii) *p* is accidentally necessary at *t*, then *q* is accidentally necessary at *t*.[5]

The third principle develops (at least to some extent) an important relationship (mentioned above) between accidental necessity and 'causal power'; Freddoso notes that this principle also appears to follow from (A):

(C) If *p* is accidentally necessary at *t*, then no agent has the power at or after *t* to contribute causally to *p*'s not being true.[6]

(Hasker 1989: 18). In a sense I do not go much beyond Hasker's point in this paper, although I hope to develop and explain it in an explicit way.

  [2] Freddoso, trans., Molina: 1988.
  [3] The argument is presented and discussed in Freddoso 1988: 53–62.
  [4] Freddoso 1988: 55.
  [5] Ibid. 1988: 55. Note that this implication presupposes that if *p* entails *q* and *p* is true at *t*, then *q* is true at *t*. Since Freddoso is working with a conception of propositions that allows them to vary in truth value from one moment to another, it would be appropriate for Freddoso to provide a defence of this presupposition.
  [6] Freddoso 1988: 55. Evidently, Freddoso is here assuming that 'causally contributing to *X*' entails that *X* occurs. One might however wonder whether this is so; perhaps one

The final principle purports to give a sufficient condition for a proposition's being accidentally necessary. Here P represents the past-tense propositional operator:

(D) If p is true at t, then the proposition Pp is accidentally necessary at every moment after t.[7]

According to Freddoso, (D) implies that 'once a proposition has been true at a given time, its having been true at that time is from then on necessary and hence, by (C), not subject to any future causal influence.'[8]

Now Freddoso is in a position to articulate a version of the powerful and perennially disturbing argument that God's omniscience is inconsistent with human freedom. Here's the argument, as regimented by Freddoso:

(1) The proposition *God foreknows, infallibly and with certainty, that Peter will sin at T* is now true. [assumption]

(2) So at every future moment the proposition *God foreknew, infallibly and with certainty, that Peter would sin at T* will be accidentally necessary. [(1) and (D)]

(3) But the proposition *God foreknew, infallibly and with certainty, that Peter would sin at T* entails the metaphysically contingent proposition *If T is present, Peter is sinning.* [assumption]

(4) So at every future moment the proposition *If T is present, Peter is sinning* will be accidentally necessary. [(2), (3) and (B)]

Therefore, no agent will have the power at any future moment to contribute causally to its being the case that the proposition *If T is present, Peter is sinning* is not true. That is, no agent (Peter, God) will have the power at any future moment to make it true that Peter is not sinning when T is present. [(4) and (C)][9]

Freddoso contends that Molina's response to the argument is to reject the inference from (2) and (3) to (4) by denying (B), the thesis that accidental necessity is closed under entailment.[10] Further, since (A) entails

---

can do things that causally contribute to, say, Bush's not being elected, and yet he is elected. (I am indebted to Jonathan Kvanvig for this point.)

[7] Freddoso 1988: 55.   [8] Ibid. 1988: 55.   [9] Ibid. 1988: 55.

[10] Freddoso 1988: 58. Freddoso here invokes the following quotation from Molina's *Disputation* 52, sec. 34: 'Even if (1) the conditional is necessary (because ... these two things cannot both obtain, namely, that God foreknows something to be future and that thing does not turn out that way), and even if (ii) the antecedent is necessary in the sense in question (because it is past-tense and because no shadow of alternation can befall God), nonetheless the consequent can be purely contingent.'

(B), Freddoso points out that insofar as Molina rejects (B), he must also reject (A). Freddoso explains Molina's reasoning as follows:

God's foreknowledge is not a cause of Peter's sinning. To the contrary, it is evident that Peter's sinful act satisfies the necessary condition for indeterministic freedom ... There is, after all, no reason to think that God's foreknowledge makes the sin occur by a necessity of nature or that it is in any way a contemporaneous cause of the sin. Yet it is also true that there is absolutely no power over the past. If God knew from eternity that Peter would deny Christ at T, then no agent can now cause it to be true that God never knew this. But if God's past foreknowledge is thus accidentally necessary and entails that Peter will sin at T, and if, in addition, Peter's action will satisfy the causal conditions necessary for it to be free, then accidental necessity must not be closed under entailment. Since this conclusion conflicts with (A), it must be the case that (A) does not correctly capture the necessity of the past.[11]

Freddoso goes on to summarize what he takes to be the Molinist's answer to the incompatibilist's argument:

So even though Peter cannot now cause it to be true that God never believed that he would sin at T, he nonetheless can now cause something, namely, his not sinning at T, such that had it been true from eternity that he would cause it if placed in the relevant circumstances, God would never have believed that he would sin at T. And, significantly, the theory of middle knowledge provides an intuitively accessible model on which both parts of this claim come out true.[12]

Freddoso thus points to the doctrine of 'middle knowledge' as a 'significant' component of Molina's response to the incompatibilist's argument insofar as it provides an intuitively accessible model on which the relevant claims come out true. It is important to note here that Freddoso's Molinism involves at least two separate components: the denial of (A) and the doctrine of middle knowledge. Below I shall consider the relationship between these two elements, but it will be useful first to explain the rudiments of the doctrine of middle knowledge.[13]

Of course, Molina's doctrine of middle knowledge is subtle and nuanced, and I am here greatly oversimplifying. I do not believe however that this will be problematic in the present context; for my purposes, all that is relevant are the bare logical bones of the position. Molina presupposes that for an act to be free, the agent must be free to do otherwise, and, further, that the act must not be causally determined by prior events. Additionally, Molina posits what might be called three 'moments' in God's knowledge: (i) His prevolitional (i.e., prior to God's willing to

[11] Freddoso 1988: 58.   [12] Ibid. 1988: 60.
[13] For more careful and comprehensive discussions, see, for example, Freddoso 1998; and Flint 1988.

actualize any particular possible world) 'natural knowledge' of metaphysically necessary states of affairs, including the capacities of all possible
free creatures, (ii) His prevolitional 'middle knowledge' of conditional
future contingents (including knowledge of what creatures would *freely*
do in all possible circumstances), and (iii) His 'free knowledge' of the
total causal contribution He himself wills to make to the created world
plus what God knows via natural and middle knowledge.[14] As Freddoso
puts it:

By (i) He knows which spatio-temporal arrangements of secondary causes are
possible and which contingent effects *might* emanate from any such arrangement.
By (ii) He knows which contingent effects *would in fact* emanate from any
possible spatio-temporal arrangement of secondary causes. By (iii) He knows which
secondary causes He wills to create and conserve and how He wills to cooperate
with them ... So given His Natural Knowledge, His Middle Knowledge, and His
Free Knowledge of His own causal contribution to the created world, He has free
knowledge of all absolute future contingents.[15]

Middle knowledge thus stands 'midway' between natural knowledge
and free knowledge. It consists (in part at least) of a set of (putatively
true) conditionals whose antecedents specify circumstances and whose
consequences specify how individuals would freely act: 'In $C1$, Agent A
would freely do X', 'In $C2$, Agent A would freely do Y', and so forth. As
I stated above, Freddoso contends that the doctrine of middle knowledge
provides a kind of model for Molinism. How exactly are we to interpret
this claim?

Freddoso points out that the Molinist will contend that (say) Peter
sins freely at T. This is (in part) because nothing causally determines or
compels him to sin at T. Thus, it appears that Peter could have refrained
from sinning at T. It follows that Peter could have done something at
T (refrained from sinning) which is such that, had Peter done it, God
would have always known that he would so act (refrain from sinning) at
T. Peter cannot at T initiate a causal chain that flows backwards in time;
thus, Peter cannot at T causally contribute to God's knowledge in the
past (in the sense of 'causally contribute' adopted by Freddoso). But Peter
can at T so act (refrain from sinning) that God would always have had
a different belief about Peter's behaviour at T from the one He actually
had. Freddoso presumably believes that this structure of claims is rendered
intuitively plausible by the theory of middle knowledge in that God would
(prevolitionally) know the relevant conditionals about what Peter would
freely do in various circumstances; He could then use this knowledge to

[14] Freddoso 1988: 23.   [15] Ibid. 1988: 24.

generate the knowledge that (in the relevant alternative possible world) Peter would freely refrain from sinning.[16]

II. CRITIQUE OF FREDDOSO'S MOLINISM

II.1a. The theory of middle knowledge

It is crucial to Molinism, as presented by Freddoso, that the following two claims can be true together: Peter can at T (or just prior to T) do other than he actually does, that is, Peter can at T (or just prior to T) refrain from sinning at T (the 'can-claim'), and 'If Peter were to refrain from sinning at T, the past (relative to T or just prior) would have been different from the way it actually was in that God would have had a different belief from the belief He actually had (the 'backtracking conditional' or 'backtracker'). But it is important to recognize that someone inclined toward incompatibilism will point out that the truth of the backtracker calls into question the truth of the can-claim. One can think of it this way: suppose it is a necessary condition of my doing something that the past be different from the way it actually was. Since the past is fixed and out of my control, it at least seems to follow from this that I can't do the thing in question. (Similarly, if it is a necessary condition of my doing something that some law of nature that actually obtains would not have obtained, then apparently I can't do the thing in question; it does not seem that the past is different from the natural laws as regards its fixity characteristics.) But if this is correct, then the truth of the backtracking conditional appears to be in *conflict* with the truth of the can-claim.

In previous work, I have argued that, although there is clearly a difference between the power to initiate a backwards-flowing causal chain (issuing in a different past) and the power so to act that the past would have been different from what it actually was (counterfactual power over the past), it is not at all clear that this difference *makes* a relevant difference (as regards fixity). Surely, anyone who believes that the past is fixed in the sense that one cannot initiate a backwards-flowing causal chain issuing in a different past will *also* contend that one cannot at some time perform an action which is such that, were he to perform it, the past would have been different from what it actually was. The point is that it is a pervasive feature of our

---

[16] When Freddoso claims that Molina's theory of middle knowledge would provide a model for a certain sort of compatibilism, I do not take it that he is contending that it is *necessary* for a defence of the relevant sort of compatibilism—and I do not find the necessity claim plausible in any case.

common-sense way of framing issues about agency that the past is fixed and out of our control; and if this intuitive idea of the fixity of the past applies to initiating backward-flowing causal chains, it would seem to apply equally to counterfactual power over the past (in which it is necessary, in order to perform some act, that the past have been different from what it actually was).[17]

I frankly do not see how Freddoso's Molinism provides the resources to reply to this incompatibilistic worry. As I mentioned above, there are two distinct elements of Freddoso's Molinism—the theory of middle knowledge and the denial of (A). It will be helpful here to evaluate the two components separately with an eye to figuring out whether we can identify a strategy of response to the incompatibilist (on behalf of Freddoso's Molinist). I shall begin with the theory of middle knowledge, and I note here that the argument with respect to middle knowledge will proceed in two steps; in this section of the paper I undertake the first step, and in the following section I take the second step.

Freddoso claims that it is 'significant' that Molinism provides an intuitively accessible model showing how certain crucial claims can be true. Given the textual passage cited above, I am not absolutely sure whether Freddoso has in mind the two claims I have isolated above—the can-claim and the backtracker. I believe however that these are the two claims to which Freddoso is referring. In any case, these are indeed the crucial claims logically speaking, from the perspective of evaluating Molinism as a response to the incompatibilist's argument.

I suppose that in some sense Freddoso's contention is correct, since Molinism—in particular, the theory of middle knowledge—provides a picture or story in which the two claims could be true, *if the sceptical worry can be answered*. But the theory of middle knowledge in itself provides no answer to the sceptic; that is, it does not even seek to explain how the can-claim is compatible with the backtracker. Rather, it takes the compatibility of these claims for granted. It is thus at best *ancillary* to an answer to the incompatibilist, and it piggybacks on such an answer. Thus, the theory of middle knowledge is not *in itself* an answer to the basic thrust of the incompatibilst's argument.

To explain. On the theory of middle knowledge, God has prevolitional knowledge of a large set of conditionals specifying how individuals would freely behave in various circumstances: 'If in circumstance $C1$, agent A would freely do X' 'If in circumstance $C2$, agent A would freely do Y', and so forth. These conditionals are supposed to be simply 'given' in the sense that they are true prior to any decree by God as to which possible world

---

[17] For this point, see: Fischer 1994: 78–83.

will be actualized. But note that it is an assumption shared by Molina and Freddoso that acting freely implies freedom to do otherwise. So, on the theory of middle knowledge, conditional truths of the form, 'If agent A were in circumstance $C1$, he would be free to do other than he actually does (X)', or 'If agent A were in circumstance $C2$, he would be free to do other than what he actually does (Y)' are simply assumed to be knowable by God prior to the relevant times (the times of the actions). Thus, it at least appears that the theory of middle knowledge simply presupposes that God's foreknowledge is compatible with human freedom to do otherwise! (I say a bit more to explain why exactly the theory of middle knowledge presupposes compatibilism in the following section; that is, I explain more explicitly why commitment to the relevant *conditionals* does indeed presuppose compatibilism.)

The theory of middle knowledge does not answer the incompatibilist's sceptical argument from the fixity of the past. The theory of middle knowledge does not even attempt to explain how the pertinent can-claims can be consistent with their paired backtracking counditionals. In assuming that God can know the conditionals in question, the theory of middle knowledge appears to be taking for granted the very question at issue in the debate between the compatibilist and the incompatibilist: it appears to be assuming that human agents can so act that the past would have been different from what it actually was.

I said above that, at best, the theory of middle knowledge is ancillary to (and piggybacks on) a genuine answer to the incompatibilist's challenge. The point is this. Given such an answer, the theory of middle knowledge provides a nice model for divine providence. My claim in this section has not been that the theory of middle knowledge is somehow incoherent or entirely useless; rather, I have contended that it doesn't help at all with the specific problem of reconciling God's foreknowledge with human freedom. However, given such a reconciliation, the theory of middle knowledge might be invoked to explain God's providence. Indeed, arguably it provides an attractive account of *how* God can know about future contingent truths without assuming causal determinism or a quasi-perceptual model (according to which God can have direct apprehension of future contingent events). But, of course, this presupposes that the basic thrust of the incompatibilist's argument can be rebutted.

The last caveat is important, and it is ignored at one's peril. When it is said that Molinism (the theory of middle knowledge) provides an account of 'how God can know future contingents', it might be thought that Molinism answers the 'how' question by providing some sort of answer to the incompatibilist. Indeed, in his otherwise superb recent book, *A Contemporary Introduction to Free Will*, Robert Kane presents Molinism (and, in particular, the theory of middle knowledge) as a response to the incompatibilist:

> The third solution to the foreknowledge problem originated with another later medieval thinker, the Spanish Jesuit philosopher and theologian Luis de Molina ... Like Ockham, Molina rejected the timeless solution to the foreknowledge problem of Boethius and Aquinas. But Molina sought a better answer than Ockham was able to give about *how* God can foreknow future free actions. To explain this, Molina introduced the notion of divine 'middle knowledge'.[18]

But, as we have seen, Molinism (the theory of middle knowledge) does not in itself provide any sort of explanation of how God's foreknowledge is compatible with human free actions—it does not address the incompatibilist's worry. Thus, contrary to Kane's presentation, Molinism does not stand on a par with the views of Boethius, Aquinas, and Ockham, which are indeed attempts to answer the incompatibilist's worries. At best, the theory of middle knowledge explains how God knows about future contingents, given that he can know about them at all (something it does not seek to address).

Kane emphasizes (as others have) that Molina sought an answer to the question of *how* God can foreknow future free actions. One might distinguish, very roughly, two interpretations of the 'how-question'. On the first, one is asking for a 'nuts-and-bolts' account of how God can know about the future; on the second, one is asking for a philosophical explanation of how God can know about future free actions, where this involves an answer to the incompatibilist's challenge. In focusing on the contention that Molina provides an answer to the question of 'how God can know about future free actions', one can conflate the two versions of the question. But it is evident that a nuts-and-bolts answer does not in itself provide a philosophical explanation, which is really what is needed, if Molinism is indeed to be considered on a par with the views of Boethius, Aquinas, and Ockham.

Perhaps I could say a bit more to bring out the distinction I have in mind between a 'nuts-and-bolts' answer and a 'philosophical explanation'. By a 'philosophical explanation' I mean an answer to the question that takes the incompatibilist's challenge seriously; it thus seeks to address a certain kind of sceptical worry. Consider the fact that one could have a perfectly good mechanical description of some physical process. As long as we bracket sceptical hypotheses, scientific testing and confirmation works pretty well, and we may have an adequate 'nuts-and-bolts' explanation of the process. But we should not confuse such confirmation with confirmation

---

[18] Kane 2005: 157.

that radical scepticism is false; we should not confuse such an explanation with a genuine philosophical explanation that takes the sceptical hypotheses seriously.

In general, it is important to distinguish knowledge that there exist 'how-to manuals' about a subject matter, and knowledge of the details of a particular how-to manual. By a 'philosophical explanation' I mean knowledge of the existence of how-to manuals about a given subject matter, and some general understanding of how such manuals can exist, despite challenges to their existence. By a 'nuts-and-bolts' answer to the 'how' question I mean knowledge of the specifics in a particular how-to manual. Clearly, having one of these sorts of knowledge does not entail having the other.

Consider the question of how time-travel is possible. A philosophical explanation would consist of knowledge that how-to manuals on time travel exist, despite the sceptical worries about the coherence of time-travel. A nuts-and-bolts answer to the question would say how to go about traveling in time—first one builds a timemachine, and so forth. Clearly, if time travel is indeed possible, one could have the latter sort of knowledge without the former: one can read the how-to manual without knowing the answers to the sceptical worries about time-travel.[19]

II.1b. A refined argument with respect to middle knowledge

In the previous section I contended that on Molina's theory of middle knowledge, God is said to know in advance a large set of conditionals of the form, 'If in circumstance $C1$, agent A would freely do X', 'If in circumstance $C2$, agent A would freely do Y', and so forth. Given Molina's assumption about the relationship between acting freely and freedom to do otherwise, I noted that truths of the form, 'In circumstance $C1$, agent A would be free to do other than he actually does (X)', 'In circumstance $C2$ agent A is free to do other than what he actually does (Y)', and so forth are simply assumed to be knowable by God prior to the relevant times (the times of the actions). I claimed that this seems to show that the Molinist is here simply assuming or presupposing what is under dispute—that God's foreknowledge is compatible with human freedom in the sense that requires freedom to do otherwise.

But the Molinist might reply as follows.[20] The template of Molinist views sketched above does *not* posit that God knows some simple, unconditional

---

[19] Here I am thankful for comments by Neal A. Tognazzini.
[20] I am indebted to Eleonore Stump for pointing out the need to address this Molinist point.

claim of the form, 'Agent *A* does *X* freely' or 'Agent *A* is free to do other than he actually does'. Rather, on this constellation of Molinist views, God is only said to know (prevolitionally) *conditionals*, such as, 'If in circumstance *C*1, agent *A* would freely do *X*,' and 'If in circumstance *C*1, agent *A* would be free to do other than he actually does (*X*)'. But certainly God can know these conditionals without knowing the unconditional truths posited in the consequents. (That is, prior to God's willing to create a particular set of antecedent circumstances, He can know the conditionals in question without knowing the unconditional truths posited in the consequents.) His merely knowing the *conditionals* does not straightforwardly involve presupposing that God can know in advance that human agents can be free to do otherwise; it is an important feature of Molina's theory of middle knowledge that it thus avoids begging the question against the incompatibilist.

I grant that this is a legitimate move on the part of the Molinist, and I grant that the argument presented in the previous section does not—apart from further considerations—decisively show the Molinist theory of middle knowledge to presuppose compatibilism; the considerations presented above are the first step in a two-step argument. The second step contends that there is no relevant difference (as regards the dialectical issues) between positing God's knowledge of the conditionals and God's knowledge of the unconditional truths specified by their consequents.

To elaborate. It should be absolutely obvious and uncontentious that in the dialectical context (in which the incompatibilist's argument is under consideration), it would be question-begging (or at least not dialectically helpful at all) simply to bring forward (without explanation) the claim that God does know in advance truths of the form, 'At some future time agent *A* will be free to do other than he actually does (*X*)'. This simply posits, without explanation, that in the actual world God knows in advance that some human agent will in fact be free to do otherwise. My contention is that it would be *similarly* question-begging (or at least not dialectically helpful at all) simply to bring forward (without explanation) the claim that God can know in advance truths of the form, 'If agent *A* were in (possible) circumstance *C*1, *A* would be free to do other than he actually does (*X*)'.

Note that God is assumed by the Molinist to know (via His natural knowledge) that (say) *C*1 is possible. So God knows that there is a possible world in which *C*1 obtains. Since (according to the Molinist) He also knows (via His middle knowledge) the conditional, 'If agent *A* were in (possible) circumstance *C*1, *A* would be free to do other than he actually does (*X*)', it follows that God knows that there is a possible world in which *A* is free to do other than he actually does. (Obviously, God's knowledge is closed under known implication.) Molinism here simply *posits* that it is possible that

God knows in advance that a human agent is free to do otherwise. But the incompatibilist's argument putatively establishes that God's foreknowledge is *incompatible* with human freedom to do otherwise—and thus that is it *impossible*—there is *no* possible world—in which God knows in advance that some human agent is free to do otherwise. And it would clearly be dialectically unfair and unproductive, within the context of a fair-minded evaluation of the incompatibilist's argument, simply to *presuppose without explanation or justification* that in some possible world (perhaps not the actual world) God does indeed know in advance that human agents are free to do otherwise.

Put slightly differently, my argument here is that if it is problematic for the Molinist simply to posit (without explanation or argument) that God *does* in fact know in advance that a human agent is free to do otherwise, it would be similarly problematic for the Molinist simply to posit (without explanation or argument) that God *can* know in advance that a human agent is free to do otherwise. If it is problematic simply to assert that the actual world contains both God and human freedom to do otherwise, it would be similarly problematic simply to assert that there exists some possible world (perhaps different from the actual world) that contains both God and human freedom to do otherwise. Within the relevant dialectical context, the latter claim is no more helpful than the former.[21]

[21] There is perhaps an unclarity in the notion of God's 'knowing in advance'. It might be useful to distinguish the following two claims: 1. In some possible world, God knows in advance that some human agent is free to do otherwise; 2. God knows in advance that, in some possible world, some human agent is free to do otherwise. My critique in the text appears to presuppose that the Molinist is committed to (1). But if the Molinist is only committed to (2), it is not clear that Molinism is open to the critique. (1) seems to assume that there is a single 'absolute' temporal framework into which both God and the various possible worlds fit; this temporal sequence exists prior to God's willing to actualize any particular world. A commitment to (2), on the other hand, seems to deny that there is such a temporal framework; on this view, it is as though God's decreeing that a particular world be actual brings into being the temporal framework—a framework that did not exist antecedently. Further, on this view there are presumably different temporal sequences associated with each possible world. On this picture, God atemporally decrees that a particular possible world come into being, along with its associated spatio-temporal framework.

I am not confident that the Molinist will wish to adopt (2) and the suggested metaphysical picture; here I simply wish to note that it may be open to a Molinist to pursue this approach. (I am indebted to Neal Tognazzini for helping me to see that the Molinist may have this option.) But I also wish to note that it is not clear that adopting (2) solves the problem, since it would seem to me that worries similar to the ones developed in my critique will arise at the point at which God wills to actualize a particular possible world, even on (2). At that point, on the Molinist assumptions, God must be assumed to have prior knowledge of human freedom to do otherwise—but this knowledge comes 'for free', as it were—the compatibility claim is simply presupposed, and no answer is given to the sceptic.

Of course, one cannot simply point out that the conclusion of the incompatibilist's argument entails something that does not fit with something invoked by a compatibilist and expect that the compatibilist will be silenced! And, in general, it is a somewhat delicate project to say what constitutes 'begging the question'.[22] Perhaps it is wiser and more careful to point out here that the basic ingredients that go into the incompatibilist's argument—including some crystallization of the intuitive idea of the fixity of the past—appear to entail a *general* incompatibility result, not a world-indexed result. Further, these ingredients should commend themselves to fair and reasonable people not antecedently committed to a position in the debate between the incompatibilist and compatibilist—they are not *only* attractive to an antecedent incompatibilist.

The Molinist reply points to the subtlety of his position. I believe however that this subtlety has perhaps blinded some of its proponents to its deeper dialectical difficulties. If it is problematic simply to presuppose that God actually foreknows that humans are free to do otherwise, it is similarly problematic to presuppose that it is possible that God foreknows that humans are free to do otherwise. If the Molinist strategy based on the theory of middle knowledge is not *straightforwardly* unproductive and question-begging here, it is nevertheless unproductive and question-begging.

I wish to end this part of the paper by being as explicit as I can be about the dialectical situation here, keeping in mind a broader perspective on the debates about God's foreknowledge and human freedom. Some have begun their analysis of the relationship between these two phenomena by noting that mere human foreknowledge does not in itself rule out human freedom to do otherwise. After all, the order of explanation when knowledge is under discussion goes from fact to mind, rather than the other way around; so it is natural to suppose that mere human foreknowledge does not threaten human freedom to do otherwise. It is then tempting to conclude that the situation is similar with respect to God' foreknowledge.

But the situation is manifestly *not* similar—or at least not indisputably similar! This is because doing otherwise in the context of God's foreknowledge (as opposed to the context of mere human foreknowledge) would arguably require so acting that some temporally genuine or non-relational feature of the past would not have been a feature of the past, whereas doing

[22] As far as I can tell, my point is not simply about the dialectical impropriety of this sort of presupposition in the context of a conversation or discussion with someone who holds the other viewpoint. Additionally, I do not see that the Molinist has sought to offer any *reason* to accept the presupposition—a reason that could be evaluated by someone trying to figure out whether the sceptical worries are decisive, quite apart from any discussion or conversation with anyone else.

otherwise in the context of human foreknowledge would not.[23] So it does not *follow* from some uncontroversial facts about knowledge (and foreknowledge) that God's foreknowledge is compatible with human freedom; and the incompatibilist is perfectly within his rights to point to the apparent asymmetry between human foreknowledge and God's foreknowledge.

Now a standard move here is to accept the distinction between temporally relational and non-relational features of the past (hard and soft features) but to take the Ockhamist position that God's prior beliefs are entirely relational or soft features of the past. On this view, the symmetry between human foreknowledge and God's foreknowledge is reinstated. Of course, Ockhamism is an important and distinctive view about the relationship between God's foreknowledge and human freedom, and I have discussed it at some length elsewhere.[24] A Molinist may well embrace Ockhamism at this point in the dialectic. But then it is crucial to see that *all* of the work of reconciling God's foreknowledge and human freedom is being done by Ockhamism, and *none* is being done by Molnism! Here Molinism would not be offering anything substantive and distinctive in the reconciliation project. Now this is not to say that Molinism is identical to Ockhamism in all respects.[25] Nor is it to say that Molinism does not offer distinctive and important contributions to our understanding of God's providential powers. But it *is* to say that (on this picture, according to which the Molinist adopts the Ockhamist move discussed above) Molinism does not offer a distinctive answer to the incompatibilist. And this is all that I've been arguing all along.

II.2. The denial of (A)

Most philosophers associate the theory of middle knowledge with 'Molinism'. But above I pointed out that there are two apparently separate components of Freddoso's Molinism—the denial of (A) and the theory of middle knowledge. Recall:

(A) p is accidentally necessary at t if and only if (i) p is metaphysically contingent and (ii) p is true at t and at every moment after t in every possible world that shares the same history with our world at t.

If one denies (A), one is willing to say that not all features of the past are fixed and out of our control in the present. As I noted above, the

---

[23] For more careful development and discussion of this point (and related points), see: Fischer (ed.) 1989; and Fischer 1992.

[24] For a systematic presentation of my critique of Ockhamism, see Fischer 1994: 111–30.

[25] For example, I do not think that Ockhamism is committed to the framework of Molinism in which there are true 'counterfactuals of freedom'.

Ockhamist also seems to deny that all features of the past are now fixed. But the Ockhamist denies only the fixity of temporally relational or 'soft' features of the past. Insofar as Molinism is supposed to be distinct here, the Molinist is taken to claim that even some temporally non-relational or 'hard' features of the past are such that we can now so act that they would not have been features of the past.

Of course, a compatibilist about causal determinism and human freedom to do otherwise may accept (and typically does accept) that humans can sometimes so act that hard facts about the past would not have been facts. I have dubbed such a compatibilist, a 'Multiple-pasts Compatibilist'.[26] What makes the Molinist denial of (A) distinct from the general doctrine of Multiple-pasts Compatibilism is that the Molinist holds that *all* causally relevant features of the past—all features of the causal history leading to the present moment—must be held fixed; according to the Molinist denial of (A), this leaves it open that non-causally relevant features of the past—features of the past that are not along the causal path to the present—need not be held fixed. So the Molinist in question here holds a restricted fixity of the past principle. He contends (as against the Ockhamist) that not all temporally nonrelational facts need to be held fixed; and he contends (as against the Multiple-pasts Compatibilist) that all features of the causal history leading to the present must be held fixed.[27]

Despite Freddoso's linkage of them, the relationship between the two components of Molinism—the denial of (A) and the theory of middle knowledge—is not immediately obvious. They appear to be separate ideas. For reasons adduced in the previous sections, it should be evident that

---

[26] See, for example, 'Introduction' in Fischer (ed.) 1986: esp. pp. 32–40; and Fischer 1994: 78–82.

[27] Freddoso puts the restricted version of (A) as follows: '(A*) p is accidentally necessary at t if and only if (i) p is metaphysically contingent and (ii) p is true at t and (iii) for any possible world w such that w shares the same causal history with our world at t, no agent has the power at or after t in w to contribute causally to p's not being true' (Freddoso 1988: 59). Here Freddoso appears to elide the distinction between causation and causal determinism; for simplicity's sake, I shall follow Freddoso in employing 'causal history' to refer to causal determination.

In the text I am assuming that the Molinist believes that causal determinism is incompatible with freedom in the relevant sense (requiring genuine access to alternative possibilities). Thus, I take it that the Molinist must hold that all causally relevant facts about the past are to be held fixed. If a theorist does not agree that all such facts are to be held fixed, then it is not at all evident how he could defend incompatibilism about causal determinism and freedom. (Of course, one could detach other features of Molinism from the view that causal determinism rules out freedom; this would be a worthwhile doctrine to explore, but it would not be 'Molinism'.)

the *mere* acceptance of the theory of middle knowledge does *not* in itself provide any justification for the denial of (A).[28]

Freddoso's point is that a Molinist *must* deny (A); but presumably the philosophically more interesting (and important) question is whether a denial of (A) *plausible*. As just noted, one cannot invoke the theory of middle knowledge to seek to justify a denial of (A). Let us consider (again) what Freddoso says in defence of the denial of (A):

God's foreknowledge is not a cause of Peter's sinning. To the contrary, it is evident that Peter's sinful act satisfies the necessary condition for indeterministic freedom ... There is, after all, no reason to think that God's foreknowledge makes the sin occur by a necessity of nature or that it is in any way a contemporaneous cause of the sin.

But I do not find it at all plausible that (A) is false; and I certainly do not find it plausible that it is false in the way required by the Molinist. I happily grant what Freddoso says here—that God's foreknowledge does not cause Peter's sinning. Indeed, I can grant that nothing causally determines it (and hence that nothing causally determines it in a problematic way). But this concession does nothing to vitiate the force of the commonsense point that the past is fixed. If the past is really fixed because it is 'over-and-done-with', then *all* of the past, insofar as it is over-and-done-with, is now fixed. If one feels the force of the idea that the past is fixed insofar as it is past, then it seems highly dubious to distinguish causally relevant from causally irrelevant features of the past (in regard to their fixity). It may well be that the fact that John F. Kennedy was assassinated in 1963 is causally irrelevant to my current state and behavior; but if the past is fixed because it is over-and-done-with, then surely the fact that John F. Kennedy was assassinated in 1963 is now fixed, quite apart from its causal relevance to me now. I cannot now perform any action which is such that were I to perform it, John F. Kennedy would not have been assassinated in 1963. So, whereas the denial of (A) would indeed allow the Molinist to respond to the incompatibilist, it is highly implausible, and such a denial certainly does not follow from the considerations invoked by Freddoso.

---

[28] Perhaps the link between the acceptance of the theory of middle knowledge and the rejection of (A) can be made more perspicuous as follows. The Molinist accepts the theory of middle knowledge together with the doctrine that God is necessarily foreknowing. Thus, the Molinist is committed to the existence of wolds where creatures act freely and God foreknows as much. But worlds where creatures act freely (taking freedom, as does the Molinist, as freedom to do otherwise) and God foreknows it are worlds in which (A) is false. And If (A) is false in some worlds, then presumably it is false in all. (I am indebted to Tom Crisp for this point.)

To help to see the extreme implausibility of the Molinist stance here, consider the position of the Multiple-pasts Compatibilist. This sort of compatibilist (like the Molinisit) is willing to say that even hard features of the past are not fixed—that agents can sometimes so act that temporally nonrelational features of the past would not have been features of the past. Such a compatibilist typically holds that one is free to do otherwise in a causally deterministic world, unless certain 'special' circumstances obtain. ('Mere' causal determination is not deemed to be a special circumstance.) Thus, this sort of compatibilist holds that the only relevance of the past is to create certain circumstances in the present (relative to the behavior under consideration). On this view, the past must cast a certain sort of *shadow* on the present, in order for it to constrain one. Keith Lehrer calls this the *Shadow Principle*.[29]

Freddoso's defence of the denial of (A) fits with the *Shadow Principle*. But it is striking that the Molinist is clearly *not* a multiple-pasts compatibilist; the Molinist insists that causal determinism is incompatible with human freedom. An incompatibilist about causal determinism and human freedom (in the sense that requires freedom to do otherwise) *rejects* the *Shadow Principle* and holds that constraints on an individual's power can arise from the *relationship* between the present and past *in itself*, rather than requiring a present shadow of indisputably freedom-undermining factors cast by the past. Thus, the incompatibilist accepts something like the *Dog's Tail Principle*: the past is viewed as like a dog's tail, which follows the [intact] dog wherever it goes.[30] A version of the *Dog's Tail Principle* is articulated rather elegantly by Carl Ginet as follows:

If I have it open to me now to make the world contain a certain event after now, then I have it open to me now to make the world contain everything that has happened before now plus that event after now. We might call this the principle that *freedom is freedom to add to the given past* ...[31]

An incompatibilist about causal determinism and freedom to do otherwise would typically accept that our freedom is the freedom to add to the given past; after all, the past is over-and-done-with and out of our control. And the Molinist is an incompatibilist about causal determinism and freedom to do otherwise. But Freddoso points out that the Molinist must deny (A)—he must deny the unrestricted fixity of the past (the *Dog's Tail Principle*). Rather, the Molinist embraces the view that only a proper subset of features of the past—the causally relevant features—are now fixed.

[29] Keith Lehrer, 'Self-Profile', in Bogdan, ed. 1981: 31; for a discussion, see Fischer 1994: 196–7.
[30] Fischer 1994: 197.   [31] Ginet 1990: 102–3.

Whereas the Molinist's position here is logically coherent, it seems to me to be highly unstable and intuitively dubious. If one rejects multiple-pasts compatibilism because the past is over-and-done-with, how could one say that only some—not all—past facts are fixed? After all, *all* past facts (temporally non-relational or hard facts) are now over-and-done with.[32] The Molinist's rejection of the compatibility of causal determinism and human freedom to do otherwise requires a principle that does not sit well with a rejection of (A); Molinism thus appears to be unstable.

It just seems highly plausible to me that our freedom is indeed the freedom to add to the given past. Of course, a compatibilist about causal determinism and human freedom to do otherwise may well deny this, contending that the *only* relevance of the past is that it leads to certain circumstances contemporaneous to the behavior under evaluation (the *Shadow Principle*). In my view, this sort of view is not particularly plausible; but it is not straightforwardly problematic or unstable. What issues in the distinctive instability of Molinism is its claim that 'causally relevant' features of the past are fixed simply because they are past (and not in virtue of casting a shadow of the relevant sort on the present), whereas causally irrelevant features of the past need not be fixed. If causally relevant facts about the past are fixed *qua* past, then so should be causally irrelevant past facts. If causally relevant facts about the past are fixed but not simply qua past, then what exactly is it in virtue of which they are fixed? Note that the Molinist, insofar as he is an incompatibilist about causal determinism and human freedom, *cannot* say that it is in virtue of those facts *casting a shadow* on the present—a shadow of indisputably freedom-undermining contemporaneous factors. For the *Shadow Principle* leads to compatibilism about causal determinism and freedom to do otherwise.[33]

In summary, Freddoso identifies two elements of Molina's views on the basis of which a Molinist may allegedly respond to the challenge posed by the incompatibilist about God's foreknowledge and human freedom (in a sense that requires freedom to do othwerwise.): the theory of middle

---

[32] Thus, insofar as what is driving one is intuitions about what is 'over-and-done-with', one should say that freedom requires different possible action with the same past—*not* different possible action with the same causally relevant past.

[33] Another way of putting the point is as follows. The Molinist, being an incompatibilist about causal determinism and human freedom to do otherwise, presumably must accept the so-called 'Consequence Argument' for incompatibilism: (Van Inwagen 1983). But if the Molinist denies (A), he cannot also accept the Consequence Argument, which employs a fixity-of-the-past principle such as (A). I suppose a Molinist could conceivably reject the Consequence Argument but accept some *other* argument for incompatibilism about causal determinism and freedom to do otherwise, but I do not see how this sort of position could be developed plausibly. For a helpful exploration of the apparent instability of Molnism here, see: Perszyk 2003.

knowledge and the denial of (A). I have argued that the theory of middle knowledge is no response at all; rather, it presupposes some antecedent and independent response to the incompatibilist. This is of course not to say that the theory of middle knowledge is not theologically interesting or important; it does provide a model for God's providence, *given an antecedent solution to the problem of the relationship between God's foreknowledge and human freedom.* I have simply sought to show that the importance of the theory of middle knowledge is here, rather than in providing a response to the incompatibilist (and thus a solution to the problem of reconciling God's omniscience with human freedom). Further, I have contended that, although a denial of (A) of the sort envisaged by the Molinist would provide an answer to the incompatibilist, it is unstable and highly implausible. If our freedom is the freedom to add to the given past, it seems very odd to suppose that we can subtract off some of the past, leaving the dog with only part of its tail.

Neither of the elements identified by Freddoso as part of Molinism is particularly promising then. Note that my critique has completely bypassed the huge literature on whether the conditionals posited by the theory of middle knowledge can be true.[34] This literature raises fascinating and complex issues. In my view, however, the problems I have pointed to are independent of these issues and raise at least as fundamental worries for Molinism, if not even more basic problems.

II.3. Molinism: the best game in town?

In his important and influential book on Molinism, Thomas P. Flint argues that Molinism is 'by far the best game in town' for a Christian.[35] More specifically, Flint argues that the 'twin bases of Molinism'—a libertarian view of human freedom and a 'traditional' view of providence—constitute the doctrine of 'libertarian traditionalism', and he says, 'Absent insurmountable problems which its acceptance might engender, libertarian traditionalism seems, if not the only, then at least by far the best game in town.'[36]

It is perhaps not surprising that I do not find that Molinism is the only or best game in town for a Christian or for anyone. And it will not at all be surprising that I *certainly* do not believe that it is 'by far' the best game in town. Flint is quite explicit that he does not think he can provide a knockdown argument for libertarian traditionalism. In contrast, he lays out three considerations that he feels should result in the conclusion that this doctrine is 'by far the best game in town,' even if it is indeed possible for a

---

[34] For just a sample, see: Adams 1977; and Flint 1998.
[35] Flint 1998.   [36] Ibid. 34.

reasonable person to reject it. I shall not address the first two considerations in detail here, although I certainly have attempted to do so elsewhere.[37] Here I shall simply summarize some of the worries I have about Flint's first two arguments, and I shall develop a critique of his third. Finally, I shall add a worry that I believe weighs heavily against libertarian traditionalism in overall assessment of the doctrine.

In presenting what he takes to be one of the two bases of Molinism — libertarian freedom — Flint lays out three propositions:

(1) Some human actions are free.
(2) All human actions are ultimately causally determined by events not under the causal control of their agents.
(3) It is not possible that a free human action be ultimately causally determined by events not under the causal control of its agent.[38]

Clearly, these three propositions, each of which has some initial plausibility, are inconsistent. Although Flint emphasizes that he does not seek to present a decisive argument, he does find libertarianism alluring, and he rejects (2), which he attributes to the compatibilist. He offers three arguments for the rejection of compatibilism and the acceptance of libertarianism, the first two of which are purportedly available even to secular philosophers.

Flint's first argument is basically the so-called 'Consequence Argument', to use Peter van Inwagen's term.[39] This argument is structurally parallel to the argument of the incompatibilist about God's foreknowledge and human freedom; of course, it employs not only the Fixity of the Past but also the Fixity of the Natural Laws. Flint's point here is that propositions (1) and (2) entail that some free human actions are causally determined (by events not under the control of the agents), and that the Consequence Argument shows (even if not decisively) that this cannot be so.

Leave aside for now whether the Consequence Argument, in any of its myriad forms, is sound; I am inclined to think it is, but we do not need to take a stand on this issue here. Rather, I would simply point out that

(1) Some human actions are free

is ambiguous. On one reading, (1) says that some human actions are free in the sense that the agent is free to do otherwise; on this reading, I am inclined to agree with Flint that (1) and (2) are inconsistent with the very impressive Consequence Argument. But on another reading, (1) says that some human actions are free in the sense that the agents act freely (and are morally responsible for what they do). Although, of course, this view is

---

[37] See, for example: Fischer 1994; Fischer and Mark Ravizza 1998; Fischer 2006.
[38] Flint 1998: 22, 23.   [39] Ibid., pp. 26–8; Van Inwagen 1983; and Ginet 1990.

contentious, I would argue that agents can act freely even in the absence of the freedom to do otherwise.[40] I am not alone in holding this view, and it (arguably) allows for a certain very attractive kind of compatibilism: a compatibilism about causal determinism and acting freely. What is striking is that Flint does not even consider such a view. He essentially assumes that free action requires freedom to do otherwise.[41]

Flint's second argument is basically the Direct Argument for the Incompatibility of Causal Determinism and Moral Responsibility.[42] This argument is parallel to the Consequence Argument, although here the relevant modality is moral responsibility, rather than power or freedom. The argument employs a crucial *Transfer of Nonresponsibilty Principle*:

(TNR) If no one is morally responsible for p, and no one is morally responsible for the truth that p leads to q, then no one is morally responsible for q.[43]

Very roughly, the Direct Argument has it that causal determinism entails that there is some (temporally non-relational) condition of the universe, C at some time prior to my birth, which, together with the laws of nature, entails that I behave as I do now. But I am not morally responsible for C, and I am not morally responsible for the fact that C together with the laws of nature entails that I behave as I do now. Given (TNR), it follows that I am not morally responsible for what I do now. Obviously, the argument generalizes.

But this is at best a highly contentious argument. I have argued that there are clear counterexamples to (TNR), and further that any attempt to modify (TNR) to yield a principle that will work successfully in the incompatibilist's argument is doomed to failure.[44] Further, David Widerker has argued that the Direct Argument depends crucially on the Consequence Argument, and thus offers no additional support for incompatibilism.[45]

---

[40] See: Frankfurt 1969; and Fischer 1994, 1998 [Fischer and Ravizza], and 2006.

[41] In fairness to Flint, he does offer an intriguing modification to the Principle of Alternative Possibilities (according to which moral responsibility requires the sort of freedom that involves access to alternative possibilities), which he suggests is immune to the sorts of objections one finds in the literature inspired by Frankfurt 1969 in Flint 1998: 165–6. And it is certainly unfair to require anyone to address this huge literature in a project such as that of Flint.

[42] Van Inwagen 1983. Flint attributes the view that many Christians would be attractive to such an argument to Alvin Plantinga (Plantinga 1984: 265–6).

[43] Fischer and Ravizza 1998: 151–69.

[44] Ibid. 1998; and Fischer, 'The Transfer of Non-Responsibility', in J. Campbell, M. O'Rourke, and D. Shier (eds) 2004; reprinted in Fischer 2006; 159–74.

[45] Widerker 2002. For further discussion, see John Martin Fischer, 'The Direct Argument: You Say Goodbye, I Say Hello', in Trakakis (ed.) forthcoming.

I cannot go into the details of the discussion here, but it should suffice simply to note that the Direct Argument is (at best) contested vigorously.

Flint's third argument is supposed to appeal to Christian philosophers.[46] Flint here points out that God is a *free* agent par-excellence. Specifically, God is a free creator of the universe, and yet there simply *are* no causes external to God which 'could, so to speak, set him in motion'.[47] Flint develops the argument as follows:

> God is a free creator. Yet it seems that the typical compatibilist complaints against the libertarian notion of a free action are (from an orthodox Christian's perspective) not applicable to God's actions. But then, if God's actions can be rational and appropriate, actions for which he is properly seen as morally praiseworthy, even in the absence of any ultimate causes beyond his control, then there clearly can be no *conceptual* problem with the notion of free, rational, responsible, but undetermined actions. And if there is no such conceptual problem, then there seems to be no conceptual problem with viewing ourselves as agents with libertarian freedom as well.[48]

I am inclined to agree with what Flint says here. But what should also be obvious is that this argument does nothing to show that compatibilism per se or (2) is false; its target is merely a particular argument for (or perhaps version of) compatibilism or (2). That is, Flint's argument only cuts against a compatibilist who contends that causal determination is *necessary* for human freedom, and whereas some compatibilists certainly believe this, it is in no way an essential part of compatibilism. For example, my view is that human freedom (in the relevant sense) and moral responsibility are compatible with both causal determinism and indeterminism. And it is clear that Flint's argument is completely orthogonal to this sort of compatibilism; it offers no reason for a Christian (or anyone) to reject this sort of compatibilism.

To take stock. I find the three arguments sketched by Flint on behalf of the doctrine that encapsulates the 'twin bases of Molinism' unpersuasive. In fairness to Flint, he does not present them as apodictic or as part of a thorough discussion of the relevant issues; and it must be conceded that many philosophers will find the considerations he adduces persuasive. But I should register my view that they fall considerably short of being compelling. And I wish to present a final consideration, which I believe should weigh heavily against libertarian traditionalism (and thus Molinism).

Note that Molinism requires causal indeterminism. But I believe that the doctrine of causal determinism is an empirical doctrine; if it is true,

---

[46] Flint attributes a similar line of reasoning to Alvin Plantinga in Flint 1998: 30; according to Flint, the Plantinga reasoning is in Plantinga 1984: 266–7.

[47] Flint 1998: 30.   [48] Ibid. 30.

it is contingently true. Presumably, it is a scientific issue whether causal determinism or indeterminism obtains. What is disturbing about Molinism is that it commits anyone who believes in God (interpreted in the relevant way) to the falsity of causal determinism. Thus, it commits any religious person—anyone who believes in God and, in particular, any Christian—to the falsity of a scientific doctrine that presumably may or may not turn out to be true. It thus commits anyone who believes in God to the view that we can know from our armchairs, as it were, that an empirical scientific doctrine is false. If in the future scientists discover that causal determinism is true, a Molinist would be committed to denying the science—to denying it from his or her armchair! Or the Molinist who accepts the scientific discovery would have to give up his belief in God. This would seem to be a dialectically uncomfortable position—to say the least.

The Molinist is in this potentially torturous place in dialectical space precisely because of his commitment to libertarian traditionalism. It is implausible to posit that we can know the falsity of some interesting and live empirical hypothesis from one's armchair; and it is unattractive that one's belief in God should 'hang by a thread'—that it should depend on whether or not the scientists discover the truth of causal determinism.[49]

I wish simply to bring out this unattractive feature of Molinism; I do not suppose that it, or even it taken together with the other objections we have considered, is a decisive reason to reject Molinism. I would however submit that it should be given significant weight in an overall assessment of Molinism. Just as we do not want our moral responsibility to 'hang on a thread'—to be dependent on whether the laws of nature are unversal or almost-universal generalizations—we do not want our belief in God to 'hang on a thread'.

It is sometimes thought that a religious person and, in particular, a Christian, must reject compatibilism. I agree that there are difficult issues here, especially as regards the Problem of Evil. But I wish here simply to show that there is another side to the story—that there are significant reasons for a religious philosopher (in the Judaeo-Christian tradition) to *want* there to be a plausible compatibilist account of freedom and moral responsibility. After all, it is an open scientific question whether causal determinism is true. If it does in fact turn out to be true, wouldn't a religious philosopher want to be able to maintain his beliefs in freedom, moral responsibility, and God? One way of putting it is that it would seem extremely attractive-indeed, important—for a (say) Christian to have a

---

[49] Similarly, I have argued that our view of ourselves as morally responsible agents should not 'hang by a thread': Fischer and Ravizza 1998: 253–4.

compatibilist view of freedom and responsibility in his breast pocket, as it were, in case it turns out that causal determinism is true. And, as I pointed out above, a compatibilist view of freedom and responsibility need not in any way *require* causal determinism; so it would be perfectly consistent with viewing God's creation of the world as a free act, and even ordinary human free acts as in fact not causally determined.

Return to the passage from Flint quoted above, 'Absent insurmountable problems which its acceptance might engender, libertarian traditionalism seems, if not the only, then at least by far the best game in town.' Taken literally, I suppose I do not disagree, but only in the sense that I am also prepared to say, 'Absent insurmountable problems which its acceptance might engender, I would put forward the claim that George W. Bush is an outstanding President of the United States'! One can perhaps interpret my arguments in this section as bringing out some arguably insurmountable problems for the acceptance of libertarian traditionalism.

III. CONCLUSION

There is much of value in the voluminous literature on Molinism and related issues. For just one example, Molinism provides an elegant picture of how God could select a particular possible world to actualize, among the various possible worlds He could actualize. It thus provides an illuminating model of Divine Providence. But many philosophers—including, most recently, Robert Kane—have thought that Molinism provides an answer to the great traditional problem of reconciling God's foreknowledge with human freedom, an answer on a par with those of (say) of Aristotle, Boethius, Aquinas, and Ockham. I have shown why this view is mistaken; Molinism presupposes an answer to the incompatibilist's challenge, but it does not in itself provide an answer.[50]

---

[50] Robert Adams has pointed out to me (in personal correspondence) that perhaps the Molinist does have something to say in order to increase the plausibility of the compatibility of the can-claim and the backtracking counterfactual. That is if one were worried that the reason why the two are incompatible is that the only way the backtracker could be true is due to clearly implausible or freedom-undermining conditions (like backward causation or predetermination), then the Molinist picture can allow us to avoid such concerns.

But in my view the fundamental worry posed by the incompatibilist stems from the fixity of the past, *not* causation or causal determination. Thus I believe that the mere truth of the backtracker would call into question the truth of the can-claim. Additionally, even if we grant the Molinist's separation of issues of causation from the grounding of the backtracker, this would at best 'pave the way' for an argument that the can-claim and the backtracker would be compatible. But of course this is a far cry from actually *offering* such an argument.

Of course, there has been much discussion of the so-called 'counterfactuals of freedom', the subjunctive conditionals (whose consequents specify that agents act freely) posited by Middle Knowledge. As is well known, Robert Adams (and others) have challenged the idea that these sorts of conditionals can be true antecedently to God's willing a world to be the actual world, and others (including Freddoso) have sought to reply to the challenges. Lots of ink has been spilled, and many trees felled. Perhaps it is now clear that, although a resolution of these issues is crucial in evaluating Molinism qua model of God's providence, it is not relevant to providing an answer to the problem of reconciling God's foreknowledge with human freedom. It is important to note that I am in no way suggesting that the debates about Middle Knowledge are not significant; I simply wish to identify their significance more precisely.[51]

REFERENCES

Adams, Robert. 'Middle Knowledge and the Problem of Evil', in *American Philosophical Quarterly* 14/2 (1977): 109–17.

Bogdan, Radu J (ed.), *Profiles: Keith Lehrer* (D. Riedel Publishers, 1981).

Campbell, J., M. O'Rourke, and D. Shier (eds), *Freedom and Determinism: Topics in Contemporary Philosophy Series Vol. II* (MIT Press, 2004).

Fischer, John Martin (ed.), *Moral Responsibility* (Cornell University Press, 1986).

—— (ed.), *God, Foreknowledge, and Freedom* (Stanford University Press, 1989.)

—— 'Recent Work on God and Freedom', in *American Philosophical Quarterly* 29/2 (1992): 91–109.

—— *The Metaphysics of Free Will: An Essay on Control* (Blackwell, 1994).

—— 'The Transfer of Non-Responsibility', in Campbell, et al. (eds) (2004): 189–201.

—— *My Way: Essays on Moral Responsibility* (Oxford University Press, 2006).

Fischer, John Martin and Mark Ravizza, S. J. *Responsibility and Control: A Theory of Moral Responsibility* (Cambridge University Press, 1998).

—— 'The Direct Argument: You Say Goodbye, I Say Hello', in N. Trakakis (ed.) (forthcoming).

Frankfurt, Harry. 'Alternate Possibilities and Moral Responsibility', in *Journal of Philosophy* 66/23 (1969): 829–39.

---

[51] I wish to emphasize that I am not suggesting that Molina himself or all of his expositers (and followers) have mistakenly supposed that his theory provides an answer to the incompatibilist. Thomas Flint, in his thoughtful book referred to above, is careful to frame Molinism as primarily an account of Divine Providence, rather than in itself an answer to the incompatibilist; I do not mean to suggest that Flint is guilty of this sort of mistake. (For relevant discussion, see Flint 1998: 229–50.) Perhaps the target of my critique are those who have *expropriated* Molina's views for purposes for which they were not, strictly speaking, intended, and to which they are not (in my view) suited.

Flint, Thomas P. *Divine Providence: The Molinist Account* (Cornell University Press, 1998).

Freddoso, Alfred J. (trans.). Luis de Molina, *On Divine Foreknowledge (Part IV of the Concordia)* (Cornell University Press, 1988).

Ginet, Carl. *On Action* (Cambridge University Press, 1990).

Hasker, William. *God, Time, and Knowledge* (Cornell University Press, 1989).

Kane, Robert. *A Contemporary Introduction to Free Will* (Oxford University Press, 2005).

Lehrer, Keith. 'Self-Profile', in Bogdan (ed.): 3–104.

Perszyk, Kenneth. 'Molinism and the Consequence Argument: A Challenge', in *Faith and Philosophy* 20/2 (2003): 131–51.

Plantinga, Alvin. 'Advice to Christian Philosophers," in *Faith and Philosophy* 1/3 (1984): 253–271.

Trakakis, N. (ed.), *Essays on Free Will and Moral Responsibility* (Cambridge Scholars Press, forthcoming).

Van Inwagen, Peter. *An Essay on Free Will* (Clarendon Press, 1983).

Widerker, David. 'Farewell to the Direct Argument', in *Journal of Philosophy* 99/6 (2002): 316–24.

3

Spirituality, Expertise, and Philosophers

Bryan Frances

We all can identify many contemporary philosophy professors we know to be theists of some type or other. We also know that often enough their non-theistic beliefs are as epistemically upstanding as the non-theistic beliefs of philosophy professors who aren't theists. In fact, the epistemic-and-non-theistic *lives* of philosophers who are theists are just as epistemically upstanding as the epistemic-and-non-theistic lives of philosophers who aren't theists. Given these and other, similar, facts, there is good reason to think that the pro-theistic beliefs of theistic philosophers are frequently epistemically upstanding. Given their impeccable epistemic credentials on non-theistic matters, the amount of careful thought that lies behind their theism, the large size of the community of philosophical theists, as well as other, similar facts, it would be surprising if all or even most of their pro-theistic beliefs were epistemically blameworthy in some or other significant sense tied to charges such as 'He should know better than to believe that' (so mere false belief need not be blameworthy in this sense; the use of 'blameworthy' will be clarified below). Of course *some* of the pro-theistic beliefs of some theistic philosophers are epistemically blameworthy; the mere large numbers of fallible theistic philosophers almost guarantees it. My point here is that it would be unexpected if most of the pro-theistic beliefs of theistic philosophers were epistemically blameworthy.

But what exactly *makes* their pro-theistic beliefs epistemically upstanding? In virtue of what combinations of epistemic items—arguments, experiences, belief formation facts, even the absences of certain facts—do their pro-theistic beliefs end up epistemically blameless?

Thanks to Duncan Pritchard, Robin LePoidevin, Mark Nelson, Philip Quinn, David Efird, Scott Shalkowski, John Greco, Brian Davies, Matthew Mullin, Jeremy Pierce, Trent Dougherty, Dylan Futter, and Colleen Keating.

I will eventually be arguing that the theistic beliefs of a significant class of philosophers are blameworthy in an interesting sense. Part of what makes the argument worthwhile lies in the theistic claims I assume to be true. For starters, I will suppose that God really exists, created the universe, and is supremely good, loving, powerful, and knowledgeable. Call the latter five features God's 'major properties'. This isn't to say that those are His most important characteristics. If you like, you can make some amendments here (in addition to substituting some other term for 'properties'). For instance, you could add that God continues to create the universe; or you could completely omit the idea that God created the universe. You could add that God is worthy of worship. My argument won't have the same strength when applied to every conception of God. It seems strongest the more person-like God is taken to be; it seems weakest when God is taken to be much more abstract (e.g., divine goo pervading the universe).

The theistic assumptions don't stop there. I will also suppose that people are often divinely 'zapped' in some kind of quasi-perceptual way so that they acquire and retain knowledge of God's existence and major properties—even high-quality reflective knowledge and understanding. If it helps, we can assume the truth of an appropriate kind of substance dualism along with immortality and an appropriate kind of Heaven. I'm happy to assume that there are knowledge-producing arguments for God's existence. Finally, and this will be an important focus of this essay, I will assume that there is some special, relatively calm (as opposed to 'zappy') cognitive state or belief-formation type G that many of us, including philosophy professors, enjoy and which has a pair of enviable properties. First, it produces theistic beliefs with oodles of high-quality warrant—perhaps as good as the warrant had by visual beliefs such as 'My socks are blue' that are acquired in the usual, maximally good ways. Second, that warrant is more than sufficient for *knowledge* of God's existence.

I make all those controversial assumptions because I want to investigate the epistemic standing of theistic belief while assuming as much as possible on behalf of the theist. One might think that making all those assumptions would not leave any question regarding the epistemic standing of theistic belief—even the beliefs of contemporary professional philosophers. For instance, the non-theistic philosopher who suspects that there is something epistemically problematic about the pro-theistic beliefs of her colleagues won't be able to mount any decent argument backing up her suspicion if forced to accept all *those* theistic assumptions! Sceptics about the epistemic merits of theistic belief typically argue that there are good arguments against theism, or that there are no good arguments for theism, or that there are no quasi-perceptual experiences that warrant theistic belief. They usually won't challenge the idea that theistic belief is warranted if forced to assume that such experiences, arguments, and warrants all exist!

However, it is surprisingly difficult to uncover the epistemic items, very broadly construed, that on balance serve to make the pro-theistic beliefs of contemporary professional philosophers epistemically upstanding—even when we grant all the pro-theistic assumptions articulated above. That is, even if *all* those assumptions are true, it remains the case that for many, maybe most, philosophers who have the right background and knowledge (and I think there are lots of us in the relevant category, to be described below), the arguments in this essay suggest that some of the most interesting supports for theistic belief are not actually had, are had but aren't sufficient for epistemically upstanding belief, or are had and sufficient but are outweighed by other epistemic factors that ruin one's chances for epistemically upstanding belief. So, if my argument is sound, it could easily be the case that you once knew that God existed, you still today believe truly and on the very same basis that God exists, but in an important epistemic sense you should no longer believe it; you should now know better than to believe that He exists.

Philosophical investigation into the epistemic status of theistic belief has focused mostly on merely possible or actually available sources of warrant, such as philosophical arguments or miracles or spiritual experiences, thereby often neglecting the actual overall status of particular theistic beliefs. It's one thing to say that theistic belief is epistemically upstanding in some non-actual but close possible world; it's another thing to say that there are ways to have such a belief in the actual world; it is still another to say that the typical philosopher's theistic belief is actually based on some of those actually available means; and, finally, it is yet another to say that the typical philosopher's theistic belief is epistemically upstanding overall. This essay focuses on the last of those four issues.

In §I I'll clarify what I mean by 'epistemically upstanding' and its opposite 'epistemically blameworthy'. In §II I'll present reasons why the contemporary philosopher needs to have some impressive epistemic items—reasons, experience, externalist epistemic facts, et cetera—in order for her belief in God to be epistemically upstanding. In §III we will take stock and summarize what will come next. In §§IV–IX I'll clarify and consider two kinds of spiritual experience or mentality: zapping experiences, and states of consciousness that result from G, mentioned above. I will argue that while the first, zappy experiences, may be sufficient for knowledge of God's existence and major properties, almost all of us rightly claim we haven't had those spiritual experiences. I'll then argue that while the second kind of spiritual mentality, connected to G, may be sufficient for theistic knowledge in many people, and philosophers might have that kind of spiritual mentality (unlike zappy experiences), the warrant provided by G is outweighed or diminished by other epistemic factors had by many although not all philosophers. The conclusion of the essay is that the two kinds of spiritual mentality often do not provide contemporary philosophers with epistemically upstanding theistic beliefs. Of course, this does not rule out those beliefs being epistemically upstanding in virtue of other factors.

A couple points before we get underway. First, a good portion of the argument I will use has nothing essentially to do with religious belief. Rather, that part of it came out of other recent work I have done regarding the epistemic position of someone who, roughly put, is no genius but who knowingly disagrees with expert opinion of a certain kind (Frances 2005a, 2005b, 2008, ms). On the face of it, such a person's belief is not upstanding even if true; and yet philosophers find themselves in this position all the time. So the argument should be of general interest. Second, although I'm not a sceptic about the epistemic upstandingness of philosophers' pro-theistic beliefs that are based on spiritual experience—as I do *not* think that there aren't many such high quality beliefs—in this essay I will speak with that voice.

I. EPISTEMICALLY UPSTANDING BELIEF

The argument I'll give concludes that for many typical contemporary philosophers, theistic belief is not *epistemically upstanding* in virtue of facts regarding certain kinds of spiritual mentality. Before I start the argument I need to clarify what I mean by 'epistemically upstanding', which is meant to be synonymous with my use of 'not epistemically blameworthy'.

Suppose professional philosopher Pam became a mind–body dualist based on her acceptance of the following argument: when I know I'm about to touch a hot surface I expect to feel pain; but in these cases I don't expect to have a certain brain process; thus, by Leibniz's Law the pain is not a brain process. Pretend further that dualism is true. Finally, pretend that there are several ways to come to *know* that dualism is true. Here is one way. Intentionally drop a brick on your toe to generate a throbbing pain. Then carefully introspect the throbbing feeling. If you now come to think that that very feeling just couldn't be a physical thing, with any physical properties—if that thought just seems irresistible to you—then you now know that dualism is true (only according to our pretense of course!). Another way is to expertly work one's way through some very sophisticated conceivability argument. Another way: die, go to Heaven, and have God tell you dualism is true. But Pam didn't become a dualist in any of those ways. She used the simplistic Leibniz's law argument given above, with a few but not many interesting elaborations. She just made a big mistake, something not uncommon in philosophy.

One problem with her belief is that the great majority of professional philosophers who have investigated these issues rightly think that *that* argument is inadequate for endorsing dualism. Most philosophers also think that dualism is false; and in our story they're wrong about that. Most philosophers also think that dropping a brick on one's toe and introspecting appropriately won't produce knowledge of dualism; and (in our story) they're wrong. Most philosophers also think the conceivability argument cannot be turned into a knowledge-producing argument for dualism; and they're wrong once again. Despite all those errors, they are right about one thing: the simplistic Leibniz's law argument is bad and no professional philosopher should be a dualist based on it. That is, any contemporary professional philosopher should not, epistemically, be a dualist based on *those* grounds. Their subsequent belief is epistemically blameworthy. We can suppose that Pam is completely sincere and reflective in holding that the Leibniz's Law argument is sufficient support for dualism. She insists that she's 'done her level best' to arrive at the truth. But she hasn't, not really. We know that she can do much better, as she has been a quality philosopher for years. Not only has she failed to live up to professional standards, she failed to live up to her own standards—standards she has had and lived up to for years. Just because you sincerely think that you've done your level best, and you suffer from no relevant memory loss, does not mean that your belief in your performance is true.[1]

When my argument of this essay concludes that many typical contemporary professional philosophers are epistemically blameworthy in having their theistic beliefs, it is making the very same charge as in the dualism case with Pam. Analogous to the dualism story, I'm assuming that theism is true and there are theistic knowledge-producing arguments and (spiritual) experiences readily available. Of course, I'm not *arguing* in this section of the essay that the theist is just like the dualist; I'm just trying to indicate the meaning of my argument's use of 'epistemically upstanding' and 'epistemically blameworthy'. I'm not saying that the theistic belief must be like the dualist belief in being based on a crude argument. The only purpose of the dualist story is to illustrate what I mean by my use of 'epistemically upstanding' and 'epistemically blameworthy'. No *analysis* of 'she shouldn't be a dualist/theist on those grounds' will be offered here; I have to stop

---

[1] The preceding argument amounts to a criticism of Plantinga's discussion in his 2000, at 99–102.

somewhere. I offer only what is a familiar kind of example. I (i.e., the sceptic I'm pretending to be in this essay) don't think that our theistic beliefs are as bad as Pam's dualistic belief. But both fail to be epistemically upstanding.

Here is another example of the same kind of blameworthiness, one I think is closer to the theist's case. Pam is walking through a forest with a group of friends. One points to a tree in the distance and asks, 'What kind of tree is that one?' Pam replies, 'It is a fir'. And she's right. But two other friends say that it's a spruce. And two more friends in the group say that it's a hemlock. And yet another says that this forest is loaded with spruces and hemlocks in addition to firs, and from their distance to the tree no one can tell firs from hemlocks or spruces by vision alone. Pam knows full well that these people are intelligent, sincere, knowledgeable, and honest (but of course some are mistaken). With the exception of the questioner all of them know about trees; no one is a novice (although they need not be experts). In this situation, in order to have an epistemically upstanding belief that the tree is a fir one has to have some significant epistemic support for one's belief. At least, one has to have significant support provided the alternative possibilities (hemlock, spruce) are 'real, live' expertly endorsed hypotheses, one is aware that they have such endorsement, and one is perfectly aware that those hypotheses conflict with one's belief that the tree is a fir. Perhaps the brain-in-a-vat possibility beloved by epistemologists doesn't pose a significant threat to Pam's belief, but the spruce and hemlock possibilities do. It might be very easy to gather that support (e.g., consult the guidebook, move closer to the tree), but it has to be obtained in any case.

Obviously, we can continue to pursue the matter, trying to further illuminate 'she shouldn't keep her belief in that situation'. I think that we can safely say that Pam is *unjustified* in some important way tied to epistemic blame, despite the fact that she sincerely says that she has tried her level best. My sceptic is making the very same claim with regard to typical contemporary theistic philosophers. However, the complex relations among different kinds of justification and epistemic blameworthiness (not to mention evidence or knowledge) prevent me from discussing the matter further; they are also the reason that I felt it necessary to illustrate rather than define or otherwise characterize how I am using 'epistemically blameworthy/upstanding'. I take it that I have said enough to clarify my use of those terms. I also assume that the clarification (in terms of the dualism-tree-theism comparisons) shows that the charge of failing to be epistemically upstanding is a serious one.[2]

---

[2] In §X I try to soften the blow imposed by my thesis of this essay.

II. WHY EPISTEMIC SUPPORT IS NEEDED

I hold that in order for a contemporary philosophy professor to have an epistemically upstanding belief that God exists and has the major properties, she needs to have some epistemic item that offers *support* for her belief. The claim is exceedingly modest, in two ways.

First, it is not demanding conclusive support. Nothing like proof or conclusive evidence is required. All we need demand of her is that she possess some kind of epistemic item that to a significant extent supports the belief. A simplistic picture will help. Think of the support for a belief on a scale from 1 to 10. At 1, the belief has no or virtually no support and is blameworthy; at 10 it enjoys the highest level of support and is not blameworthy. What we need in order to avoid a blameworthy belief is support to level 7. Conclusive proof and no-reasonable-doubt might come in at levels 8 or 9 or 10, but the kind of epistemic upstandingness illustrated in the previous section is not so demanding, or so I'm willing to assume on behalf of the theist I'm criticizing.

Second, I am being as liberal as possible as to what form the elements of the support have: arguments, pure experiences, testimony, reliability facts, or whatnot. I will call these elements *epistemic items*. Since I'm granting epistemic supporting roles to pure experience (and not merely: to beliefs about or immediately generated from such experience) and many externalist sources of warrant, my argument will not rely on any evidentialist or internalist assumptions (but neither does my argument reject evidentialism or internalism).

Let me elaborate on the 'pure experience' point, as it will be important in the latter sections of the essay. Suppose you have an agonizing toothache. You go to several dentists and doctors and they can't find anything wrong with your teeth or any other relevant part of your body. Eventually you generate enough interest in the medical community that the best doctors in the world spend all their time examining you. They still can't understand what's wrong with you. They say, 'You *can't* be in pain! You're just faking it!' That is the majority expert opinion. You only know so much about pain and nerve endings. Even so, you do *know* that you're in pain, or so I believe. On the doctors' advice you may have given up your belief that it's your *tooth* that's in pain, but you insist—and know—that you are in pain. The hypothesis that you aren't in pain is 'live', you're a typical person with respect to it (meaning roughly that you have no special expertise about pain and nerve endings), you need to have some epistemically impressive item in order to have an epistemically upstanding 'I am in pain' belief, but you *have* it via some special experiences (the painful ones, naturally). It simply doesn't matter whether your experiences provide you with anything recognizable as a *reason* that supports your belief. The experiences themselves are sufficient support.

At least, I'm willing to allow all that for the sake of argument (in order to give the theist every possible avenue of epistemic support), even if it's false. What is important about the toothache story is this: *it shows that we're allowing that there can be serious expert doubt cast on your belief, you are no genius in rebutting those experts, and yet your belief is epistemically upstanding anyway if it comes from experience in the right way*. Similarly, even if all the experts in philosophy were screaming at you with one voice 'God doesn't exist!', you were an argumentative loser, and you needed something epistemically impressive in order to have an upstanding belief that God exists, you could still *know* that God exists because, for instance, God could zap you appropriately in some quasi-perceptual way (more on that possibility in §IV). That would amount to an appropriately strong epistemic item making your belief upstanding. In the interests of giving the theist every opportunity for epistemic upstandingness, I'm willing to allow for that possibility, for who knows the bounds of experience, really?[3]

Thus, it should be uncontroversial that a belief needs some support in order to be epistemically upstanding. (Another argument for this claim: some theistic beliefs are not epistemically upstanding; they need something to make them upstanding; call that something 'support' and be almost ridiculously open-minded as to what form the support might take.) However, I'm also saying that we need *significant* support, which is a further and stronger claim (if a vague one) requiring argument.

One could give several reasons for this claim. I'll give just one.[4] In the intellectual community of philosophers who have thought hard and expertly about the possibility of God's existence, the atheistic hypothesis ~T ('T' for

---

[3] This is not to say that the existence of such experiences isn't problematic! If one hasn't been zapped, it might (or even should) sound ridiculous to think that some kind of experience—of any kind—could warrantedly convince someone that some thing exists that: is wholly good, powerful, and knowledgeable; and, especially, is the creator of the universe. However, some theists would insist that even the most amazing religious experiences don't do that all by themselves; they get you part of the way and some additional epistemic items—arguments, testimony, et cetera—provide the bridge to the warranted belief that the universe was created by the object of the experience. But whether there is any such bridge is of course *highly* controversial as well. Obviously, some theists will deny that God created the universe; they have less of a gap to fill.

[4] Many readers will think it's abundantly clear that any contemporary philosopher needs significant support for her theistic beliefs in order for them to be epistemically upstanding. In fact, it's so clear that no argument is needed. They can skip to §III.

theism, the claim that God exists) is a 'real, live' socio-epistemic possibility in the sense characterized by (a)–(c).

(a) ~T has been through a thorough (not to say exhaustive) evaluation by a large group of well informed, well respected, and highly intelligent professional contemporary philosophers over many years. I take it that this claim is perfectly obvious. For instance, it says nothing regarding what conclusions anyone has made. And of course one can be a member of this group even if one hasn't published on the topic!

(b) ~T is judged actually true or quite likely to be true by a huge number of the well informed, well respected, and highly intelligent professional contemporary philosophers mentioned in (a). I'm not saying that they are right, or that they are the very best judges of those matters, or that their opinion is justified in any way; I'm just pointing out their considered view. This is a perfectly obvious sociological fact.

(c) Those philosophy professors mentioned in (b) typically reached that favourable opinion of ~T based on ~T's apparent merits in a familiar, epistemically responsible way. In addition, their opinion typically remains epistemically responsible (that is, it doesn't merely *start off* epistemically responsible).

Claim (c) can be questioned, as it makes a substantive claim about the epistemic quality of the atheistic opinions of philosophers. In fact, it might seem thoroughly unfair: here I am in the midst of presenting an argument against theistic belief and yet I assume without any argument that atheistic belief is perfectly OK!

Well, that's clearly overstated, as I think that the atheistic opinions of *some* philosophers fail to be epistemically upstanding for an interesting reason (I won't go into it here), and more to the point I'm definitely *not* arguing that theistic belief in philosophers isn't epistemically upstanding (I'm merely arguing that if they are upstanding, then often enough it's in virtue of epistemic factors other than the kinds of spiritual mentality I examine in this essay). Even so, I think it's easier to see why atheistic belief among contemporary professional philosophers is epistemically upstanding than it is to see the same result for theistic belief. Atheistic philosophers typically work in the following way. First, as teenagers, they see that lots of people have theistic beliefs merely because they are told theism is true (roughly put). They find this distasteful, which of course is reasonable. Then over many years they look at the evidence for theism that they can understand to any significant degree; they are underwhelmed with its quality. They have sincerely and expertly looked at the epistemic items claimed to support theistic belief, with an open mind, and they just don't think they are any good. Keep in mind that almost all contemporary philosophy professors have read about and think about theistic belief off and on for *many* years, and they continue to do so on a regular basis, as it is one of the first topics we study as students and one of those topics that comes up all the time in undergraduate classes. It is hard to *avoid* the philosophy of religion if you're a philosophy professor (whereas it is much more common for a professor to not encounter analytic metaphysics or metaethics or nineteenth- century philosophy, for instance, nearly as frequently). If one of these philosophers is any good at philosophy she will admit the *possibility* that theistic people have some kind of special spiritual and epistemic access to God and theistic facts—an access that she lacks or is dormant or blocked in her. But she will think that this possibility is pretty unlikely (more on this in §§IV–VI). So she settles on atheism as most probable. Her doing so would be epistemically blameworthy if it were *clear* that there was *excellent and publicly available* evidence for God's existence, but I am assuming, without argument, that this isn't the case (I don't think that that's a controversial assumption; neither does it conflict with the other pro-theistic assumptions I have already made and will articulate further in §§IV–VI).

I'm not saying that the philosophical atheist is right about any of this! I'm just saying that this is a roughly accurate description of many atheistic philosophers and that it is an epistemically upstanding way to go. They really have looked long and hard at lots of evidence they thought had any real chance of supporting theism. That's not enough to *prove* (c), but I'm hoping that the reader will simply go with me here!

One might suspect that it is particularly difficult to think of these weighty religious matters with anything like an unbiased eye; so (c) is false. But keep in mind that all I'm demanding in (c) is a relatively unbiased eye, a standpoint of evaluation about as objective and thorough as those we take towards other hypotheses of contemporary philosophical debate. I don't know what perfect objectivity would be, but for the purposes of this essay I don't care; neither do I care that there certainly are many philosophical theses that are evaluated more objectively than atheism. Premise (c) is actually quite modest.

In endorsing (c) I'm not denying that there is a cognitive capacity that is devoted to experiencing, or quasi-experiencing, God. There might be such a faculty and it might be dormant or blocked or fouled up in atheists. Even so, I don't see any good reason to think that being in such a situation would mean that one's atheism isn't epistemically upstanding in the ordinary sense illustrated in the previous section; the standards for the latter aren't *that* high. I admit that there might well be an important notion of epistemic upstandingness that few or no atheists achieve with respect to their atheism. For instance, perhaps the only way atheistic belief can arise is if one's cognitive system is damaged in some way, perhaps by sin (of course, this idea will seem ludicrous to most atheistic philosophers). Even so, there is another notion of epistemic upstandingness, an ordinary one, that many atheists, including philosophy professors, do achieve.

In addition to (a)–(c) being true, we know that they are true (set aside forms of general scepticism). For instance, those of us who are theists know perfectly well that loads of very competent and epistemically virtuous philosophy professors think, after much expert reflection, that our theistic belief isn't true. Given that we are perfectly aware of the fact that so many epistemically excellent philosophers disagree with us, it seems to me that if our theistic belief is epistemically upstanding, then it must have some *significant* support. A piddling amount of support won't suffice for epistemic upstandingness. I hasten to add that this claim doesn't imply that it's *difficult* to supply the support. Indeed, I'm assuming on behalf of the theist that for *a significant number of* people it's *very easy* to do so (more on that in §§IV and V). All the claim says is that there's a need for *significant* support; it says nothing about whether the support is easily had by many people due to their having some heavy-duty epistemic item.

So, my argument thus far runs like this:

1. Hypothesis ∼T (the negation of theism) is live in current professional philosophy as a whole since it satisfies (a)–(c).

2. Many contemporary professional philosophers know (a)–(c).

3. If (1) is true and (2) applies to someone (so she knows (a)–(c)), then in order for her to have an epistemically upstanding belief in T (theism), she must have some significant support for her theistic belief. After all, since (1) and (2) are true of you, it follows that you *know* perfectly well that *lots* of frighteningly smart and epistemically virtuous folks think your belief is just plain false; so *if* your belief is epistemically okay anyway, *then* it must have some pretty good support behind it! And please remember that I'm being as generous as possible with the potential kinds of support and not asking for anything as potent as proof.

4. Thus, by (1)–(3) for many of us contemporary professional philosophers, if we have an epistemically upstanding belief in T, then our belief has significant support.

Let me make it crystal clear that premise (3) is not being defended with the lukewarm 'Well, atheism is contrary to theism; so in order to have a respectable belief in theism one must rule out, to some significant extent, atheism'. That kind of argument is frequently rejected among contemporary epistemologists, and with good reason. It is sometimes said that one need not, in order to know (or have an epistemically upstanding belief in) P, rule out counterpossibility Q provided Q is appropriately 'irrelevant'.[5] For instance, I can know that I have children without being able to rule out (in any sense of 'rule out') all sorts of outrageous hypotheses (e.g., 'I have been a brain in a vat for over ten years'), at least for most contexts of evaluating my true belief. That epistemological claim might be right, but it is hard to see how this would apply if Q were widely endorsed by philosophical experts and you were aware of the inconsistency of Q and P as well as the liveness of Q. Imagine a scenario in which each of the following hold, where you believe the truth P while hypothesis Q is the live contender to P.

(i) virtually everyone believes (correctly) that Q is inconsistent with P;
(ii) you've actually put together P and Q and are aware as anyone is that P is inconsistent with Q;
(iii) Q is a real, live contender in our intellectual community;
(iv) in fact, many if not most contemporary philosophy professors believe Q; and
(v) you're aware that Q is a real, live possibility actually endorsed by plenty of philosophical experts.

It will seem clear to many epistemologists that under these circumstances in order for your belief in P (theism) to be epistemically upstanding you need to be able to rule out Q (atheism); this is what I'll call the 'Ruling Out' claim. Note the significance of (iii)–(v): if we take them out, then the Ruling Out claim is much more doubtful. Arguably, even if (i) and (ii) hold, Q need not be ruled out in order for one to know P. Such a situation may obtain when P is 'I got these blue socks today for my birthday' and Q is 'I became a brain in a vat last year and have remained that way since then, with no birthday presents.' But when we have all five conditions (i)–(v) obtaining, then the Ruling Out claim is plausible. Conditions (i) and (ii) boost the threat posed by Q against P to level 1 out of 10 only; but the remaining three conditions boost the threat to level 8.

Think for a minute about traditional hypothesis-based scepticism. Those of us who take such scepticism seriously typically have two relevant beliefs: (a) it's plausible (even if false) that in order to know that I have hands I have to be able to epistemically neutralize, to some significant degree, some sceptical hypotheses, such as the brain-in-a-vat (BIV) one; and (b) it's also plausible (even if false) that I can't so neutralize those hypotheses. There is no reason for us to also think (c) that the BIV hypothesis, for instance, is *plausible or probably true*. In order to take scepticism seriously it's sufficient

---

[5] I have in mind contextualist and relevant alternative theories primarily. For an excellent but slightly out of date introduction with references, see Duncan Pritchard (2002).

to hold (a) and (b); one need not hold (c). Indeed, philosophers who accept (a) and (b) *never* endorse (c).

That's one thing that bothers undergraduates in philosophy. They object: why on earth do some philosophers take the BIV hypothesis to pose *any* threat at all to our beliefs given that those very same philosophers think that there's *no* real chance that the BIV hypothesis is true? Sure, the BIV hypothesis is *formally inconsistent* with my belief that I have hands, so if the former is true then my belief is false. But so what? Why should that bare inconsistency matter so much? Is this strange attitude amongst philosophers the result of some logic fetish infecting the philosophical community?

The students would understand the fuss over the BIV hypothesis if there were some decent reason of some kind to think that the BIV hypothesis was really true. If you believe P, a contrary hypothesis Q has some reasonably good backing—perhaps endorsement by many legitimate experts in the relevant field—and you are quite familiar with Q's good status as well as the conflict between P and Q, then the Q possibility *does* seem to mount a threat to one's belief in P, a threat that if left unneutralized does ruin one's chance at knowledge of P's truth. If the BIV or evil demon hypotheses were like Q, then we would have a real threat to our belief that we have hands.

I take it as obvious that atheism is like Q: it's a 'live' hypothesis in a sociological sense. Thus, one would think that we who are fully aware of atheism's highly respected standing among many excellent philosophers would need to be able to rule out the atheism hypothesis. Even so, *I don't need a premise that strong*. All I need for my argument is a *weaker* claim, one that has nothing to do with 'ruling out'. So I do not rely on the Ruling Out claim. All I am claiming, with my premise (3), is that when (i)–(v) hold (as they do when P is theism and Q is atheism) then in order to have an epistemically upstanding belief—in the sense illustrated in §I—one needs significant, not piddling, support for that belief; so I'm setting aside the demand for an ability to rule out atheism (as the Ruling Out claim has it). Obviously, 'significant' and 'not piddling' are awfully vague! But I think the vagueness won't matter to my arguments below.

So the crucial question is now this: what epistemic items do contemporary philosophers *actually* have that *on balance* make their theistic beliefs epistemically upstanding?

III. TWO SPIRITUAL SOURCES OF SUPPORT

Let's take stock. I have argued that professional contemporary philosophers need some impressive epistemic items in order to have epistemically upstanding theistic beliefs; that's the inference from the first three premises. In what follows I'm going to focus on spiritual mentality, broadly construed, and completely ignore other potential sources such as philosophical arguments. The structure of the rest of my argument, after claims (1)–(4) given earlier, is this:

5. Our theistic beliefs are not epistemically upstanding in virtue of spiritual mentality.

6. Thus, for many contemporary philosophers, if our theistic beliefs are epistemically upstanding, it's in virtue of something other than spiritual mentality.

Clearly, the interesting part of the argument is the defence of (5); this defence will take up the remainder of the essay. As was mentioned in the Introduction, I will now examine two broad kinds of spiritual mentality. I will grant that the first one provides knowledge of God's existence, but most of us simply don't have it and don't even claim to have it. I will then argue that even if the second one sometimes provides us with *initial* knowledge of God's existence and other features, the warrant it provides us is *then, later on* cancelled out by other epistemic factors so that the belief ends up blameworthy—at least, this is true for many of us philosophers. Thus, if our theistic beliefs remain epistemically upstanding anyway (I won't dispute this assertion), they must be so in virtue of something other than, or in addition to, spiritual mentality.

IV. ZAPPY SPIRITUAL EXPERIENCES

Very roughly: a spiritual experience of and in a sense partially coming from God is *zappy* only if it could only be depicted in a children's animated Walt Disney movie, if it could be put on a screen at all. Being zapped isn't just having a feeling of love or forgiveness that happens while or immediately after 'acting theistic', after prayer for instance. It isn't just a 'voice' that one can 'hear' in one's head accompanied by moving experiences. It isn't merely some life-altering event that gives one's life meaning (although it will probably do that as well). Those are mere *garden-variety* spiritual experiences (if spiritual at all), not zappy ones. A zapping experience is like a mind-blowing miracle that is somehow experientially private. Every zappy experience contains some intense mental fireworks—like the staggering *kensho* in Zen, although I suppose it need not be that intense. Take some public event or series of events that would truly be miraculous in the sense that many atheistic and agnostic philosophers would become theists if they saw or perceived them. Now somehow make them private experiences. That is the type of thing we mean by a zapping experience.

Obviously, that isn't a very informative characterization; in fact, it's *pathetic*. Without being zapped it's pretty hard for the writer to describe zappiness; without the audience being zapped they have a hard time understanding the writer describe zappiness; and in any case there isn't much non-metaphorical language around to work with.

However, we need not puzzle over zappiness. For the sake of argument I'll admit that it's as easy as pie to demolish the atheism possibility: God zaps you and you're done. I suppose that many theistic philosophers claim to have had some sorts of genuinely spiritual experiences, such as special feelings of love or forgiveness, but nothing out of a Walt Disney movie. If you have, then you're off the hook as far as my argument in this essay is concerned. If you haven't been zapped but you *think* you have, then my argument applies to you.

V. A SECOND SPIRITUAL WAY

Maybe there's a second general type of spiritual experience, or cognitive state, or cognitive capacity, or belief-formation type—or whatever; *I want to leave open as many possibilities as we can that might be helpful to theistic belief* —that makes the typical philosopher's theistic beliefs epistemically upstanding. For all I've argued thus far, each of the following is true regarding some spiritual quasi-perceptual state of mind or belief-formation type or cognitive capacity or whatever G ('G' for 'God') that philosophical theists sometimes, perhaps even often, find themselves in or employ.[6]

(i) If you 'use' G to come to believe that God exists, then you at least initially know that God exists (remember that among our assumptions is the claim that God exists).

(ii) G is great (see (i)) but isn't accompanied by cognitive fireworks in the sense that one who has enjoyed G can produce a lot of cognitively illuminating (to people who haven't enjoyed G) descriptions of what goes on when one is in this state or uses it to form a belief. All one can really say about G is that when one is in it one knows, immediately and with perfect clarity, that God is speaking to one, is present, is comforting one, etc. Perhaps one even somehow (although this is

---

[6] A certain kind of theist might claim that *all* experiences are experiences of God. But G is supposed to be special in that these are somehow 'direct' experiences of God that satisfy (i) – (vii) in the text.

much harder to believe) immediately knows that God has the five features mentioned earlier. In any case, no Walt Disney fireworks goes on; this isn't zapping.

(iii) Claims (i) and (ii) show that G is at least a bit relevantly similar to (but don't get carried away with the comparison) the state of 'just seeing' that *modus ponens* is valid, or that 1 + 1 = 2, or that I myself believe P or feel happy. They are similar in this relevant way: no fireworks, but high-grade knowledge nonetheless.

(iv) Coming to believe that God exists based on being in G not only secures knowledge—the belief amounts to knowledge—but upon production the belief is also epistemically non-blameworthy. (I'm not cleverly suggesting that there are cases in which one knows P even though one is blameworthy in believing P; I'm just trying to be thorough in describing G.)

(v) There is no easy to follow set of instructions for getting into or using G to generate theistic beliefs (e.g., drop a brick on your toe while singing *Ave Maria*).

(vi) However, and this might strike an outsider as incredible, being in or using G, even repeatedly, doesn't confer one with any special cognitive or other power or capacity or whatnot that a person who hasn't been in or used G can detect (restricting investigation to mortal life). More to the point, someone who hasn't ever enjoyed the state or belief-formation type can't see any direct evidence that any state or type satisfying (i)–(v) exists. Of course this is annoying to those people. They have some indirect evidence—the considered word of some generally very upstanding philosophical folk who claim to have enjoyed G—that something satisfies (i)–(v), but this testimonial evidence isn't great. This makes G quite different from ordinary cognitive capacities. Blind people can find out that those who claim to have the special cognitive power of sight definitely have some extra power that blind people do not have. Those without the power can definitely detect a big difference between those who claim to have the power and those who claim to not have it. This isn't so for G; that's one reason why it's so odd.

(vii) There is no good reason for thinking that no state satisfies (i)–(vi).

So the theist can always say to the atheist and agnostic,

Well, I hate to tell you this, but there's this special calm spiritual mental state or process or whatever G that has allowed me and millions of others to come to know that God exists, and until you get it you may (just 'may') never find any epistemic item—argument or whatnot—that provides any decent support (evidentialist or internalist or otherwise) for theism. I know that stinks, from your perspective, and I know it stinks from the perspective of philosophical discussion. In fact, if I were in your shoes I might well find theistic belief positively nuts! But those are the facts about G. I wish I had better news for you. My apologies!

The non-theist can protest that it's hard to believe that anything could satisfy (i)–(vii), but we already know that experience can be pretty amazing, so those objections won't be compelling. This is especially so since there will probably (I'm willing to assume for the sake of argument) be some naturalist premise somewhere in the objections. That is, any prima facie good argument against the conjunction of (i)–(vii) will probably have some naturalist (not to say physicalist) premise. And the only way that that premise could be adequately defended would be to show that the conjunction of (i)–(vii) is false. The circle is vicious.

This would be a truly horrible state of affairs! The theist's claim that G exists and satisfies (i)–(vii) looks like the response of a truly desperate and epistemically vicious person. It seems as though we have arrived at the most absurd defence possible: I have a special way of knowing things that you don't have, and the only evidence you have is my word for it coupled with my good epistemic reputation. How is this different from just saying 'Nyah, nyah'? Imagine trotting out the same defence when challenged on some belief that you can't defend. 'Well, you see, I have this special cognitive access to a realm of facts that you just don't have, and you'll just have to take my word on it.' Think of all the nonsense that would be generated if we took this route generally. Indeed, think of the patent nonsense that *really is* generated by some of the people who take routes similar to this one.

VI. ALTERNATIVE SPIRITUAL HYPOTHESES

At this point in the dialectic I will once again be as accommodating as possible to the theist: G exists, it satisfies (i)–(vii), the theistic beliefs of many, perhaps most, contemporary philosophy professors are based on (come from the employment of) G, and initially at least those beliefs are epistemically upstanding and amount to *knowledge*. My worry now is that there is enough expertly endorsed and highly public (to philosophical theists) epistemic items that go against certain theistic ideas (to be described below) to make the warrant or epistemic goodness produced by G no longer sufficient for epistemic upstandingness. A simplistic but helpful model: G produces 2,000 warrant units for one's belief that He exists (or is speaking to me); one needs 1,000 for upstandingness; but certain facts, to be described below, produce 1,500 negative warrant units, thereby knocking the total held to a mere 500.

Some philosophers have mounted similar arguments (e.g., the debate in Alvin Plantinga 1986, Philip Quinn 1993, and William Hasker 1998).[7] They argue that if someone is sufficiently aware of the problem of evil, or contemporary scientific explanations of the origins of humans and the universe, or Freudian or Marxist anti-theistic explanations of the origins of religious belief, or other religious traditions, and yet she can't cast sufficient doubt on those problems or explanations or traditions, then if she persists with her theistic belief she is blameworthy. I won't be arguing that way. To a first and very rough approximation, I'll be arguing that if she is aware of such-and-such views on spirituality, views held by contemporary experts regarding spirituality (who are rarely philosophers), and she can't do anything to cast much doubt on those views, then if she persists in her theism she is blameworthy. I hasten to add that no principle such as 'You shouldn't disagree with people you know full well to be experts regarding the belief in question unless you possess some evidence (including experience) they don't have or have insufficiently appreciated' will be used. There are about a million exceptions to that rule, some of which will be described below. My argument will appeal only to an exceedingly sophisticated and staggeringly urbane principle.

One of the key parts of my argument lies in what the spiritual views in question say about G. The *rough* idea is this. There are spiritual experts who say that your spiritual experiences were not experiences of God even though the experiences are in some sense very advanced, novel, knowledge-producing, not delusional, and deserving of the title 'spiritual'. You are aware that these people are spiritual *experts*, and not mere atheistic blowhards talking out of their hats. Finally, since you can't do anything to cast doubt on their considered opinion on the matter, and you need to cast doubt on their considered opinion in order to avoid blame, you are blameworthy.

Thus, I am *not* arguing this way:

Such-and-such non-theistic explanation of your G-based spiritual experience is true; thus, we shouldn't believe the theistic explanation.

That would be incoherent, as we're assuming your spiritual experiences are G-based and (i)–(vii) are true. Neither will I argue in this coherent, intriguing, but ambitious manner:

Such-and-such non-theistic explanation of your G-based spiritual experience is more likely to be true than (or is otherwise evidentially superior

---

[7] In this essay I do not address the arguments of those essays, nor the highly relevant work of William Alston (Alston, William P. *Perceiving God*. Ithaca, NY: Cornell University Press, 1991, chapter 7). I do this not out of disrespect but out of the belief that adequately addressing this work would make this already long essay just too damn long.

to) any theistic explanation of that spiritual experience; thus, we shouldn't believe that the theistic explanation is correct.

Instead, to a first approximation I'll be arguing in this way, which is clearly less ambitious:

Your awareness of the expertly endorsed status of particular alternative explanations of your spiritual experiences negates or counteracts or severely diminishes (or however one wants to put it) the epistemic support for theistic belief supplied by those G-based spiritual experiences.

On to the argument.

For the rest of the essay let's pretend that you are the theistic philosophy professor who has employed G in coming to your theistic beliefs. You say to us: 'Through my spiritual experiences or states of consciousness (or whatever you like) it has been revealed to me that P.' What you say is correct: P is true, you *knew* P, and you did indeed acquire that knowledge through G (or some other kind of spiritual experience roughly like G and not like the zappy experiences; I'll omit this qualification in the remainder of the essay). So far, so good.

I assume you are aware of people who are experts regarding spiritual experience who claim that the experiences you had, although genuine spiritual experiences, were not of God at all. I take it the people with the most plausible claim to be spiritual experts are the ones with lots of spiritual experience, especially advanced spiritual experiences, and lots of competent reflection on spiritual experience, usually via helping others develop their spiritual capacities. And I take it that most of those people will be advanced members of meditative disciplines, since these are the disciplines devoted to developing spiritual experience. For instance, the meditation masters/mystics of various forms of Zen, Christianity, Vajrayana Buddhism, and many other traditions or disciplines will count as spiritual experts (I'll partially defend this claim below). These experts are, to all appearances, as epistemically and morally and psychologically upstanding as you like. They say all sorts of very intelligent and informed things about religious experiences or states of consciousness. But *many* of them say, based on their genuine expertise on these matters, that the spiritual experiences you (and many other relatively ordinary people who aren't part of some meditative discipline) have had weren't of God. Instead, these spiritual experts say, the correct explanation of your religious experiences or states of consciousness is non-theistic, and people who form theistic beliefs upon having such experiences are victims of a particularly interesting and pervasive illusion typical for beginners at spiritual experience. The religious experiences or states of consciousness you had are very advanced, in the evolutionary psychology sense. That is, the spiritual states of consciousness are in some sense more advanced than any of those states of consciousness most of us live through in our ordinary lives. When developmental psychologists make the concerted effort, they will discover that there are stages of psychological development *far* beyond those typically studied in psychology; and it turns out that these stages are the home of spiritual experiences. People who have them, including you, are not deranged in the least; on the contrary, you're evolutionarily advanced in virtue of having those experiences. You are a beginner, yes, but what you're doing is beginning to explore the intricacies of the 'higher realms' of psychological development, not regressing to the womb or other such nonsense that applies to the deranged preachers on television such as Pat Robertson. The spiritual experts in question aren't saying anything insulting or condescending to you! They aren't saying, for instance, that you're really just deluded and deeply yearn for a supreme father figure (although such an explanation does of course apply to many people). But they are saying that those experiences don't signal the existence of any being other than the one having the experience. Given any of a fairly large range of appropriate cognitive backgrounds and expectations, one will have experiences *as if* there is a non-physical and roughly person-like being in their presence; the experiences are 'malleable' as we might put it. And one can eventually realize that fact, but only after one has had more mature spiritual experiences—in fact, this realization almost never happens unless one takes up some meditative practice in a serious way for several years. Eventually, with more advanced spiritual experiences had years later, one can see one's earlier mistakes. Indeed, there are testimonials from spiritual experts describing how their initial spiritual experiences were deceptive in many ways in spite of being illuminating. These experts say that the spiritual experiences you have had are somewhat akin to the visual experiences had by someone who was congenitally blind but who has just had an operation to gain the power of sight. She is having genuinely new and visual experiences. But her experiences are those of a novice, and novices make lots of perceptual mistakes.

Let me make it clear that I'm not picking on spiritual experiences that seemed to be of supernatural entities. Even Zen masters often say that initial 'awakenings', called *kensho*, are typically shallow and highly misleading. The misleading nature of immature spiritual experiences is certainly not confined to experiences that suggest supernatural entities to the experiencers.

This short description is pretty vague, but it can be and has been filled out in detail; and surely as a contemporary philosopher with some knowledge of spirituality you can't plead ignorance of these ideas,[8] even if you don't know their details![9]

You might say that the spiritual experts are wrong when they claim that your spiritual experiences weren't experiences of God. And I'm assuming that you'd be correct to do so! I'm assuming you have experienced Him, through G, and you know, at least initially, of His existence (as well as other facts about Him, such as the fact that you were in His presence, or He was speaking to you, or that He was comforting you). Even so, the disagreeing experts are spiritual experts anyway. Being wrong, even on some fundamental issues, clearly doesn't make one a non-expert. Whatever we end up saying about these matters, Zen masters must count as experts on spiritual experience if anyone is such an expert! Having fundamentally wrong views does not, of course, preclude one from being an expert.[10] Otherwise, Ted Sider, David Lewis, Timothy Williamson, David Chalmers, and Paul Churchland would fail to count as experts on material composition, modality, vagueness, phenomenal consciousness, and propositional attitudes, respectively (I'm not picking on them; we can make this point by pointing out highly distinguished experts on those topics who have the opposite fundamental beliefs). Perhaps better: just about the most popular view among colour experts is colour eliminativism (no ordinary objects are coloured; more on this theory below), but I think it's not difficult to imagine that that kind of eliminativism is false anyway.

The spiritual experts who offer what I'm calling 'alternative' explanations of your spiritual experiences all hold that your experiences were not experiences of God or any other supernatural being (or 'force', or whatever); that's all I mean by 'alternative' in 'alternative explanation'.[11] And we'll agree that if your experiences weren't of God at all (as those spiritual experts claim but we're assuming to be false) but your belief that God exists is based on those experiences alone (with the possible addition of a trivial

---

[8] I don't want to overstate the point: I'm certainly not saying that all living theistic philosophy professors are aware of these matters. But surely many are.

[9] For a somewhat dated but still valuable and highly ambitious collection see Wilber, Engler, and Brown 1986. One needs to keep in mind that the people who undertake these studies, like the spiritual experts, aren't philosophers. Some of them, like Ken Wilber, attempt some philosophy, but for the most part don't produce much of value. In particular, in my judgement Wilber is simply horrible at philosophy, even though he is worth studying for philosophically relevant data and ideas.

[10] I don't think an informed philosopher can, today, say that there simply are no spiritual experts. I would even go further, and claim that there are such experts even if God doesn't exist. In any case, one who believes G exists and satisfies (i)–(vii) probably won't say there are no spiritual experts, and recall that we are assuming the truth of that belief.

[11] Once again, I set aside the alleged sense in which every experience, even of backing up one's hard drive, for instance, is an experience of God.

inference, say from 'God has been speaking to me' to 'God exists'), then your belief that God exists is blameworthy. But these spiritual experts need not be atheists; in fact, they can be and actually sometimes are theists—even theists who believe that we can know God through spiritual experiences. Just like we sometimes say to an undergraduate,

I agree with your conclusion. And I think your argument is sophisticated, illuminating, and worth an A. Unfortunately I also think your argument doesn't really support your conclusion,

some actual spiritual experts will say to you,

I agree that God exists. And I think one can experience God, come to know God through spiritual experience, and your experience was extraordinary and meaningful. So we agree on some quite fundamental matters. Unfortunately I also think that you have not really experienced Him.[12]

Many others will be agnostics who say that your experience was extraordinary and genuinely spiritual but didn't come from God, regardless of whether He exists, because these experiences are indicative of the higher realms of human experience, and not experiences of divine entities. They take no stand on God's existence but just hold that your experiences have non-divine sources and explanations. And of course many of the spiritual experts will be atheists (of a great variety of kinds). But they aren't any old atheists, like the ones you will find down the hall from your office in the philosophy building: they acknowledge the 'legitimacy' and extreme importance of spiritual experience but don't think it is experience of any supernatural entity. Finally, some but not all Christian meditative souls will say that your spiritual experiences were indeed of God (or some supernatural entity); you'll find them to be the agreeable ones!

You might think that you simply can't have any disagreeing epistemic superiors when it comes to certain theistic beliefs generated from certain spiritual experiences. You might think that your spiritual experiences are so epistemically wonderful that you can safely conclude that anyone (short of the divine) who disagrees with the beliefs naturally produced by those experiences is epistemically inferior to you with respect to those beliefs (e.g., Plantinga 1997: 296). You agree that there are lots of spiritual experts, and you agree that many of them know a lot more about God and spiritual experience than you ever will. You are thus immune to certain charges of arrogance. But you hold that there are some 'litmus tests' for determining whether someone is in as good an epistemic position as you with regard to

---

[12] In making this comparison I am not suggesting that the spiritual expert's disagreement with you has anything to do with an *argument*, either yours or hers. More on this point below.

belief P: if they disagree with it, then you can be epistemically upstanding in concluding, without the slightest investigation, that their epistemic position with respect to P is inferior to yours. This might hold for some experientially based beliefs, for instance the beliefs that I'm hungry and warm. More interestingly, perhaps it holds for philosophically general beliefs like 'No contradictions are true' (but probably not; see, for instance, Priest 1987; Priest and Smiley 1993). Thus, maybe this 'Intolerance' view can hold for certain theistic beliefs generated through something like G-based spiritual experiences.

For the sake of argument I'll admit that the Intolerance view is true for theistic beliefs produced via zappy spiritual experiences (although I don't believe it). Furthermore, I think it's right when a spiritually experienced person encounters 'dismissive' views about spiritual experience. That is, the spiritually experienced person can dismiss without further investigation, Freudian, for instance, views about spiritual experience. So I won't discount the Intolerance view entirely; let's allow that 'intolerance' is permissible in some cases. However, I want to make two points about making the analogous move for non-zappy spiritual experiences. First, if your philosophizing lands you with the view that you can be epistemically upstanding in concluding, without the slightest investigation, that regarding some highly controversial philosophical issue the epistemic positions of a great many contemporary philosophy professors are inferior to yours, then you had better rethink your philosophizing that landed you there. It's extremely unlikely that this behavior of yours is epistemically upstanding. That's just a piece of advice! My second and more important point is that when the people who disagree with you are obviously spiritual experts (some of whom are theists), and you admit that your excellent epistemic position derives from your spiritual experiences, and these spiritual experts are saying things like

Yes, many of us have had those spiritual experiences too, as have many of our students, and after many years of study and further and more mature spiritual experience we think that those experiences you had don't support what you think they support—even though we're aware that they certainly seemed to at the time,

well, then it's time to forgo the litmus test and start listening.

When made familiar with some of the contents and credentials of these expertly endorsed alternative spiritual hypotheses, what is a theistic philosopher supposed to do? On the face of it, it seems that the considerable support (externalistically construed if one likes) given to her theistic beliefs by her G-based spiritual experiences is severely diminished. She had an epistemic item that strongly supported her theistic belief, and yet she then became aware of many genuine spiritual experts, of a variety of backgrounds and belief systems, who hold that her epistemic item does not support that belief (whether or not they agree with theism is neither here nor there). Of course, the person might not be able, psychologically, to take the alternative spiritual hypotheses seriously. Her experience was so divinely clear, even if non-zappy, that she is psychologically unable to seriously consider the possibility that those alternative ideas might be right (even though she is aware of them and the superb credentials of their supporters).[13] I suspect that she is not blameworthy for at least the duration of her spiritual experience: it is hard to blame someone who is in the thick of things. However, I think that after she 'sobers up a bit' if she continues with her belief then she is blameworthy in that she should have the good sense or intellectual maturity to take such alternative hypotheses seriously and adjust her beliefs accordingly by withholding judgement (setting aside alternative epistemic supports she may have for her theistic beliefs). Such a requirement on epistemic upstandingness would, I suspect, be inappropriate for most people. But my argument deals only with professional philosophers who have and often use the ability to take seriously expertly-endorsed hypotheses that are quite different from what they're initially inclined to believe. (And if they don't have that ability, then they are blameworthy for *that*.) Furthermore, the alternative spiritual hypotheses are not *terribly* different from the hypothesis that the spiritual experiences are revealing the existence of God. Most philosophical arguments against the epistemic credentials of theistic belief based on spiritual experience are so dismissive of the latter that a person with such experiences has a hard time thinking that those arguments have any plausibility. After all, many such criticisms depict spiritual experience as pure hogwash. Such a sceptical reaction to those criticisms seems reasonable to me.[14] Part of the interest in my argument is that it views spiritual experience in a very favourable light.

---

[13] It is easy to be distracted by the doxastic voluntarism issue. But I assume that it is obvious that the epistemic charge 'You should not continue with your belief' is often true. When it comes to scientific matters, for instance, we change our beliefs accordingly all the time when we discover that the experts disagree with us; and if we don't do so we are being epistemically naughty. For instance, on Monday you believe that Jupiter has about twenty moons. You've believed this for years, based on what you read about astronomy a long time ago. Then on Tuesday you talk to your friend the physics professor who tells you that astronomers have now catalogued over forty moons of Jupiter. Obviously, you should give up your old belief; you should know better than to stick with your old belief; if you stick with your old belief then you're blameworthy (unless of course you know the physicist is joking, etc). I will simply assume that such 'blame' judgements are often true.

[14] However, I don't think it's epistemically permissible to automatically discount spiritual experience traditions different from one's own—not if one is a philosophy professor anyway. One looks askance at Freudian explanations of spiritual experience and thinks, in an epistemically upstanding way, that those explanations 'just can't be right' because they leave no room for accounting for the rich, epistemically coherent

And yet, all we have seen thus far is that the blameworthiness of the theistic philosopher is present 'on the face of it'. In the remainder of the essay I will try to determine whether the epistemic goodness supplied by the philosopher's G-based spiritual experience *really is* severely diminished by her awareness of the contents and good credentials of expertly endorsed alternative spiritual hypotheses.

VII. SPIRITUALITY, VISION, AND COLOUR, PART 1

One might think that the reliability of (or other epistemically relevant facts about) G is *so* potent that the theistic beliefs end up with so much warrant as a result of those G-based experiences that the epistemic sin in not having any epistemic item that counters the alternative spiritual hypotheses isn't enough to drop the beliefs down to the status of being blameworthy. The facts about belief production via G supply 4,000 warrant units; the unsavory facts about the circumstances of your belief retention—you're familiar with the alternative spiritual hypotheses, you are familiar with their respected standing among epistemically reputable societies, you have no counteritem to them, etc—take away 1,000 warrant units, thereby producing a net of 3,000 units; but one needs just 1,000 units for upstandingness.

Alternatively, one might think that G is epistemically potent in a slightly different way: true beliefs that come from its operation under the best circumstances are immune to defeat. No matter what information one gathers after the belief has been formed, retaining the belief remains epistemically permissible.

In either case, I take it that G is supposed to be akin to vision under the *best* of circumstances. If in perfectly normal and optimal circumstances I see a blue sock (from just two feet away, in perfect light, I'm sober, I have 20/20 vision, etc.), and I form in the entirely ordinary and optimal way the true belief that the sock is blue, then I know that the sock is blue. If anyone tries to cast doubt on my belief, and I go look at the sock again under the same optimal circumstances (external and internal), I will be epistemically a-okay if I retain my belief; in fact, I'd probably be a-okay even without the second look. The belief-formation facts are *so* epistemically great that my belief retains its upstandingness even if I can't say anything clever or even mediocre in response to the genius-sophist trying to cast doubt on my belief.

phenomenology of spiritual experience had by adults who are fully functioning, well adjusted, intelligent, etc. One cannot do the same with the alternative spiritual hypotheses we are considering.

I will bend over backward once more: *cognitive type G really is as great as vision in the best of circumstances.* We can construe this as an eighth condition on G, adding to (i)–(vii). However, I suspect that that won't suffice to save the upstandingness of our theistic beliefs, as even the best ordinary colour beliefs can be rendered blameworthy through the addition of misleading evidence from genuine experts.

Consider this example (in §VIII I'll look at another that makes the same point). You see a sock in the usual excellent viewing conditions: just two feet away, in perfect light, etc. It looks, and is, blue. But it's your colleague's sock, and his wife is a colour scientist and he insists that he is wearing some of her 'trick' socks she uses in her experiments, in that although they look blue and normal, they're actually very weird and really green. We can suppose that he's made an innocent mistake in that the socks he is wearing are his entirely normal, blue socks. You mistakenly think he trying to fool you even though he's actually a pillar of honesty, so you persist in your belief that the socks are blue. Suppose his wife comes in and says 'Well *there* are those trick socks! We were looking for them all morning in the lab! What are you [your colleague] doing with them on?' Other people concur with her (her lab assistants and children say). She and other colour theorists have created various other strange objects, strange in ways having to do with their colour appearances. You are somewhat aware of these objects, involving rapidly rotating disks with special holes in them, unusual materials, and the like. So you know of the existence of such highly unusual objects. Your blue-socks belief is true and reliably produced in the entirely ordinary way, but is this belief epistemically upstanding once you've encountered the weird-socks story, especially given that you've heard and understood loads of intelligent, sincere, and honest experts saying that the socks are really green—not just his wife, but her assistants, other professors, etc.? Don't you have to rule out, at least to some significant extent (to ask for proof seems to be asking too much) the weird-socks hypothesis to retain the upstanding status of your belief that the socks are blue? I think you would be committing some significant epistemic crimes if you retained your belief. You believe the truth, you acquired the belief in just about the *best way possible*, you initially *knew* that the socks are blue, but in circumstances such as these that isn't enough for upstandingness.

I just described a case with the following features: one acquires a true belief under *virtually the best* circumstances possible, the belief-formation type was nearly the most reliable there is, the belief initially amounts to knowledge, and yet the subsequent awareness of some information that is ultimately misleading but justifiably endorsed by relevant professionals ruins the epistemic upstandingness of the belief (when the belief is retained

even after the additional information has been encountered). The socks case
and the spirituality case are analogous in some interesting ways (I'll look at
some key ways they are not analogous in §VIII).

First way. In the socks case, I believe that the socks are blue, and I believe
it based on my experience of them. In the spiritual case, I believe that God
is here or is speaking to me (or whatever), and I believe it based on my
experience of Him.

Second way. In the socks case, the scientists in question say to me things
like the following:

I agree that your experience seemed to be of blue socks. Many, perhaps most, of
us (who hold that the socks aren't blue because they are trick socks that are really
green) had pretty much the same experience as you did when looking at them. But
more careful empirical examination will show that your experiences were misleading
in that they were not of blue socks but really of some weird green socks. The
experiences you had were genuine visual perceptions, but were somewhat crude.
Further visual experience will show you your error!

In the spiritual case, the naysayers in question say to me analogous things
such as the following:

I agree that your experience seemed to be of God. Many of us (who hold that you
didn't experience God) had pretty much the same experience as you did at that stage
in our spiritual development. But more careful empirical examination (involving
more mature spiritual *experience*, which is why the examination is empirical) will
show that your experiences were misleading in that they were not of God but
instead were the beginnings of some levels of consciousness that are more advanced
than those we have in most situations (and that merit the title 'spiritual') but don't
call out for the existence of a god. The experiences you had were genuine spiritual
perceptions, but were somewhat crude. Further spiritual experience will show you
your error!

Third way. In the socks case, as far as I have determined the scientists in
question are about as expert regarding colour, bizarre colour illusions, etc.,
as anyone. Never mind whether there are other colour experts much more
expert regarding colour; I don't know about those matters. In the spiritual
case, as far as I have determined the naysayers in question are about as
expert regarding spiritual experience as anyone. Never mind whether there
are other spiritual experts much more expert regarding spirituality; I don't
know about those matters.

Fourth way. In the socks case the colour scientists are mistaken; in the
spiritual case the naysayers are mistaken. But this stipulation really isn't
very important.

Fifth way. Neither the colour nor the spiritual experts are saying that you
have gone insane, or that you are temporarily deranged or having a seizure or

anything like that. They aren't saying you are 'screwed up'. Your perceptual and spiritual faculties are working fine; it's just that circumstances are odd and you've erred in coming to the naturally produced belief. The naysayer isn't disrespectful, so to speak, of spiritual experience. I will return to this point later.

Sixth way. In the socks case, you had some utterly typical visual experiences and *immediately* formed the belief that the socks are blue. We can suppose, if you like, that the same happened in the spiritual case. Hence, I'm not saying that the move from the spiritual experience to the theistic belief such as 'God is here' or 'God is speaking to me' amounts to any more of an 'interpretation' or 'inference' than in the socks case. In the spiritual case there is *no more* of an argument to the best explanation or inference than in the socks case.

Let me emphasize that I'm not arguing as follows: (a) the socks case is just like the spirituality case; (b) in the socks case the person who persists in his belief is blameworthy; thus, (c) in the spirituality case the person who persists in his belief is blameworthy. That would be a little too fast for my taste anyway. I think (b) is true, and (a) is true to some extent (the slippery 'is just like' muddles things). My essay's argument concludes that (c) is true (modulo other sources of epistemic support) but it doesn't do so based on (a) and (b). I bring up the socks story for four other reasons.

First, in the socks case one is epistemically blameworthy if one retains one's blue socks belief and has no counter to the contrary experts. Of course, one could easily get a sufficient counter and avoid the blame. For instance, you could observe the main colour scientist discovering the true location of the real trick socks and thereby giving up her belief that your colleague is wearing the trick socks.

Second, through the six-point comparison given above, the socks case helps one *understand* what the spiritual experts are saying.

Third, the socks story shows that a tempting defence of G-based theistic belief in the face of the expertly endorsed alternative spiritual hypotheses is inadequate:

The reason Fred's G-based belief continues to be epistemically upstanding even in the face of recognized expert contrary evidence is that it is a non-inferentially formed belief that started out as knowledge and was formed in just about the best perceptual circumstances possible.

The reason for the inadequacy: your socks belief was a non-inferentially formed belief that started out as knowledge and was formed in just about the best perceptual circumstances possible and via one of the most reliable belief forming procedures there is, and yet it ended up blameworthy. There might be a perfectly adequate defence of G-based theistic belief held in the face of recognized alternative expert spiritual opinion, but it will have to do more than what appears above.

Fourth, the socks story helps me motivate a nice, simple, compact principle that will be a focus of the remainder of this essay.

Experiential Expertise: If all the following hold:

(a) You're no expert about X (God; colour),

(b) You have a belief P ('God spoke to me'; 'The socks are blue') about X based at least in part on your experiences E (the ones from the employment of G; visual experiences),

(c) You're no expert about E's genus (spiritual experiences; visual experiences),

(d) There are lots of genuine experts about E's genus who believe ~P and that E provides insufficient basis for P ('It is not the case that you were being spoken to by God (even though He may exist and can be experienced), and your spiritual experience was illusory in one respect'; 'The socks aren't blue and your visual experience of them was illusory in one respect'),

(e) These experts base these opinions of theirs on their long familiarity with experiences (their own and their students) of the genus of E,

(f) These experts are aware of the E experiences you have had (although they may or may not have personally had tokens of the very same type as you had),

(g) You're aware of their expert credentials and contrary opinion,

(h) and you're a philosopher used to dealing with contrary views in a serious manner,

Then if you don't have some special information those experts lack that in some way undercuts their expert opinion, your P belief is not epistemically upstanding in virtue of E (although of course it might be upstanding in virtue of other epistemic items you have, such as knockdown arguments for P).[15]

In the trick socks case you may well have some 'special information' the experts lack and that undercuts their opinion: you might see some odd looking socks in a box in the corner of the room marked 'trick socks', and you know that none of the experts has seen that box. In such a case it seems to me that you do know P (the socks your colleague is wearing are blue) and your knowledge is based *almost entirely* on E (your ordinary visual experiences of the socks), although of course we must credit an assist

---

[15] I'll be offering a minor amendment to the consequent of the consequent in §VIII.

to your 'special' knowledge about the box, the knowledge that defeats the testimony of the experts. The upshot is that the antecedent of the consequent of Experiential Expertise is important.

The 'undercutting' of the expert opinion can take a variety of forms. You might have some crucial bit of evidence about E that they lack. Or, you might know of some mistake they made in reaching their opinion. And this might be the case even if (a)–(h) are all true. I'll leave open what forms the undercutting might take by sticking with the highly general 'undercuts their expert opinion'.

Experiential Expertise is false! It has exceptions. We'll get to a couple simple ones in §IX. So, I'm not relying on its truth. But it's a pretty good rule anyway; it's almost true. Since you satisfy the antecedent of the rule, or so I believe is the case for an interesting number of theistic philosophy professors, then if you're *not* blameworthy in your theistic belief based on your G experiences then either (i) there is some good explanation of why you're one of the happy exceptions to Experiential Expertise, (ii) your theistic belief is upstanding in virtue of something other than G-based experiences, or (iii) you falsify the antecedent of the consequent of Experiential Expertise. With that said, I can at last formulate the structure of my argument for the crucial premise (5) (but here I ignore the bit about zappy spiritual experiences).

A. Experiential Expertise is true with few exceptions.

B. The antecedent of Experiential Expertise is true for an interesting number of contemporary professional philosophers (with the substitutions for 'E', 'P', and 'X' given above).

C. Thus, if the consequent is false for them, then they must fall into one of the exception classes.

D. But they don't.

E. And unfortunately they *do* satisfy the antecedent of the consequent of Experiential Expertise.

F. It follows from (A)–(E) that they satisfy the consequent of the consequent of Experiential Expertise: their theistic belief is not epistemically upstanding in virtue of G-based spiritual experiences (and we have already set aside zappy spiritual experiences). This is premise (5).

Burden-of-argument moves are for losers. Unfortunately, it looks as though I have to join the group of losers here, because I can't help but think that the burden is on the denier of (5) to show us the error in the conjunction of (A), (D), and (E). I don't see any serious doubt for (B), given that we're assuming God exists, we can experience Him, and G exists and satisfies (i)–(vii). So the critic of (5) has to find a mistake in

[(A) & (D) & (E)]. Showing that (A) is false is tricky for a reason I'll bring up in §IX and that suggests the burden is on the denier of (A). As for (D), if you think it is false then you should be able to show why the spiritual case falls into one of the exception classes: *which* class is it and *why* does the spiritual case fall into it? Otherwise I don't see how your rejection of (D) could be a justified one. As for (E), if you think it is false, then you should be able to *reveal* the 'special information' in question. If you can't, then it doesn't seem to me that you have any case against (E).

I won't defend either (D) or (E). The only way I could adequately defend (D) is list all the classes of exceptions and show that the typical theistic philosophers this essay is about don't fall into those classes. But I certainly don't know all the classes so I won't get very far on that project. The only way I could convincingly argue for (E) is list all the possible kinds of 'special information' and then argue that the typical theistic philosophers in question don't have those kinds of information. But just as before, I don't know all the kinds of special information.

That leaves (A). Once more we encounter disappointment: I know of no way to directly argue for (A) (how many is 'few'?). For what it's worth, I haven't been able to think of many exceptions to Experiential Expertise. My defence of Experiential Expertise, if you can even call it that, will consist of just looking at a single case (but a very good one) meant to clarify it, especially one of its key components. Thus, my 'argument' for (5) amounts to little more than a *challenge*: find the mistake in [(A) & (D) & (E)], if you think there is one.

VIII. SPIRITUALITY, VISION, AND COLOUR, PART 2

The socks-spirituality analogy has its limits. For one thing, in the spiritual case the experts are telling you that all your spiritual experiences are those of a beginner, are somewhat (not entirely) confused or crude, and naturally produce a few mistaken beliefs. In the socks case the experts are not saying that you're a beginner or that your colour experiences are *systematically* flawed; instead you have made a very limited error (just those socks). But there is another case that provides an analogy with spirituality that is significantly better than the socks one. I bring it up here because it gives a nice illustration of what Experiential Expertise really says and why it's so plausible.

As mentioned earlier, colour eliminativism is as well respected as any view on colour (see Byrne and Hilbert 2003 for an introduction and some references). It's been around for hundreds of years and is now endorsed by many philosophers who are experts on colour as well as many expert colour scientists. It's far from being some fringe view that a few philosophers are interested in but don't believe to be true; and it might actually be the favourite view of colour scientists. These colour experts insist that visual experiences are genuine experiences, are unlike other experiences, are reliably used to reveal a tremendous number and variety of facts about the world, are evolutionary advanced, etc. These experiences are simply wonderful! The only problem with them is that they almost always lead to false *colour* beliefs among people who haven't studied the matter very thoroughly. (Not all ordinary colour beliefs will be false: even if colour eliminativism is true you still know perfectly well that the table looks red and that red is darker than yellow.) This is a practically unavoidable and perfectly natural mistake; no one said evolution was perfect. Upon mature investigation, one can realize one's initial mistakes regarding colour, and in those cases one will alter one's colour beliefs. Obviously, visual experiences provide us with much more than colour beliefs (e.g., they tell us how big things are, how far away they are, etc.). According to the experts the problem with visual experiences is *quite limited*: they systematically produce false beliefs just about the colours of ordinary objects; other than that they are great.

The spiritual experience/colour eliminativism analogy is superior to the spiritual experience/trick socks analogy, as both the spiritual experts and colour eliminativists are saying that all your (but not everyone's) spiritual/visual experiences are systematically misleading in *one* particular way even though they are genuinely new and different from experiences of other kinds, knowledge producing (perhaps not propositional, when it comes to spirituality, depending on how various kinds of knowledge (propositional, ability, acquaintance, etc.) are related), evolutionarily advanced, etc. Visual experiences do much more than generate beliefs about the colours of ordinary objects; similarly, spiritual experiences do much more than generate beliefs such as 'God is speaking to me'. The colour experts in question are really making a rather minor objection to the epistemic import of your visual experiences; similarly, the spiritual experts in question are really making a rather minor objection to the epistemic import of your spiritual experiences (recall that they need not deny that God exists, deny that we can experience Him, etc.). In fact, the alternative spiritual explanations need not claim that spiritual experience is unreliable for forming beliefs. The colour eliminativists don't say that vision is unreliable, at least not generally; they just say that certain judgements based on vision (viz. most but not all colour judgements) go wrong. Similarly, the spiritual experts need not, and do not, say spiritual experience is unreliable.

It seems to me, for reasons I have detailed elsewhere (with maximum strength, wit, and elegance in Frances 2005a), that most of us philosophers who are thoroughly informed of colour eliminativism as well as its highly respected status as a philosophical and scientific theory should give up our ordinary colour beliefs such as 'Fire engines are red'. This is not to say that philosophers shouldn't believe that fire engines are red. It's not to say that contemporary philosophers shouldn't believe that fire engines are red. It's not to say that contemporary philosophers who are aware of colour eliminativism shouldn't think that fire engines are red. It is to say that contemporary philosophers who are fully aware of colour eliminativism *and* its status among genuine experts, philosophical *and* scientific, shouldn't believe that fire engines are red.

Actually, I don't think that that conclusion is exactly right either, although it's awfully close. It might be the case that we simply cannot *stop* ourselves from having certain beliefs even when our theorizing convinces us that those beliefs are false. Ted Sider and David Braun (forthcoming) think that no thoughts expressed with vague concepts are true (including that one!); Peter van Inwagen (1990) thinks that there are no chairs; Patricia S. Churchland (1986) and Paul M. Churchland (1989) believe that there are no beliefs. Despite those theoretical views, these philosophers might not be able to avoid forming beliefs obviously inconsistent with those views. Belief is biological, at least in part. What I suspect is the correct conclusion in the colour eliminativism case is this: contemporary philosophers who are fully aware of colour eliminativism and its status among genuine experts shouldn't *assert or avow* that fire engines are red, at least when doing philosophy and not merely educating children about fire engines, say. Call those 'theoretical assertions' as opposed to 'everyday assertions'. Even more carefully: if a contemporary philosopher aware of the content and credentials of colour eliminativism makes a theoretical assertion such as 'Fire engines as well as many other ordinary physical objects are red', then their theoretical assertion or avowal isn't epistemically upstanding largely in virtue of their colour experiences (although it might be upstanding in virtue of other factors, e.g., they are geniuses regarding colour and have refuted colour eliminativism in their unpublished works).

Now, maybe something similar is true for the spiritual case: some of us simply can't avoid forming various pro-theistic beliefs (any more than the Churchlands can avoid coming to have positive beliefs about beliefs). I think this won't apply to many philosophers (in spite of what they may say), but let's allow for the possibility anyway. In that case, my argument regarding G-based experiences should really conclude that the theistic philosophers who satisfy (a)–(h) shouldn't make theoretical assertions or avowals that God has spoken to them (or that they have experienced Him, etc.). Even more carefully: if (a)–(h) are true for some contemporary philosopher regarding the theism case and 'God has spoken to me' ('I have been in

His presence', etc.), then their theoretical assertion or avowal of 'God has spoken to me' or 'God exists' isn't epistemically upstanding in virtue of their G-based spiritual experiences. I'll ignore this belief/avowal/assertion wrinkle in what follows.

Of course, some people just can't 'put up with' strange theories such as colour eliminativism. They just can't take seriously philosophical error theories for instance. For them, scepticism about knowledge, moral truths, colours, character traits, free will, and a large number of other anti-commonsensical theories (not all of which are error theories) are beyond the pale—even though they are fascinating to study. These philosophers will reflexively reject any theory that goes against common sense—although they will make exceptions for well-established scientific theories.

Speaking for myself, I don't have much respect for that attitude. But it hardly matters because colour eliminativism is a scientific theory endorsed by scientists for scientific reasons. For one thing, there's no more a priori thought behind it than behind other popular scientific theories. For another, the main supports for colour eliminativism are hardly a priori. I'm not saying that there is *no* a priori reasoning behind the acceptance among scientists of colour eliminativism; I'm saying that if there is, it isn't exceptional in any way.

In any case, contrary to what you might have been recently suspecting I'm *not* going to argue this way: since we are blameworthy to retain our 'Fire engines are red' belief in the colour eliminativism case, we are likewise blameworthy to retain our 'God spoke to me' belief in the G-based spiritual case. I think that conditional is true, when construed as a material conditional, and I think it forms the basis for a decent argument for (5), but my argument for (5) in this essay doesn't rely on it in any way. Instead, I bring up the eliminativism-spirituality comparison in order to help *explain* Experiential Expertise. For one thing, it provides a nice, interesting case very similar to the spirituality case, thereby helping us better understand the latter. More to the present point, it draws our attention to the important conjunct (e) of the antecedent of Experiential Expertise:

These experts base these opinions of theirs (viz. against your belief P) on their long familiarity with experiences (their own and their students) of the genus of E.

The colour experts who think fire engines aren't red are doing so based largely (not entirely) on some advanced and difficult arguments, arguments contemporary colour experts who are colour realists don't accept. A philosopher might be wary of any highly advanced, relatively abstract argument that attempts to overthrow a whole class of commonsensical beliefs—even if the argument is mostly a posteriori and has excellent scientific as well as philosophical credentials. But please notice that none of this applies to the spiritual case! In the latter case the spiritual experts reached their opinion that is contrary to yours *based on experience, not argument*. These experts have had a great number and variety of spiritual experiences, have taught many pupils regarding their own spiritual experiences, etc. *That's* the basis for their contrary opinion. I think this shows the great plausibility of Experiential Expertise: it's one thing for experts to disagree with you based on their highly abstract arguments; it's another thing entirely for them to do so based on their years of experience.[16] That's why I put 'experiential' in the name of the principle. In reality, Experiential Expertise doesn't even apply to the colour eliminativism case, as condition (e) is not satisfied, even though the colour eliminativism and spirituality cases are quite similar.

IX. EXCEPTIONS TO EXPERIENTIAL EXPERTISE

If I make one worthwhile point in this section, let it be this: even if I miss out on some important exceptions to Experiential Expertise that doesn't mean that (A) is false or my argument for (5) thereby fails. I say: lawnmowers fall to the earth if you drop them out of flying airplanes. And I think the same will hold true of your lawnmower, which we just happen to have with us as we fly over the Atlantic Ocean. It won't do you any good to point out that the lawnmower won't fall to earth if we attach enough balloons to it, or that there might be a hole all the way through the earth and your lawnmower might fall straight into the hole. Or that your lawnmower has magical powers, or that it might land on and stick to another plane. Some counterexamples are irrelevant: your lawnmower has no balloons, no magical powers, there are no holes through the entire world, and there is no chance that your lawnmower will stick to another airplane.

Similarly, if there are exceptions to Experiential Expertise it has to be shown that the spiritual case falls within them. Otherwise all we have is misdirected cleverness. One thing we emphasize to students about the nature of argument is that one can't defeat an argument until one knows it can't be *repaired* to get around one's criticisms. Speaking from personal experience, I know this is a tough rule to follow, and philosophy professors would do well to remind themselves of it from time to time!

---

[16] I'm not suggesting, absurdly, that there is no reasoning or theorizing behind the spiritual expert's contrary opinion. When I say, as a parent, that baby bibs that are hard plastic with a scoop for catching food are better than other bibs, I do so 'on the basis of experience'. Of course I reached this expert opinion with the aid of reflection on my many relevant experiences, but it's the experiences that are doing most of the epistemic work in making my opinion expert.

Here's one exception to Experiential Expertise: although you can identify 100 spiritual experts, you know full well that only 7 think P (your theistic belief) is false while 88 think it's true and 5 are undecided. In that case, (a)–(h) are true, the antecedent of the consequent is true, and yet the consequent of the consequent is false.[17] Or so I'll allow.

Another exception: although you can identify 100 spiritual experts, and eighty-five of them say P is false while you say it's true, you know perfectly well that the remaining fifteen think P is true and that everyone including the first eighty-five agrees that those fifteen are the spiritual superiors of the eighty-five. You know that the eighty-five experts are your spiritual superiors, but you also know that the fifteen are far and away the spiritual superiors of the eighty-five superiors. In this case it seems to me that you're epistemically a-okay in sticking with your belief in P.

There are many other classes of exceptions to Experiential Expertise if we alter it to focus on disagreement due to arguments and omit the business about experiences. I claim without offering justification: often one is epistemically blameless in retaining one's belief in P even when one is *fully aware* that there are loads of people who think P is false and whom one *fully admits* are one's epistemic superiors regarding the topics that P belongs to (for enlightenment on these cases and the general issue see Frances ms.).

X. SUPPOSE (6) IS TRUE...

Suppose that I accept the main argument of this essay, so I hold that the typical theistic philosophy professor is not epistemically upstanding in virtue of spiritual mentality (even though God exists, G exists and satisfies (i)–(vii), etc.). Even so, we have argued against the epistemic goodness of (a certain interesting class of) theistic belief without arguing against the truth of that belief. A theistic philosopher could fully endorse the main argument of this essay and be epistemically upstanding in retaining her theistic belief.

In addition, even if my argument is successful, all is not lost. You might have a wonderful philosophical argument for God's existence. Or maybe you have some other epistemic item that adequately supports your belief. But even if you don't, things are *still* not that bad, for five reasons.

First, the blameworthiness need not be permanent. You could get zapped. Alternatively, you could become a spiritual expert, through years of spiritual

---

[17] Your knowledge of the sociological facts (involving the numbers) doesn't do anything to *undercut* the opinion of the experts, at least not in anything even close to a direct manner, which is why the antecedent of the consequent of Experiential Expertise is not falsified. The same point holds for the next exception case.

discipline, and rightly come to regard the disagreeing spiritual experts as epistemic peers instead of epistemic superiors.

Second, even if you have to withhold belief in order to avoid blame you're still on the path towards spiritually based knowledge of God. That's a big point in your favour. You're still *spiritually better off* than you were before you had any spiritual experience, even if you don't yet have much spiritual knowledge as a result of those experiences. As I pointed out before, you might be akin to the congenitally blind person who has just gained the power of sight but who needs some more visual experience in order to start gathering knowledge via vision.

Third, maybe a lot of philosophically fundamental belief is blameworthy. That is, perhaps almost all beliefs on fundamental philosophical issues are blameworthy due to expert disagreement (roughly put). In that way there is nothing special about theistic belief. For one thing, it doesn't mean that theists are much worse, epistemically speaking, than other philosophers who have beliefs on fundamental and controversial matters such as compatibilism, physicalism, etc.

Fourth, you still have all the positive warrant for theistic belief gained through your admittedly immature spiritual experiences. The warrant is still *there*, so to speak, and has as much epistemic goodness as it has always had; it's just been counteracted (by awareness of contrary expert spiritual opinion) in such a way that it's no longer sufficient to underlie epistemically upstanding theistic belief. There might not be a great deal of positive warrant for theistic belief generated by the spiritual experiences, but no one has argued that the positive warrant doesn't exist at all. This is yet another way in which my sceptical argument is kind to the theistic philosopher: I'm not saying that it fails to generate warrant for theistic belief.

Finally, no one has said that you shouldn't continue to develop your spiritual life, assuming you have some control over it. All the argument says is that you should 'go agnostic' as to what the import of your spiritual experiences is (setting aside other epistemic supports you may have). If anything, the contrary spiritual experts would encourage you to further your spiritual development. This is yet another way in which my sceptical argument is different from similar arguments. So: by all means vigorously continue your 'spiritual path', just suspend judgement on what it means!

REFERENCES

Byrne, A. and D. Hilbert, 'Colour Realism and Colour Science', *Behavioral and Brain Sciences* 26 (2003): 3–21.

Churchland, P. M., *A Neurocomputational Perspective: The Nature of Mind and the Structure of Science* (MIT Press, 1989).

Churchland, P. S., *Neurophilosophy: Toward a Unified Science of the Mind-Brain* (MIT Press, 1986).

Frances, B., 'Who Am I to Disagree with David Lewis?' (ms).

—— *Scepticism Comes Alive* (Oxford, 2005a).

—— 'When a Sceptical Hypothesis is Live', *Noûs* 39 (2005b): 559–95.

—— 'Live Sceptical Hypotheses', in J. Greco (ed.), *Oxford Handbook of Scepticism* (Oxford University Press, 2008).

Hasker, W., 'The Foundations of Theism: Scoring the Quinn-Plantinga Debate', *Faith and Philosophy* 15 (1998): 52–67.

Plantinga, A., 'The Foundations of Theism: A Reply', *Faith and Philosophy* 3 (1986): 298–313.

—— 'Ad Hick', *Faith and Philosophy* 14 (1997): 295–8.

—— *Warranted Christian Belief* (Oxford University Press, 2000).

Priest, G., *In Contradiction: A Study of the Transconsistent* (Martinus Nijhoff, 1987).

Priest, G. and T. Smiley, 'Can Contradictions Be True?', *Proceedings of the Aristotelian Society, Supplementary Volume* 68 (1993): 17–54.

Pritchard, D., 'Recent Work on Radical Scepticism', *American Philosophical Quarterly* 39 (2002): 215–257.

Quinn, P., 'The Foundations of Theism Again: A Rejoinder to Plantinga', in L. Zagzebski (ed.) *Rational Faith* (Notre Dame University Press, 1993), 14–47.

Sider, T. and D. Braun, 'Vague, So Untrue', *Noûs* (forthcoming).

Van Inwagen, P., *Material Beings* (Cornell University Press, 1990).

Wilber, K., J. Engler, and D. P. Brown, *Transformations of Consciousness* (New Science Library, 1986).

4

Are Miracles Chimerical?

Alan Hájek

I. INTRODUCTION

Hume's notorious essay 'Of Miracles' (1902 [1748]; 1986) is as cheeky as it is problematic. A centrepiece in his ongoing attack on theism, it has outraged many, and perplexed still more; it has thus been both denounced with missionary zeal, and scrutinized in countless scholarly works. In this paper, I will scrutinize it further. I will challenge two readings of it by noted Hume scholars, which I regard as uncharitable, offering in their place my own reading. I will also clear it of a prevalent charge. Along the way, however, and especially in the final section, I will level some further charges against it.

In more detail: Hume argues that belief in a miracle report is never justified. According to Flew's (1985) reading of the argument, Hume gives an a priori argument that defines miracles out of existence. I find this reading hardly sympathetic: it portrays Hume as employing an overly strong premise, and as settling for a strangely timid conclusion. Furthermore, on Flew's reading, Hume's lengthy ruminations about testimony would be quite otiose. I have a similar complaint about another reading of the argument, given by Coleman (1989). As my own reading of the argument makes clear, it does have a substantial a priori component, but it is not as

I presented a much shorter, early ancestor of this paper—featuring its exegesis of Hume's argument and its discussion of his balancing principle—at the Australasian Association of Philosophy conference, and at the Australian National University's philosophy department, both in 1994. I am grateful for comments from both audiences. Many thanks to Donald Baxter, Dorothy Coleman, Fiona Cowie, Jennifer Saul, Dorothy Stark, Eric Steinhauer, and Margaret Wilson, for comments on another early version of this paper; and to Alex Byrne, Fiona Cowie, Ned Hall, David Hilbert, Ralph Miles, James Woodward, and Lyle Zynda for comments on its various resurrections.

trite as Flew would have it. Moreover, the argument has an important and clearly demarcated a posteriori component that turns on certain empirical facts about testimony, which finds no place in Coleman's reading. The argument does, however, have some significant shortcomings, as I hope my analysis will reveal.

The most prevalent charge against Hume's argument is that a key principle of his linking belief and probability is flawed. He has us balance the probability of a miracle's occurrence against the probability of its being falsely attested to, and he argues that the latter must always be the greater; thus, Hume argues, reason requires us to disbelieve any miracle report. The 'flaw' in this reasoning is supposedly that it proves too much—if it were any good, it would supposedly counsel us to reject the claims made by historians, to reject newspaper reports of lottery results, and so on; and this is clearly absurd. This charge is misguided: far from providing counterexamples to *Hume's balancing principle*, as I will call it, these cases actually confirm it.

Having cleared Hume of this charge, I will relocate the Achilles heel of the argument: the problem is not with the balancing principle, but rather with the probabilities being balanced. Hume argues that miracles are, in a certain sense, maximally 'improbable'. Our search for just what that sense is leads us to his notion of probability as *strength-of-analogy*: miracles are incredible according to Hume because they bear no analogy to anything in our past experience. Now, strength-of-analogy does not seem to be a genuine sense of 'probability' at all. However, it may feed in as one input in the formation of a rational agent's overall state of belief, which we can model with a probability function. To the extent that it does, I believe that Hume's argument is exposed to further charges, with which I will conclude.

II. HUME'S ARGUMENT—AND OTHER ARGUMENTS

II.1. Flew's reading

There are many readings of Hume's argument to be found, but I want especially to distance myself from two of them. I begin with:

The 'miracles are contradictory' reading

A miracle is a violation of a law of nature. But a law of nature is, among other things, a regularity to which there are no exceptions. It is thus impossible for any event to occur that falsifies this regularity—any such putative 'exception' is really proof that the supposed law did not in fact obtain. That is, it is contradictory to say that a miracle has actually occurred. Thus, belief in testimony to the occurrence of a miracle is never justified.

I take this to be Flew's (1985) reading of the miracles argument. He writes that Hume's argument:

takes off from the observation that there cannot but be a conflict, even a contradiction, within any suitably comprehensive case for saying that a miracle has actually occurred. Such a case has to show: first, that the supposed laws, of which the actual occurrence of the putatively miraculous events would constitute an overriding, do in fact obtain; and, second, that the overridings have in fact occurred.

All evidence for the first proposition, however, is at the same time evidence against the second; and the other way about. For *to say that a law of nature obtains just is to say that it is* (not logically or apriori (*sic*.), but naturally and practically) *impossible for any events to occur such that these events would by their occurring falsify the* universal and nomological (law-stating) *proposition which expresses that law of nature. Thus, to show that a law of nature obtains just is to show that the occurrence of exceptions is naturally impossible; while to show that even one 'exception' has occurred would be to show that that law, at least in that formulation, did not obtain.* (8, my emphases)

A few pages earlier, Flew states that 'Hume's prime concern here is with knowledge, and hence with evidence rather than fact. He is not asking whether any miracles have occurred or do occur …' (4). 'Knowledge' is surely the wrong word; Hume's argument is all about rationally weighing probabilities in the face of evidence that pulls in opposing directions. But at least Flew realizes that the conclusion of the argument concerns the *epistemic attitude* that one should take to miracles, rather than their ontological status: while Hume may be prepared to concede that a miracle is in some sense possible, *rational belief* in a miracle is *not* possible (especially on the basis of testimony). Miracles are, according to Hume, what Sorensen (1988) would call 'blindspots' for rational believers.

However, Flew's reading quoted here then becomes quite perplexing. It portrays Hume as regarding a miracle's occurrence as an *analytic* false-hood—on a par with the death of an immortal being—as if he had simply defined miracles away. One is left wondering why Hume would settle for a merely epistemological conclusion, why he thinks he has merely ruled out rational belief in miracles, when really he has (on this reading) ruled out the miracles themselves. Miracles are contradictory—belief need not enter the picture. Flew, then, implicitly attributes a glaring oversight to Hume, and charity alone should make us hesitate to join him, unless there is good evidence on his side. I find no such evidence.

But one might press the point that Hume is still guilty of an over-sight—less glaring perhaps, but an oversight nonetheless. 'Granted', the point-presser allows, 'this "incoherence" argument against miracles is not

Hume's. But it is a good argument that was available to him, and it could have saved him a lot of work.' Even this I find untenable: contrary to Flew's version of the argument, the notion of a violation of the laws of nature is arguably consistent. For example, it might be thought that the laws of nature govern or describe the workings of *nature*, understood as a closed system, when left to its own devices; but they can be violated by the intervention from the outside of some *super*natural agent.[1] I suspect that Hume was aware of this position himself, and he would thus have been chary of any argument that simply defined miracles away, if only to avoid begging the question against an opponent who held this position.

The 'miracles are contradictory' reading of the argument presupposes a certain view of what laws are: exceptionless regularities, with possibly some further features. While this view has strong support (Mill, Ramsey and Lewis providing much of it), there are analyses of lawhood that deny it (for example, certain subjectivist analyses).[2] And Hume does not presuppose such a view in the miracles argument. He *does* presuppose, of course, that there are such things as laws of nature. Note that someone like van Fraassen (1989), who finds the very notion of the 'laws of nature' incoherent, would have another snappy argument against violations thereof—but again, it wouldn't be Hume's.

Furthermore, Hume's argument famously has more than a little to do with *testimony*, and Flew obviously recognizes this elsewhere in his article. After all, the entire Part II of Hume's essay—by far the longer part—is a sustained harangue on the wretched historical track record of actual testimony to miracles. But on Flew's reading above, it is mystifying what role could be left for any discussion of testimony to play; and note that the word 'testimony' does not appear in this reading, nor any mention of that track record. Given the death blow that miracles have putatively been dealt already, Hume's subsequent pontifications on testimony ought to seem utterly puzzling. Compare the following argument:

Part I A bachelor is an unmarried man. Thus, there cannot but be a conflict, even a contradiction, within any suitably comprehensive case for saying that a particular married man is actually a bachelor.

Part II There have been numerous instances of people claiming to be married bachelors; but they all turned out to be unreliable. (Insert here various stories of false claims to married bachelorhood through the ages.)

---

[1] Mackie (1982: 19–23), among others, makes a similar point.

[2] Aficionados of the lawhood literature will recognize the entailment from a law to the corresponding regularity as van Fraassen's (1989) 'inference' condition. And van Fraassen argues that various accounts of lawhood fail to meet this condition.

Conclusion
Testimony to a particular married man's being a bachelor should not be believed.
Your reaction should be: utter puzzlement.

II.2. Coleman's reading

Similar puzzlement is generated by another reading of the argument.

The 'we were wrong about the laws' reading

To the extent that we seem to have evidence that a supposedly 'miraculous' event has occurred, we really have evidence that the putative 'law' that this event contravened was not in fact a law at all—in which case, the event wasn't really a miracle at all. That is, on the basis of this evidence, we should conclude that we were mistaken about what the true laws are, and not that a miracle has occurred. Thus, belief in testimony to the occurrence of a miracle is never justified.
Coleman (1989) puts the argument this way:

> one must ask if it is always more likely, i.e., conformable to experience, that those claiming the event to be a miracle are mistaken rather than that the event is a genuine violation of a law of nature. Counter-instances of what are taken to be natural laws are not by themselves evidence establishing that no natural law could possibly explain them: at most they provide grounds for revising our formulations of natural laws or seeking an improved understanding of the nature of the phenomena in question ... On the other hand, *past experience shows that what are at one time considered violations of natural laws are frequently found at some later time not to be so. Proportioning belief to evidence, therefore, it is more reasonable to believe that the claim that an event is a miracle is mistaken than it is that the event is a violation of natural law.* (338–9, my emphasis)

Again, one is left wondering why Hume bothered to write the second part of the essay—why all those pages on testimony's checkered history? After all, on this reading, wariness of testimony to a certain anomalous event's occurrence is not an issue. On the contrary, we are enjoined to believe that *the event attested to really happened*—we should just be cautious not to *regard* it as a miracle, cautious not to believe claims that this particular event is in fact miraculous.
   Distinguish:

1. *disbelieving* testimony to an event's occurrence, when that event really would be miraculous;
2. *believing* the testimony to the event's occurrence, but interpreting that occurrence as non-miraculous.

I must stress that I find no ambiguity in Hume on this point: he is arguing for the rational requirement of 1, not of 2. And convincing us of this is the purpose of his lengthy treatment of testimony in the second part of the essay. Hume is *not* enjoining us, for example, to believe Tacitus's reports of Vespasian curing 'a blind man in ALEXANDRIA, by means of his spittle, and a lame man by the mere touch of his foot' (122),[3] as long as we revise our formulations of the relevant natural laws. Quite the contrary.

So I do not find the arguments above in section X of the *Enquiry*. I will offer in their place the argument that I do find, spelling out its premises in detail. Doing so will also give me something definite at which to aim my own criticisms later on: fixing my target will, I hope, make it easier to hit.

II.3. My reading

One of the problems in coming up with a reading of Hume's argument is that there are tensions within the text itself. Hume says at one point 'the proof against a miracle, from the very nature of the fact, is *as entire as any argument from experience can possibly be imagined*' (76, my emphasis), which supports a 'hard-line' reading: no testimony could ever justify belief in a miracle, even in principle. However, he says later:

I beg the limitations here made may be remarked, when I say, that a miracle can never be proved, so as to be the foundation of a system of religion. For I own, that otherwise, there may possibly be miracles, or violations of the usual course of nature, of such a kind as to admit of proof from human testimony. (127)

This suggests a 'softer-line' reading: testimony could in principle justify belief in a miracle, as long as it is not a 'religious' miracle, and as long as the testimony is stupendously good. Mackie (1982) opts for such a softer-line reading. Note that we saw neither reading above: Flew opts for a *diamond-hard-line* reading that banishes the very notion of a miracle, and for Coleman the rejection of the testimony is not even an issue.

I favour the hard-line version, mainly because I find Hume's concession to 'non-religious' miracles somewhat baffling: the argument seems to go through just as smoothly whatever the nature of the miracle in question may be.[4] In any case, I am happy to allow that there may be more than one coherent reading of the miracles argument to be extracted from Hume's

---

[3] All page references are to the classic Selby-Bigge (1902) edition of Hume's *Enquiries*.

[4] While I do not want to detain myself here on this point, I offer further defence of my reading in footnotes 5 and 9 for those who are interested. Note that it is only at premise 9(d) below that talk of religion comes into the argument—which is to say, *after* the first main conclusion.

text. I simply want to insist that the reading I offer below is one of them, and that the readings above are not.

Hume's argument: my reading

1. A miracle is a violation of the laws of nature.
2. A law of nature is, *inter alia*, a regularity to which no exception has previously been experienced.

Thus,

3. There is as compelling a 'proof'[5] from experience as can possibly be imagined against a miracle.
4. In particular, the proof from experience in favour of testimony of any kind cannot be more compelling.
5. There is no other form of proof in favour of testimony.

Therefore,

6. The falsehood of the testimony to a miraculous event is always at least as probable as the event attested to (however good the testimony seems to be).

However,

7. *(Hume's balancing principle)* The testimony should be believed if, and only if, the falsehood of the testimony is less probable than the event attested to.

Therefore, (by 7 and 8):

8. (Conclusion 1) Testimony to a miraculous event should never be believed—belief in a miracle report could never be justified.

This defeats the best case for believing in miracles that could be made.

9. As a matter of fact, we are never faced with the best case, for testimony in favour of miracles (particularly those associated with religions) is never the best possible. After all,

---

[5] I put 'proof' in scare quotes since the word is to be understood in Hume's sense, one which some would find idiosyncratic: 'By proofs meaning such arguments from experience as leave no room for doubt or opposition' (37, fn 24). Thus, it is hard to see how Hume can really mean it when he makes the concession that I adverted to earlier: 'there may possibly be miracles, or violations of the usual course of nature, of such a kind as to admit of proof from human testimony'. How can there be arguments from experience that leave *no* room for doubt or opposition for contrary propositions—both for a given law of nature, and its violation? I thus take Hume's concession to be something of a slip, and I regard this as further support for my hard-line reading of the argument.

(a) There has never been an instance of a miracle report made under such circumstances as to guarantee its trustworthiness.

(b) People have a natural inclination to believe in miracles on the basis of meagre evidence.

(c) The more civilized a nation is, the less frequent are its accounts of miracles.

(d) Every religion abounds with alleged miracles, but to the extent that these religions are contrary to each other, reports of miracles in one religion destroy the credibility of those in another.

Therefore, (by 3 and 9)

10. (Conclusion 2) Any actual miracle report (particularly one associated with a religion) should be outright disbelieved.

Figuring out just what Hume means by 'improbable' here will require some more excavation in his writings, and I will undertake this task in §IV. But before moving on, let us look at the textual support for this reading.
Hume writes:

A miracle is a violation of the laws of nature; and as a firm and unalterable experience has established these laws, the proof against a miracle, from the very nature of the fact, is as entire as any argument from experience can possibly be imagined. (114).

From this I glean the first three premises. The inference to premise 4 is obvious. Premise 5 summarizes this passage:

It being a general maxim, that no objects have any discoverable connexion together, and that all the inferences, which we can draw from one to another, are founded merely on our experience of their constant and regular conjunction; it is evident, that we ought not to make an exception to this maxim in favour of human testimony, whose connexion with any event seems, in itself, as little necessary as any other. (111)

Premise 6 makes explicit the bridge Hume implicitly assumes between evidence and probability, applied to the special case of a miracle report—we will return to it at length in §IV. I call premise 7 *Hume's balancing principle*, a much maligned centrepiece of the argument. He gives an example of the principle, then articulates it, as follows:

When any one tells me, that he saw a dead man restored to life, I immediately consider with myself, whether it be more probable, that this person should either deceive or be deceived, or that the fact, which he relates, should really have happened. I weigh the one miracle against the other; and according to the superiority, which I discover, I pronounce my decision, and always reject the greater miracle. If the falsehood of his testimony would be more miraculous, than the event which he relates; then, and not till then, can he pretend to command my belief or opinion. (116)

Hume's talk of rejecting 'the greater miracle' is a little infelicitous, suggesting as it does that contravening a law admits of degree. His point is better expressed as involving a comparison of two probabilities; and various remarks in the neighbourhood of this quote convince me that this is in the right spirit. Furthermore, this is how his critics standardly understand him.

I have distinguished conclusions 8 and 10 to facilitate my later discussion, but they should be familiar to any reader of the argument. Premise 9 is a summary of part II of Hume's essay.

II.4. Commentary

I hope that it is perspicuous how the parts of the argument cohere, and that Hume does not simply define miracles away—this is only underscored by his attention to *experience* and *observation*. But more than that: he does not even define away the *observability* of miracles. In footnote 43, he surmises: 'The raising of a house or ship into the air is a visible miracle.' Miracles, and even observations thereof, are coherent alright, as these examples make clear.

What, if anything, *does* Hume define away? The following, I submit:

(i). a miracle that has been previously observed (that is, up to but not including the time of the miracle report);

(ii). an (empirical) proof more compelling than the proof against a miracle;

Hence,

(iii). a proof in favour of an item of testimony more compelling than the proof against a miracle;

and, in particular,

(iv). a proof in favour of a miracle report more compelling than that against the miracle itself.

Let's take these points in turn:

Regarding (i): I see no room for flexibility here. How else could Hume say: 'the proof against a miracle is as entire as can possibly be imagined'? If there had been even a single observation of a miracle previously, a stronger proof against this miracle could easily be imagined—namely, if that observation had not been made. I add the word 'previously' here, for if I didn't I would be saddling Hume with another argument that simply defines observations of miracles out of existence. Note that many a theist will baulk at (i). The transubstantiation, for example, is thought by many to be a miracle that is observed at every mass.

Regarding (ii): this involves Hume's inference from 1 and 2 to 3. Every step is problematic. Arguably, a miracle need not violate the laws of nature; it might suffice for it to be extremely improbable, but nonetheless consistent with the laws. As Hambourger (1980) has noted, the parting of the Red Sea can be regarded as the law-abiding conjunction of many small events: this droplet of water moving one way, that droplet of water moving another, and so on. And some might allow for there to be *ceteris paribus* laws—ones that might admit of exceptions when *ceteris* is not *paribus.*

But we should especially question the validity of the inference. Grant Hume 1 and 2 for the sake of the argument. It is consistent with a law being a regularity to which no exception has previously been experienced, that it is *also* a regularity of which no *instance* has previously been experienced. Tooley (1987) countenances the possibility of uninstantiated laws; we might, for example, think of laws of radioactivity that cover non-existent atoms (although they could exist). But even if laws must be instantiated (as Armstrong 1983 would require), that does not mean that they must be instantiated *much.* A law might govern a particle that is instantiated exactly once. Hume moves all too swiftly from the *absence* of counterevidence against a law to the *presence* of supporting evidence for the law, and thus the *presence* of counterevidence against a miracle that violates it—indeed, a maximal amount of it. But there may be laws, and corresponding miracles, for which there is very little evidence on either side. More generally, thanks to the underdetermination of theories by evidence, many incompatible theories have admitted of no observed exceptions, but this hardly means that they are all maximally confirmed, and that their violations are maximally disconfirmed. 'All emeralds are green' and 'all emeralds are grue' are both regularities to which no exception has previously been experienced. But nobody thinks that the proof from experience against a violation of the 'grue' regularity is as compelling as can possibly be imagined.

Regarding (iii) and (iv): their support from (ii) thus undercut, they are on rather shaky ground. Note also that it is consistent with all that Hume has said in his argument that miracles enjoy some *further* source of support that testimony does not—as it might be, some immediate revelation to us. In that case, even granting (as I have not) that the empirical proof against a miracle report is as strong as can be, there may still be a *non*-empirical proof in favour of a miracle report that makes it compelling. But of course this notion would fly in the face of Hume's empiricism, and for now, I am happy to let it pass.

Continuing with Hume's argument: premise 5 might be questioned by someone who thinks that as well as the empirical basis for judging testimony, there are further a priori considerations that support at least somewhat the veracity of testimony—perhaps interpretivist considerations, especially those involving some principle of charity (see, e.g., Lewis 1974). I am prepared simply to grant this premise. The status of premise 6 will be the subject of §IV. I will defend premise 7 (at least in the 'only if' direction, which is all that Hume needs) in the next section.

There has been much dispute about whether Hume's argument is meant to be a priori or a posteriori.[6] In my opinion, it is surely *both*. It is a priori up to and including the first conclusion; a posteriori from then on. Incidentally, this division of labour is neatly drawn by the two parts of the essay. But what are the distinctive contributions of these two parts?

The first part establishes that even the best testimony imaginable cannot outweigh the case against a miracle, from the very nature of a miracle. At best, the case for the testimony is also 'as entire as can possibly be imagined'. Hume does seem to admit this as at least a conceptual possibility: 'In the foregoing reasoning we have supposed, that the testimony, upon which a miracle is founded, may possibly amount to an entire proof' (116)—but even then it is not sufficient to justify belief in the miracle itself.

To see why not, imagine that we are faced with powerful testimony, of a kind that has had a distinguished and totally unblemished track record, to a miracle M. (If this is not the best case, what is?) M belongs to two different reference classes, which incline us in opposing directions. Qua event attested to by this (up till now) uniformly reliable testimony, M is highly probable; qua event that violates another regularity of which we have had (up till now) uniform experience, M is highly improbable. In Hume's words, 'here is a contest of two opposite experiences; of which the one destroys the other, as far as its force goes, and the superior can only operate on the mind by the force, which remains' (113). If, then, we suppose these opposite forces to be exactly equal (and we may as well stipulate it to be so in our imaginary case) then they exactly annihilate each other. We are left with a stalemate. Nevertheless, Hume's first conclusion still follows: the testimony to M should not be believed—belief in M is not justified. Rather, *agnosticism* is surely the appropriate state of mind (although Hume does not spell this out in so many words).[7]

---

6 See, for example, Levine's discussion (1989: 13).

7 Mackie (1982: 17) has made the gist of this last point before me. As he says, when the improbability of the miracle's occurrence equals the improbability of the testimony's being false, 'we must simply suspend our judgement until some fresh consideration tips the balance either way; but in the meantime we cannot rationally accept the report'.

But, as Hume remarks (116), 'we have been a great deal too liberal in our concession' to miracles up to this point. As a matter of empirical fact, the case against actual miracle reports is stronger than it is in our imaginary case—and showing this is the business of the second part of the essay. So now Hume goes for the jugular, driving home just how *un*distinguished the track record of testimony to miracles actually is. And a veritable hall of shame it is. It is clear that his target here is testimony to *religious* miracles; but the considerations that I have labelled (a) to (c) seem to be equally telling against miracle reports in general, irrespective of their affiliation.

In fact, there are two respects in which Hume could have strengthened his conclusions at no extra cost. Firstly, his first and second conclusions could cover even the 'testimony' of one's own senses to a miracle. For such testimony cannot in principle outweigh the evidence in favour of the relevant law of nature; and as a matter of empirical fact, such testimony has also had a tarnished past (witness optical illusions, magicians' tricks, our theory-laden perceptions leading us astray ...). When it comes to miracles, seeing is not believing, or at least by Hume's lights it shouldn't be. (Note, however, that the evidence in favour of a law is merely provided by another body of sensory testimony, and the testimony of other informants. That's another respect in which the 'proof' in favour of a given law *could* be stronger, besides those adduced in my discussion 'Regarding (ii)' above: your senses, and your informants, could be more trustworthy!)

Secondly, thanks to the a posteriori part of the argument, we could go back and allow a more liberal definition of 'miracle' than Hume's, which will in turn produce a stronger second conclusion. For example, let's define a miracle to be a violation of a law of nature *or* an exceptionally improbable event. This new definition would embrace various events that one might want to call miraculous, even though strictly speaking no law of nature is violated. Again, the parting of the Red Sea is consistent with the laws that we believe obtain, despite having staggeringly low probability. This loosening up of the definition will still sustain Hume's final conclusion, now read with the more liberal sense of 'miracle' in mind. For presumably no actual testimony could have such exceptionally small probability of falsehood, given the empirical facts about past testimony that Hume cites. So we simply run the argument again: balance the

However, he goes on to make more of a concession to miracles than I think Hume would allow: he imagines a case in which 'the occurrence of the miracle is intrinsically less unlikely than the testimony's being false: in this we are rationally bound to accept the miracle report'. Hume, on my hard-line reading, would deny that such a case could arise, even in principle. This is the upshot of premise 6.

probabilities, and incline our belief (and disbelief) accordingly, just as Hume says.

Be that as it may, let me sum up Hume's actual argument. The first, a priori part of Hume's essay, shows that one is never justified to believe a miracle report, even in the best case—for at best only agnosticism could be justified. The second, a posteriori part, shows that the actual case for (religious) miracle reports is far from the best, and thus disbelief in them is an obligation of rationality.

III. THE CHARGE: 'HUME'S BALANCING PRINCIPLE IS FLAWED'

Recall Hume's balancing principle, which was premise 7 of the argument:

The testimony should be believed if, and only if, the falsehood of the testimony is less probable than the event attested to.

Stated this way, the principle is surely too strong—the 'if' direction is implausible. Suppose that the falsehood of the testimony is *very slightly* less probable than the event attested to; that is, that the miracle's occurrence is *very slightly* more probable than not. It is surely hasty to *believe* the testimony. (You should not *believe* that you will win a 100-ticket lottery if you hold fifty-one of the tickets. You should have degree of belief greater than half—but that is something else.) But in fact the 'if' direction plays no role in Hume's argument; indeed to the extent that it is plausible, it only *improves* the case for miracles, since it allows one to believe a miracle report on the basis of a very slight balance of evidence in its favour. All the action really concerns the 'only if' direction:

The testimony should be believed only if the falsehood of the testimony is less probable than the event attested to.

This has as an immediate consequence:

If the probability that the testimony is false exceeds the probability of the event attested to, the testimony should not be believed.

Any counterexample to this will therefore be a counterexample to Hume's balancing principle. It is to putative counterexamples to this that I will now turn.[8]

---

[8] See my (1995) for a fuller treatment; the following four paragraphs are largely lifted from that paper.

And there is quite a tradition of them. We may trace them back to contemporaries or near-contemporaries of Hume's, starting with Butler (1736; reprinted 1961). His discussion does not address Hume's argument specifically—in fact it predates the argument—but it has proved influential on subsequent critics. Responding directly to Hume, they include Price (1811), and fast-forwarding to contemporaries of ours, they include Hambourger (1980), Burns (1981), Brown (1984), and Langtry (1989). Since the objections are variations of a theme found in Butler, I will call them *Butler-style objections*. We see, then, that there is no denying their prevalence; in fact, it is fair to say that they collectively form the single most common sort of objection to Hume's argument.

The Butler-style objection that I want to consider first is none other than Butler's. He argues that miracles are no more improbable than specific historical events. Setting aside the truth or falsehood of that claim, let us just grant him that certain historical events are, a priori, extraordinarily improbable. (What probability would *you* have given, before the fact, to that exact conjunction of battles, retreats, victories, and defeats, that we call the Napoleonic wars—not to mention their exact dates?) Now, we usually accept testimony to such events—in fact Hume himself discusses in the *Treatise* (1739–40; 1975: 46) why we should—even though we know that testimony of this sort has a non-negligible probability of being false. We may quickly turn this into an argument against Hume's balancing principle: it seems that according to that principle we are never justified in believing historians. *Reductio ad absurdum!*

Hambourger ushers in other examples of this ilk in his attack specifically on Hume's balancing principle. His main one is a focused version of an example given by Price. He imagines a lottery in which there are one million entrants, and that the *New York Times* reports that the winner of the lottery is Smith. He supposes that *The Times* misreports the winner one in ten thousand times. Hambourger says 'it is even more unlikely that Smith should win than that the *Times* should make a mistake, and, therefore, on balance, it is more probable that Smith lost the lottery, and the *Times* misreported the winner than that Smith won the lottery' (p. 592). Thus, it is an unwelcome consequence of Hume's balancing principle that we should not believe the testimony of *The Times*—or so Hambourger argues. Thus, the principle proves too much and should be rejected, according to Hambourger.

I do not find these criticisms to be damaging to Hume's balancing principle. The 'unwelcome consequences' of the principle, while undoubtedly unwelcome, are in fact not consequences of the principle at all.

Of course it is sometimes rational for you to believe a historian, or the *New York Times* lottery report. But on those occasions, *pace* Butler and

Hambourger, you must regard the probability of the truth of what is said to exceed the probability of its falsehood. On the other hand, if you really think (and Hambourger claims you do, in the example) that 'it is more probable that Smith lost the lottery, and *The Times* misreported the winner, than that Smith won the lottery', then surely *you should not believe that Smith won the lottery.* Just try saying out loud: 'I believe that Smith won; but I think it is more likely that he lost'. Or try saying it this way: 'I believe the report; but I think it is more likely to be mistaken than correct'. Far from being reasonable things to say, they are tantamount to reports of contradictory beliefs.

The point is that you *don't* think that it is more probable that *The Times* misreported the winner than that Smith won the lottery; you *don't* think that it is more likely that the report is mistaken than that it is correct. In my (1995) I work through the lottery case with detailed calculations. But their upshot can be seen very quickly. Suppose that *The Times* reports that Smith won, and assume (as Hambourger does) that there is no reason to think that this report is special—that is, as usual, there is a probability of 10^{-4} that this testimony is false. Then there is a probability of $1-10^{-4}$ that the event really occurred as attested. Thus, the probability that the testimony is false is far *smaller* than the probability of the event attested to. But remember that a Butler-style counterexample has to be a case in which the probability that the testimony is false *exceeds* the probability of the event attested to, and yet the testimony should be believed. Clearly, the lottery example is no such case: the inequality in the probabilities goes in the way congenial to Hume. To be sure, the probability that you *used to* give to Smith winning (10^{-6}) is smaller than the probability that you gave then and give now to *The Times* report being mistaken (10^{-4}). But this innocuous fact cannot be parlayed into a counterexample to Hume's balancing principle concerning the probability you give *now* to Smith's winning, post report ($1-10^{-4}$), without the wildly implausible premise that you cannot rationally update your probabilities. That would *really* prove too much!

I submit that all the Butler-style cases go the same way. The calculations are not quite as straightforward, but the relevant points carry through.

Advocates of the Butler-style objection would have our beliefs, and presumably our actions, ill reflect our probabilities—after all, they think that it is sometimes reasonable for one to believe a particular proposition, despite assigning greater probability to some contrary proposition. I find it ironic that it should be Butler, of all people, who proclaimed that 'probability is the very guide of life'.

IV. ANALOGICAL PROBABILITY

IV.1. Miracles and absence of analogy

So let us be quite clear about this: there is nothing wrong with the 'only if' direction of Hume's balancing principle, which is all his argument needs. If there is anything wrong with that argument, it must be in his claims about the quantities being balanced. Can Hume really show that the probability of a particular miracle's occurrence must always be less than the probability that the testimony to it is mistaken?

It seems he has his work cut out for him. For I don't see how Hume can give a general argument here that *any* (rational) agent is constrained to assign subjective probabilities that balance the way he says they should: towards the falsehood of a miracle report, as opposed to the miracle actually occurring. He will certainly find no support from modern Bayesianism, which requires only that one's degrees of belief obey the probability calculus, and that they update by conditionalizing on one's evidence. The probability calculus is silent on such inequalities regarding contingent matters, and conditionalization need not drive the agent's degrees of belief the way that Hume wants. For example, the agent might give a high prior probability to God existing, and to God intervening in the world in miraculous ways; and a generously low probability to humans deceiving each other, or being deceived. And this agent could always interpret the events of the passing show in such a way that these prior beliefs are only confirmed by experience—seeing God's hand in everyday happenings, and so on. To be sure, Hume would find such an agent irrational for other reasons, such as those he gives in the *Dialogues Concerning Natural Religion* (2006 [1779]), but the miracles argument is supposed to be self-contained, independent of those other considerations.

So why does Hume think that miracles should be assigned such a low probability? Consider firstly his remark that 'the evidence, resulting from the testimony, admits of a diminution, greater or less, in proportion as the fact is more or less unusual' (113). Miracles, then, must be the most *unusual* of events, for they diminish the evidence resulting from testimony to the greatest degree. 'Unusual' certainly seems to imply 'infrequent'—but perhaps it implies something else as well. It had better do so, since Hume recognizes a distinction between 'extraordinary' events and 'miraculous' events, even though the former may happen no more frequently than the latter (indeed, even many events that we would call 'ordinary' never happen). The distinction must therefore be based on something other than a comparison of frequencies. In a later passage, Hume clarifies how it is that miracles are unusual in a way that merely extraordinary events are not—and thus why one could rationally believe testimony to the extraordinary, but never to the miraculous. He imagines firstly testimony to an extraordinary event:

suppose, all authors, in all languages, agree, that, from the first of January 1600, there was a total darkness over the whole earth for eight days: Suppose that the tradition of this extraordinary event is still strong and lively among the people: That all travellers, who return from foreign countries, bring us accounts of the same tradition, without the least variation or contradiction: It is evident, that our present philosophers, instead of doubting the fact, ought to receive it as certain, and ought to search for the causes whence it might be derived. (127–8)[9]

---

[9] I should forestall a particular objection to my reading this as the description of an extraordinary event. You might point to the text that immediately precedes this passage: 'I beg the limitations here made may be remarked, when I say, that a miracle can never be proved, so as to be the foundation of a system of religion. For I own, that otherwise, there may possibly be miracles, or violations of the usual course of nature, of such a kind as to admit of proof from human testimony.' What follows are the two examples that I discuss in the main text. You might say that the eight-day darkness is thus seen by Hume as an example of a miracle that one could rationally believe. I reply that this passage is a little mystifying, quite apart from any stake I might have in explaining it away. Hume has just primed us to expect an example of a *non-religious miracle* that could be believed if the testimony in its favour were spectacularly good, followed by an example of a *religious miracle* that could not be believed, however good the testimony seemed. But in fact, what we find is quite different: The eight-day darkness is a merely 'extraordinary' event—the text is quite explicit on this, as we have seen—a *non-miracle*, apparently; and the resurrection of Queen Elizabeth is a *non-religious miracle*. To be sure, Hume then goes on to imagine the resurrection as being 'ascribed to any new system of religion'. But he has already dismissed the possibility of rationally believing in it while it was being imagined as a *non-religious* miracle: 'the knavery and folly of men are such common phenomena, that I should rather believe the most extraordinary [that word again!] events to arise from their concurrence, than admit of so signal a violation of the laws of nature.'

Furthermore, I don't think that the passage is a special problem for my hard-line interpretation of the argument, because it is *internally* dissonant. My best attempt to explain it away, for what it is worth, is that Hume strangely concedes more to his opponents than he needs to. After all, it is not even implicit in any of the premises in the 'a priori' argument that I presented on his behalf that the miracles he is concerned with must be used to found religions. Whether the argument stands or falls is independent of reading 'miracle' as 'religious miracle'. Rather, this point only enters when he shows that the case for belief in testimony to a miracle is particularly poor when the miracle concerned is religious—but he has already established that the case is poor enough for miracles in general. Indeed, how else could Hume have felt justified in saying at the beginning of the argument that it will 'be an everlasting check to all kinds of superstitious delusion'? After all, not all superstition is religious. In short, the rider 'so as to be the foundation of a system of religion' seems to be a red herring—or a snide dig at Christians. So here again I claim support for my hard-line reading of Hume's argument.

Why should this event be regarded as extraordinary rather than miraculous, and thus the testimony acceptable? The answer comes in the crucial sentence that immediately follows:

The decay, corruption, and dissolution of nature, is an event *rendered probable by so many analogies,* that any phenomenon, which seems to have a tendency towards that catastrophe, comes within the reach of human testimony, if that testimony be very extensive and uniform. [my italics]

Despite the exceptional nature of the eight-day darkness, we have sufficient experience of *analogous* events to accept testimony to it.

Next comes a description of an event that would be truly miraculous, and which Hume thinks ought not to be believed on the basis of testimony: the resurrection of Queen Elizabeth. Unlike the eight-day darkness, there are no 'analogies' to a resurrection in our experience.[10] Thus, he explicates *unusualness* in terms of *absence of analogy* to our past experience. It is now clear why miracles are unusual, according to Hume. They bear *no resemblance* to events of which we have had experience.

As I read him, Hume's idea is the following. In the past, we have had a number of experiences of events of type A followed immediately by events of type B. A miraculous occurrence would be one in which an event of type A is immediately followed by an event M, *where M bears no analogy whatsoever to B.* It remains to be seen how all of this is related to Hume's belief that miracles are so *improbable* that testimony to them should not be believed. How are the notions of probability and analogy connected? To solve this last stage in the puzzle, we need to leave the *Enquiry,* and look to the *Treatise* instead.

IV.2. Improbability and absence of analogy

In section XII of Book 1 of the *Treatise* (1739–40/1975) Hume introduces us to his notion of analogical probability:

there is a third [species of probability] arising from ANALOGY ... all kinds of reasoning from causes or effects are founded on two particulars, viz. the constant conjunction of any two objects in all past experience, and the resemblance of a present object to any one of them ... If you weaken either the union or resemblance, you weaken that principle of transition, and of consequence that belief, which arises from it. The vivacity of the first impression cannot be fully convey'd to the related idea, either where the conjunction of their objects is not constant, or

---

[10] That is, whereas the eight-day darkness is a token of a reasonably common event-type, Queen Elizabeth's resurrection is not. I must confess I don't find Hume's remarks about the eight-day darkness completely convincing, partly because his talk of the 'decay, corruption and dissolution of nature' is rather vague.

where the present impression does not perfectly resemble any of those, whose union we are accustom'd to observe ... in the probability deriv'd from analogy, 'tis the resemblance only, which is affected. Without some degree of resemblance, as well as union, 'tis impossible there can be any reasoning: but as this resemblance admits of many different degrees, the reasoning becomes proportionably more or less firm and certain. An experiment loses of its force, when transferr'd to instances, which are not exactly resembling; tho' 'tis evident it may still retain as much as may be the foundation of probability, as long as there is any resemblance remaining. (142)

I contend that Hume regarded miracles to be maximally improbable in this third sense of probability: they bear no analogy whatsoever to anything in our past experience.

Actually, 'analogical *probability*' is not a happy name, because strength-of-analogy does not seem to be a probability. (It would be a two-argument probability, for starters. Conditional probability comes to mind, but it can't be that, for strength-of-analogy is the same irrespective of the order of the arguments, but that's typically not true of conditional probability.) Nevertheless, Hume has surely captured something important about the way that we typically *think* about probabilities. Kahneman and Tversky (1973, 1982) have shown that people tend to rely heavily on judgements of similarity when attempting to form judgements about probability. Specifically, we tend to estimate the probability that an individual object belongs to some class by simply estimating how *similar* that object is to a stereotype of that class, the so-called 'representativeness heuristic'. (For example, when asked to estimate the probability that a person described as shy, helpful, tidy ... is a librarian, subjects systematically give high answers—apparently explained by the fact that the described person resembles to a high degree the stereotypical librarian.)

This only underlines the point that strength-of-resemblance is not probability—in fact, the use of this very heuristic goes a long way to explaining why people's intuitions about genuine probability are so poor. For instance, unlike genuine probability, strength-of-resemblance is insensitive to so-called 'base rates', the prior probabilities of the classes in question. (The fact that librarianship is a relatively improbable profession for a randomly selected member of the population seems not to diminish at all the subjects' probability judgement that the person described is a librarian, when in fact it should.) But we should not be overly critical of Hume's usage of the word 'probability' here. After all, Hume is in large part concerned with the psychological forces that operate on us when we come to form probabilistic judgements. And on this point I submit that Hume has to a great extent anticipated Kahneman and Tversky's findings.

Be that as it may, I think Hume's position will sound better to the modern philosopher's ear if I say it this way:[11] We represent a rational person's overall state of opinion with a probability function. That function is arrived at by a complex process that involves prior opinions, modified by the influx of evidence. Hume stresses the importance of analogies as determinants of that function. Up to a point, this is familiar enough even to those of us ignorant of Kahneman and Tversky's findings—witness the importance of symmetry considerations in the calculation of probabilities (like the lottery example), and symmetry and analogy go hand-in-hand. But Hume's associationist psychology has a distinctive role for the effect of analogy on opinion. You have witnessed A's constantly followed by B's in the past. You see an A now. How strongly should you expect C, some new event, to follow—that is, how probable should you regard C? According to Hume, it depends on how analogous C is to the B's. Weaken the analogy, and you lower the probability. And when it comes to miracles, the probability gets lowered all the way.

V. FURTHER CHARGES

We must assess whether the notion of 'analogical probability' can bear the burden that the miracles argument seems to require of it.

Here is a source of suspicion that it cannot. It appears that the miracles argument can be all too easily rewritten so as to give an 'epistemological' solution to the problem of induction. Hume challenged us to justify our belief that the future will resemble the past. But what is medicine for miracles is equally medicine for violations of induction. So we could reply to Hume's challenge: to be sure, the future may *not* resemble the past; but it would never be rational for us to *believe* this to be the case. Suppose, for example, that it appeared to me as if bread failed to nourish me. There is absolutely uniform experience—as compelling a 'proof' from experience as can possibly be imagined—against this really being the case. On the other hand, I have been fooled by appearances in the past, so the 'proof' from experience against my being mistaken is less compelling. Hence, I should not believe that this violation of induction has actually taken place. And so it is with other putative violations of induction. (This recalls my earlier discussion of how Hume could have strengthened his conclusion to cover even the 'testimony' of one's own senses to a miracle.) Put in terms of analogical probabilities: A particular violation of induction

[11] Here I depart from Dorothy Coleman's (2001) reading of analogical probability as being a sense of probability in its own right.

does not resemble anything in my past experience, whereas a deceptive appearance does, so the analogical probability of the former is smaller than the analogical probability of the latter—whence Hume's balancing principle does the rest. There's a quick solution to the problem of induction for you—a little too quick.

In any case, Goodman (1954) taught us that the notion of 'resemblance to the past' is problematic to say the least. He famously wrote: 'Regularities are where you find them, and you can find them anywhere' (82). A corollary to that is that analogies are where you find them, and you can find them anywhere. The Eiffel Tower and my left shoe resemble each other in being terrestrial objects, in being artfacts, in being smaller than a pulsar but bigger than a quark, in being spatio-temporally connected to me, and so on. And while commonsense undoubtedly tells us that certain respects of similarity are more salient than others, this is highly context dependent; yet Hume's argument purports to be quite general, and thus context independent. By focusing on certain respects of similarity at the expense of others, very familiar events can be regarded as disanalogous to past events (for example, focus on the times of the events in question). Conversely, by focusing on certain respects of similarity at the expense of others, putative miracles can be regarded as analogous to past events—they occur in space and time, they are visible on Earth, they are the result of some agent's action, and so on. Perhaps some brand of anti-nominalism (such as an appeal to universals, or 'natural' properties and relations) could support the claim that analogy is not just in the eye of the beholder; but that is an injection of metaphysics that would sit somewhat uncomfortably with Hume's empiricism. And some miracles bear significant natural resemblance to non-miracles: arguably, a person walking through a wall is significantly analogous to an electron passing through a tin foil. Indeed, all miracles had better bear at least *some* natural resemblance to our ordinary experience—otherwise, like a Jackson Pollock painting, we could not even make sense of them.

Or perhaps Hume could appeal to the distinctions drawn by science: we could regard a property or relation as 'natural' if it is recognized in our best scientific theories. But this only brings me to another problem for Hume's argument. Let us set aside the considerations just mentioned, and grant Hume that miracles bear no analogy to anything in our past experience. The trouble is that this is true to the same extent of other events as well. Science tells us that there are events that happen so rarely that they have not yet fallen under our experience—certain astronomical phenomena, for example. And other new phenomena may be quite commonplace, and yet have gone unnoticed—this was once true of the effects of magnetism, for instance, and more recently of various quantum mechanical phenomena—and indeed it is one of science's tasks to discover them. Put simply, if miracles get vanishingly small probability because they are so disanalogous to our past experience, then so should these events. However, Hume would hardly want us to remain sceptical about all such scientific findings.

To sum up: there is nothing wrong with Hume's balancing principle (in the 'only if' direction that he needs for his argument). There *is* something wrong with Hume's claims about the magnitudes of the probabilities being balanced. He surmises that the probability of a miracle's occurrence must always be vanishingly small—in particular, always smaller than the probability of falsehood of the testimony to that miracle. He believes that miracles are rendered so improbable because they are utterly disanalogous to anything that we have experienced. I have argued that this will cut no ice with a person who has high prior probabilities for God's intervening in the world in various ways. Furthermore, even granting him his somewhat problematic notion of 'strength-of-analogy', whether or not miracles count as analogous to familiar events will depend on which respects of analogy are focused upon. In any case, if strength-of-analogy is such a crucial determinant of a reasonable person's probability function, then that person should also be a sceptic about all spectacular scientific discoveries. And that is absurd.

REFERENCES

Armstrong, D. M., *What is a Law of Nature?* (Cambridge: Cambridge University Press, 1983).

Brown, Colin, *Miracles and the Critical Mind* (Grand Rapids, MI: Eerdmans Publishing Co., 1984).

Burns, R. M., *The Great Debate on Miracles: From Glanville to David Hume* (Lewisburg, PA: Bucknell University Press, 1981).

Butler, Joseph, *The Analogy of Religion* (Frederick Ungar Publishing Co., 1961). Originally published as *The Analogy of Religion, Natural and Revealed, to the Constitution and Course of Nature* (Philadelphia: Lippecott, 1736).

Coleman, Dorothy P., 'Hume, Miracles and Lotteries', *Hume Studies* (1989), pp. 328–46.

—— 'Baconian Probability and Hume's Theory of Testimony', *Hume Studies* 27/2 (Nov. 2001): 195–226.

Flew, Antony, introduction to Hume (1985).

Goodman, Nelson, *Fact, Fiction and Forecast* (Harvard University Press, 1954); 4th edn. 1983.

Hájek, Alan, 'In Defense of Hume's Balancing of Probabilities in the Miracles Argument', *Southwest Philosophy Review* 11/1 (January 1995): 111–18.

Hambourger, Robert, 'Belief in Miracles and Hume's Essay', *Nous* 14 (1980): 587–604.

Hume, David, *Enquiries Concerning the Human Understanding and Concerning the Principles of Morals*, ed. L. A. Selby-Bigge (Oxford: Clarendon Press,

2nd edn. 1902). (*An Enquiry Concerning Human Understanding* originally published 1748.)

—— *A Treatise of Human Nature*, ed. L. A. Selby-Bigge, 2nd edn. (Oxford: Clarendon Press, 1975). (Originally published 1739–40.)

—— *Dialogues Concerning Natural Religion* (London; New York: Dover Publications, 2006). (Originally published 1779.)

—— *Of Miracles* (Chicago, IL: Open Court Classics, 1985).

Kahneman, Daniel and Amos Tversky, 'On the Psychology of Prediction', *Psychological Review* 80 (1973): 237–51.

—— 'Judgment Under Uncertainty: Heuristics and Biases', in *Judgment Under Uncertainty: Heuristics and Biases*, ed. Daniel Kahneman, Paul Slovic and Amos Tversky (Cambridge University Press, 1982).

Langtry, Bruce, 'The Use of Probability Theory in Some Recent Defences of Hume on Miracles', Preprint 1/89, Department of Philosophy, University of Melbourne, June 1989.

Levine, Michael, *Hume and the Problem of Miracles: a Solution* (Dordrecht, Holland: Kluwer, 1989).

Lewis, David, 'Radical Interpretation', *Synthese* 27 (1974): 331–44; reprinted in *Philosophical Papers*, Vol 1 (New York and Oxford: Oxford University Press, 1983).

Mackie, J. L., *The Miracle of Theism* (Oxford: Oxford University Press, 1982).

Price, Richard, 'Dissertation IV on the Importance of Christianity, the Nature of Historical Evidence, and Miracles,' in *Four Dissertations*, 5th edn. 1811.

Sorensen, Roy, *Blindspots* (Oxford: Oxford University Press, 1988).

Tooley, Michael, *Causation, a Realist Approach* (Oxford: Clarendon Press, 1987).

van Fraassen, Bas, *Laws and Symmetry* (Oxford: Oxford University Press, 1989).

Wittgenstein, Ludwig, 'A Lecture on Ethics', *Philosophical Review* 74 (1965): 3–12.

5

Epistemological Foundations for the Cosmological Argument

Robert Koons

I. INTRODUCTION

The cosmological argument—the argument from contingency to the existence of a necessary First Cause—forms the core of a long-standing research programme in philosophical theology. Even if such theistic arguments are, as Plantinga has demonstrated, unnecessary for the reasonableness of theistic belief, a successful proof would by all accounts have considerable significance. The cosmological argument has in recent years garnered considerable respect, both from theists and agnostics. However, the central assumption of that argument, a principle of sufficient reason or general causation, has failed to win universal acceptance. A recent book by Alexander Pruss (2006a), *The Principle of Sufficient Reason*, has addressed this question with a number of ingenious appeals to our metaphysical intuitions. In this paper, I will attempt to complement Pruss's efforts through an appeal to epistemology.

In the early modern period (from Descartes through Kant, at least), the epistemological need for a principle of general causation was a commonplace. However, the collapse of Cartesian foundationalism in the first half of the twentieth century resulted in a general neglect of the role of such a causal principle in accounting for our empirical knowledge. I will not argue for a return to Cartesian assumptions: I accept a broadly common-sense, Reidian or Moorean approach to epistemology. However, I will argue that the need to secure knowledge against the possibility of undermining defeaters leads to the restoration of the principle of general causation to an exalted status in epistemology.

Any plausible principle of general causation must fall short of absolute universality. If everything must have a cause, then this would apply to the whole of reality, including the supposed First Cause itself. A coherent principle must admit of exceptions. However, not all exceptions are equal in respect of their epistemological implications. I will argue that any exception to the principle of general causation that is narrow enough to avoid a collapse into global scepticism about empirical knowledge is also narrow enough to permit the construction of a successful proof of God's existence (in something like the classical Anselmian and Thomistic sense of 'God').

Quite a few defenders of theism (Augustine, Anselm, Descartes, Chesterton, C. S. Lewis, Plantinga), have claimed that a theistic metaphysic affords an unusually coherent foundation for epistemology. It is no mystery to theists that human cognitive capacities are well designed for the task of acquiring truth, including both a priori and a posteriori capacities. However, the high ontological price of theism has seemed to many to be too high a price to pay for the admitted virtues of theistic epistemology. I will attempt here to make a necessity of virtue.

II. COSMOLOGICAL (FIRST-CAUSE) ARGUMENTS

The cosmological, first-cause argument has, of course, a long history, appearing in the work of Plato, Aristotle, Plotinus, al-Farabi, ibn Sina, Aquinas, Scotus, Leibniz and many others. In the latter half of the twentieth century, it has experienced something of a renaissance among analytically oriented philosophers of religion (Reichenbach 1972; Rowe 1975; O'Connor 1993; Pruss and Gale 1999; Pruss 1998). I have written three times on the subject (1997, 2000, 2001), relying on a version of the argument developed by ibn Sina and Leibniz, in which there is no assumption that infinite causal regresses are impossible, but in which instead there is the assumption that the causal principle applies to arbitrary aggregations of wholly contingent events and situations. The aggregation principle enables us to assert the existence of the Cosmos (the aggregate of all wholly contingent situations). I was able to prove, using standard modal logic and the calculus of mereology, that the Cosmos, so defined, is itself a wholly contingent situation. The cause of the Cosmos must be wholly separate from the Cosmos itself and so must consist entirely of necessarily existent situations.

The formal framework I employed in 'A New Look at the Cosmological Argument' (1997) was a modal logic supplemented by the Leoniewski–Goodman–Leonard calculus of individuals ('mereology') (Leonard and Goodman 1940). By way of pure modal logic, I needed only the axioms and rules of T.

Axiom 1 *x is a part of y iff everything that overlaps x also overlaps y.*
Axiom 2 *If there are any φ's, then there exists a sum of all the φ's. For any x, x overlaps this sum iff x overlaps one of the φ's.*
Axiom 3 *x = y iff x is a part of y and y is a part of x.*

Axiom 1 defines the part-of relation in terms of overlap, and Axiom 2 is an aggregation or fusion principle: if there are any situations of type φ, then there is an aggregate or sum of all the φ situations. Axiom 3 guarantees that the part-of relation is reflexive and anti-symmetric.

We need some sort of term as a name for the relata of causation. I have chosen the relatively neutral word *situation* to fill this role. Situations are worldly, coarse-grained states of affairs. Events and states are species of situations. I assume that we can meaningfully quantify over a domain of possible situations, some of which have actuality or actual existence. I also assume that situations can have other situations as proper parts, in such a way that standard mereology can apply. I require two axioms that combine modality and mereology. Axiom 4 asserts mereological essentialism with respect to situations: a situation has its parts essentially, in the sense that a situation cannot be actual without all its parts also being actual. Moreover, an aggregation of situations is nothing over and above its parts: if all of the part of such a sum are actual, so is the sum itself.

Axiom 4 *Situations necessitate the actual existence of their parts.*
Axiom 5 *The actual existence of all the members of a sum necessitates the actual existence of the sum.*

Only three axioms about causation itself are required: the actuality of the relata of actual causation (Axiom 6), a Humean principle of the separate existence of cause and effect (Axiom 7), and a principle of general causation (Axiom 8). A situation is *wholly contingent* iff it has no parts that are necessary.

Axiom 6 *Causation is a binary relation between (actually existing) situations.*
Axiom 7 *Causes and effects do not overlap (have no parts in common).*
Axiom 8 *For any given wholly contingent situation x, there is a (defeasible) presumption that x has a cause.*

From these axioms, I was able to prove the following theorem (employing a defeasible or nonmonotonic logic):

Theorem 1 *If there are any contingently existing situations, then there is a necessarily existing situation that is the cause of the Cosmos (the sum of all wholly contingent situations).*

Of course, there is evidently a significant gap between proving the existence of such a necessary First Cause and proving the existence of God. Much of Aquinas' *Summa Contra Gentiles* is devoted to bridging that gap (Kretzmann 1997), and I made some further suggestions in 'A New Look'. (See also Tim O'Connor's very interesting piece on Scotus' efforts to move from First Cause to God (1996), as well as a recent paper by Jerome Gellman (2000).) Interestingly, the overwhelming majority of objections to the cosmological proof have targeted the principle of general causation (Axiom 8) rather than the various assumptions needed to get from Theorem 1 to the existence of God.

III. RESTRICTIONS ON THE PRINCIPLE OF GENERAL CAUSATION: THE NEED AND THE CANDIDATES

As I mentioned in the introduction, an axiom asserting the existence of a cause of every actual situation is incompatible (in the presence of Axioms 1–7) with the existence of any actual situations. If there were any actual situations, there would be a maximal situation, Reality, that was the aggregate of all actual situations.[1] Reality would have to have a cause, which would have to be both actual (Axiom 6) and wholly separate from Reality (Axiom 7), a conclusion that is inconsistent with the definition of Reality.

Therefore, the principle of general causation must be restricted. But how? Here is a list of six possible candidates that have been proposed or could plausibly be proposed by non-theists:

1. All non-first situations have causes (Graham Oppy 1989). A situations has *non-firstness* just in case there is an actual situations wholly located at an earlier time than it is.
2. All situations with finite temporal duration have causes.
3. All situations that don't occur at a first moment of time have causes.
4. All situations that don't include infinite causal regresses have causes.
5. All situations that aren't both extremely simple and cosmic in scale have causes.
6. All situations that could (*de re*) be caused have causes.

---

[1] If we suppose that mereological universalism about situations is false, there might not be any such aggregate. However, we would still have to restrict the principle of causation, in the sense that we would have to deny that every plurality of situations have (collectively) a separate cause.

Each of these would block the derivation of the existence of a necessary first cause. The first was proposed by Graham Oppy (1999). The second, third and fourth could be gleaned from Hume's *Dialogues*. The fifth is close to what Quentin Smith (1997) has proposed. Each of these is clearly compatible with a fully contingent and finite cause of the universe's present existence. The sixth version (suggested by Alex Pruss (2006b)) is also compatible with a wholly contingent cause, since it is plausible (on Kripkean grounds) to think that *any* uncaused situation is uncaused of necessity (*de re*).

The crucial question is this: what are the implications of these and all similar exceptions for empirical epistemology? I will argue that all of these lead inevitably to global scepticism.

IV. THE FALL AND RISE OF THE NOTION OF CAUSE

With the resurgence of a Humean empiricism in the first part of the twentieth century came typically Humean doubts about the legitimacy of the notion of *cause*. In fact, these doubts went further even than Hume had taken them, reaching to the question of the indispensability and even the usefulness of the notion. The causation's fortunes reached their nadir with the publication of Bertrand Russell's (1913) classic paper, 'On the Notion of Cause', in which the idea of causation was compared with that of the hereditary monarchy: on outmoded idea that had survived only because it was (wrongly) believed to do no harm.

The notion of causation has experienced a remarkable resurgence in vigour since then, triggered by Edmund Gettier's (1963) refutation of the justified true belief theory of knowledge. As epistemologists have responded to Gettier's challenge, they have found the assertion of a causal element to knowledge to be unavoidable. Reliabilists, proper-function theorists and other contemporary contenders agree in supposing there to be some sort of causal connection between a state of knowledge and the state of the world that is known thereby, at least in the case of empirical or a posteriori knowledge.

Russell had argued that modern science no longer requires the notion of cause, because its work can be taken over entirely by the functional laws of physics that constrain the evolution of systems over time. However, we have excellent reason to believe that there is no such substitute for causation in accounting for our empirical knowledge. All of the laws of physics (with the possible exception of the decay of the insignificant kaon particle) are time-reversible. The direction of time seems to depend on purely statistical factors (the increase in entropy) that depend on contingent features of the initial conditions of the universe (or of our *branch* of the universe). This fact has profound implications for our knowledge of the past. The apparent history of the world that presents itself to us in memory, testimony and physical traces is a highly improbable one (involving extraordinarily low entropy). As Huw Price (1996: 34–6) has observed, it is far more likely, given the time-reversible laws of physics, that the present state of our memories and traces emerged spontaneously from a high-entropy precursor than that they faithfully represent the world's history.[2] Thus, if we were, even implicitly, relying on the retrodiction of the past on the basis of physical laws alone, we would be forced to reject all of our memories as non-veridical.

If we are to avoid global scepticism about the past, we must be justified in taking our memories at face value, despite the physical improbability of the world they represent to us. We must approach our memories with a Reidian or Moorean presumption as to their accuracy, treating them as innocent until proven guilty. However, this common sense approach to knowledge of the past brings with it a commitment to causation, since it is part of our common-sense view that our memories are reliable *because* they have been caused, in the right way, by the situations they represent. A realist epistemology of the past carries a tacit commitment to certain causal generalizations about the production of human memories and other traces.

V. TWO POSSIBLE CONNECTIONS BETWEEN CAUSATION AND EMPIRICAL KNOWLEDGE

Alvin Plantinga's proper-function epistemology could be summarized by the assertion that there are at least four necessary conditions for knowledge: a state of knowing *p* must be:

1. a true belief that *p*,
2. formed by cognitive processes that are functioning normally, and in circumstances for which they were designed,
3. formed by cognitive processes that have the proper function of producing and sustaining true beliefs, and
4. immune to internal defeaters.

This Plantingan account seems to be fundamentally sound, at least as a good first approximation (Plantinga 1993). Given this account of knowledge,

---

[2] This is true, almost by definition, since states with lower entropy are more improbable, and by positing a still lower entropy in the past, we would be merely digging ourselves deeper into a thermodynamic hole.

there are two ways in which a principle of general causation could be connected to the possibility of empirical knowledge: (i) as an objective fact needed as the ground for the reliability of our cognitive processes, and (ii) as a subjectively required presumption needed for immunity to internal defeaters. Let's explore each of these in turn.

Suppose that there were a significant probability that any one of our empirical beliefs occur without cause, or that some of the states that intermediate between our beliefs and their objects so occur. In such a world, the occurrence of those belief states would not reliably indicate their truth, since the occurrence of an uncaused state would be probabilistically independent of the occurrence of those states which might have caused it.[3]

I would like to introduce here the term 'knowledge-net' for the sake of simpler exposition. A person's knowledge-net consists of all of his[4] belief-states, together with their objects and those states, if any, that both cause one of those belief-states and intermediate causally between it and its object (or between it and the common cause of it and its object). For example, if S has perceptual knowledge of the fact that p by vision, then S's knowledge-net includes his belief that p, the fact that p, and those states that are causally intermediate between these two, such as the reflection of light by the objects involved in the fact that p, the transmission of that light to S's eyes, the occurrence of nerve signals between S's retina and brain, and S's visual impressions as of the truth of p.

S's actual knowledge-net is a part of the actual world that varies from one possible world to another. In order for S to have empirical knowledge, it must be that a principle of general causation applies with high probability to the situations that make up S's knowledge-net. For this fact of high probability to be knowledge-enabling, it must not be merely accidental or coincidental that nearly all the situations in S's knowledge-net are caused. Therefore, it must be at least nomologically necessary (if not metaphysically necessary) that situations of the kinds making up S's actual knowledge-net be caused, i.e., nomologically impossible for situations of those kinds to occur without a cause.

However, although there must be something like a law of nature guaranteeing that the scope of causation include nearly everything in S's knowledge-net, and this law of nature must apply to those situations

---

[3] My argument is intended to be entirely neutral between the various competing metaphysical accounts of the nature of causation, whether nomological-deductive, regularity-based, counterfactual, singularist or what have you. It may be that the conclusion of the argument will have significant implications for the metaphysics of causation (indeed, I am quite certain this is so), but I am being careful not to beg any such questions in the setup of the argument itself.

[4] For the sake of simplicity, I use the generic masculine pronoun throughout.

non-accidentally, it could be that the law applies to those situations by virtue of some feature that is essential to *S* as a particular individual: that is, the applicability of the principle of causation to *S*'s knowledge-net could well turn on features of that net that are necessary *de re* of *S* himself. Since it is not at all obvious what features might be necessary *de re* of *S*, it is difficult to know what exactly the scope of causation must be in order for *S* to be *de re* reliable with respect to the formation of his beliefs.

There is, however, a second possible connection to explore: the need for immunity to *internal* defeat, in the form of a justified presumption of a principle of general causation. This, I will argue, is a much more promising route to take.

VI. IMMUNITY TO DEFEAT AS A NECESSARY CONDITION FOR KNOWLEDGE

VI.1. What are internal defeaters?

A *defeater* is a proposition belief in which rationally *defeats* one's grounds for believing another proposition. The notion of a defeater was introduced to epistemology by Roderick Chisholm and plays a central role in the epistemologies of John Pollock (1987) and Alvin Plantinga (1993). In this section I will give my own account of defeaters, drawing heavily on Plantinga's discussion in *Warrant and Proper Function*.

First, following Pollock, we can distinguish two kinds of defeaters: rebutting and undercutting. A rebutting defeater for a belief that *p* constitutes grounds for believing *p* to be false; and undercutting defeater does not do so but instead provides grounds for believing that one's prima facie reasons for believing that *p* are epistemically faulty.

Definition 1 *A proposition q is a* rebutting defeater *of proposition p for S iff S believes q and q provides S with adequate grounds against judging that p is false, even when combined with S's evidence for p.*

Definition 2 *A proposition q is an* undercutting defeater *of proposition p for agent S iff S believes q and q provides S with adequate grounds for judging that it is not highly likely that the processes that led to his*[5] *disposition to believe p are warrant conferring.*

As Pollock and Plantinga observe, defeaters can themselves be defeated. I will call a defeater defeater a *neutralizing* defeater:

---

[5] I follow Castenada's convention of adding an asterisk to pronouns corresponding to *de se* belief.

Definition 3 *A proposition q is a* neutralizing defeater *of q in relation to p for S iff S believes r and q, q is a defeater of p for S, and (r&q) is not a defeater of p for S.*

To ignore the epistemic upshot of one's defeaters is itself a serious cognitive malfunction. Evidently, our *design plan* (insofar as that plan is aimed simply at truth) includes an unvarying disposition to give up beliefs that one knows have been defeated, unless one knows that those defeaters have themselves been neutralized by further beliefs. Respect for rebutting defeaters embodies a kind of principle of total evidence: one must not form beliefs based on an arbitrarily selective consideration of available evidence.

Respect for undercutting defeaters embodies a commitment to good probabilistic reasoning and a refusal to rely blindly on a supposition of sheer good luck. There is a kind of probabilistic incoherency in believing both that p and that there is a low objective probability that one's belief that p is true. Rationality demands a match between one's lower-order and higher-order probabilistic judgements; a match that Brian Skyrms (1984: 23) labelled *Miller's principle*. Following Miller's principle involves transcending an unjustified egocentricity, treating oneself as a typical member of one's kind (in the absence of evidence to the contrary). Since internal justification is such an important part of our cognitive design plan and the respect for defeaters an important aspect of internal justification, knowledge is impossible in the presence of unneutralized defeaters.

Proposition 1 *S knows that p only if every rebutting or undercutting defeaters of p for S is neutralized for S.*

VI.2. Why immunity to defeat is needed

However, knowledge requires more than merely the absence of actual defeaters. One must be in a state of belief that is in certain respects *immune* to defeat. If S believes that p merely because he has not inferred certain propositions that one would be fully justified in inferring, then S's continuing to believe p is simply a matter of dumb luck, which is incompatible with knowledge. Moreover, one must be, at least to some extent, resistant to misinformation and misleading suggestions that would undermine one's internal justification. If the mere suggestion that S might not be warranted would be sufficient to defeat his belief that p, then S's belief that p doesn't have the kind of stability and robustness that is required for knowledge.

Proposition 2 *S knows that p only if S is in a position to believe that p with internal justification.*

Proposition 3 *S is in a position to believe with internal justification that p only if S is in a position to believe with internal justification that it is very unlikely* *that q is true, for every available q that would, if believed, be an unneutralized undercutting defeater for S of p.*

In particular, in order to know that p, one must be in a position to disbelieve with justification any possible *undercutting* defeater of *p*. As Plantinga has argued, the warrant for one's belief that *p* is undercut if the probability that one's belief that *p* is warranted is either low or *inscrutable*. If a reasonable doubt about the epistemic status of one's belief that *p* can be raised, and one is not in a position to judge with reason that the probability of a failure of warrant is low, one would be unjustified to persist in believing that *p*. Suppose, to use Plantinga's example, that one has conflicting evidence that is hard to assess concerning whether or not the lighting on the widget factory floor is tinted. Even in the absence of positive belief that the lighting is tinted, one's putative knowledge about the colour of the pink-looking widgets is undercut so long as one cannot justifiably assign a low probability to the condition of abnormal lighting.

By *being in a position* to believe *p* with justification, I mean that one can arrive (through the competent exercise of one's inferential capacities) in a stable noetic state in which one believes that *p* and in which one has access to exactly the same evidence as one has in one's actual noetic state. The *noetic state* of a person includes everything about him that is relevant to the internal justification of his beliefs: what the person believes, together with all of the relevant perceptual and mnemonic appearances. A noetic state is *stable* it contains no beliefs that would be defeated by further competent ratiocination.

Proposition 4 *S is in a position to believe with internal justification that p only if S is in a position to believe with internal justification that it is highly likely that his* belief that p is warranted.*

This proposition doesn't give us closure of knowledge under the necessary-condition relation. If one knows that *p* and the fact that *q* is a necessary condition of one's knowing that *p*, it does not follow that one knows that *q*. I can know that I am seeing a chair without knowing that I'm not a brain in a vat, even if my knowing that I'm seeing a chair implies that I'm not a brain in a vat.

The immunity-to-defeat condition also falls short of what Timothy Williamson (2000) labelled the *KK* principle, and it does so in three ways: (i) actual belief is not required: one must merely be in a position to believe something; (ii) it is not necessary that one be in a position to *know* anything but merely to be justified in believing it; and (iii) what one must be in a position to believe is not that one is warranted, but only that it is *highly likely* that one is warranted.

Thus, it's enough if I can rationally assign a very low probability to the failure of a necessary condition of knowledge. Thus, to know that I am seeing a chair, I must be in a position to judge it very unlikely that I'm a brain in a vat. I needn't *know*, or even believe, that I'm not. The probabilities involved are subjective in nature but correspond to the probability judgements of an ideal, rational agent. In order to be in a position to believe that there is a high probability that I am not a brain in a vat, I must believe that the world has been so constituted as to make the objective probability of my having become a brain in a vat quite low. Otherwise, the possibility that I might be a brain in a vat would have an inscrutable probability, and so would be a successful undercutting defeater.

In the case of empirical knowledge, one must be justified in believing that there is a high objective probability that any of the situations making up one's knowledge-net—one's belief-states that constitute ordinary empirical knowledge and any of the epistemically mediating events (events belonging to the causal chain that connects those belief-states with their objects, or to the common cause of the states and their objects)—are caused in an epistemically appropriate, normal way. Let's call the set of S's beliefs about his* knowledge-net S's *conception* of his* knowledge-net. Here we encounter another paradox: the richer and more detailed is S's conception of his* knowledge-net, the greater is his potential vulnerability to undercutting defeaters.

VI.3. Strong vs. weak a priori justification

There are at least two categories of beliefs that must be distinguished from our ordinary empirical beliefs: beliefs that are justified in a *strongly a priori* way, and self-verifying beliefs.

There are, in turn, two kinds of a priori justification: weak and strong. Weak a priori justification requires the occurrence of a certain kind of non-sensual experience: a cognitive or intuitive experience, in which a proposition somehow presents itself to the mind as apparently true, or a felt inclination, by which holding the belief in question seems natural or normal. In contrast, a belief is justified in a strongly a priori way if the belief is justified without reference to any kind of experience or inclination whatsoever, whether sensual or purely intellectual.

Weakly a priori knowledge would seem to be subject to undercutting defeat along lines very similar to those that pertain to ordinary empirical beliefs. If I were to believe that one of my beliefs that I took to be justified in a weakly a priori way was actually uncaused, or that the cognitive experience or inclination on which that belief was based was uncaused, this would seem to constitute an undercutting defeater. This would apply also to those beliefs that are justified because we have a natural inclination to have them, of the kind that Thomas Reid described. If, in my estimation, this inclination to believe flows not from a human nature designed by God or by natural selection to grasp the truth reliably but is simply uncaused, then I would have a defeater for the Reidian justification of such a belief. In the case of intellectual experience, it may be unclear how exactly our intellectual intuitions are connected to the situations which are their subject matter, but it seems clear that an uncaused intuition has not been formed in a normal or reliable way. Hence, it is only the *strongly* a priori beliefs that are intrinsically immune to such defeat.

VI.4. Self-verifying beliefs

There is another category of belief intrinsically immune to defeat through doubts about the scope of causation: self-verifying beliefs. A belief is self-verifying if its occurrence satisfies its own truth-conditions (like believing that I am believing something). I will also exclude beliefs that are causally upstream of their truth-conditions, such as beliefs about what I will do or ought to do. It seems plausible to suppose that I can know what I will do without making any assumptions about the causes of that belief, so long as I believe that it will have its usual effects.

Beliefs about one's current phenomenal state or about the contents of one's current thoughts fall into a similar category. It's reasonable to suppose that these beliefs in some way incorporate their objects, in such a way that the belief-state as a whole includes the truthmaker for the proposition believed. Such reflective, introspective beliefs are thus also immune to defeat due to doubts about their causes.

VI.5. The principal argument

To summarize what I have claimed so far, ordinary empirical knowledge is subject to the condition that it be immune to undercutting defeaters. In particular, we must be in a position to believe that it is highly likely that our ordinary empirical knowledge is caused, and this latter belief must not depend for its justification on the empirical knowledge whose causal status is in question. If such circular immunity were allowed, few empirical beliefs would ever be vulnerable to undercutting defeaters, since we could always appeal to the belief itself, along with similar beliefs, to justify a belief in the reliability of the process leading to it. For example, to return to the widget factory, if circularity were permitted, I could justify my belief that my perceptual beliefs were reliably (and therefore probably normally) caused by simply relying on my perceptually formed beliefs in the pinkness of the observed widgets to verify that my perceptually formed beliefs about the widgets are all true. To avoid such vicious circularity, we must posit a kind of asymmetric dependence between the actual justification of an empirical belief and the potential justification of a hypothetical belief in its probable warrant.

This asymmetric dependency relation should not be confused with a different, distinct relation: that of believing one proposition *on the basis of* one's belief in another proposition, *inferring* one belief from another, or, conversely, one belief's providing one with *evidence* for a second belief. However, we should not assume that this evidential/inferential relation is the only form of justification-dependency. Providing immunity to defeat is a distinct form of dependency.

Proposition 5 *If S's belief that p is not strongly a priori justified or self-verifying (i.e., if S's belief that p is an* ordinary empirical belief), *then S is in a position to believe with internal justification that p only if S is potentially in a position to believe with internal justification that it is highly probable that his* belief in p is warranted (formed by a normal and alethically reliable process), and in such a way that S's belief that p would depend for its internal justification on the justification of the latter belief.*

Proposition 6 *It is evident that (with the possible exception of strongly a priori justified beliefs and self-verifying beliefs) any belief that is uncaused or whose epistemic grounds are uncaused is not warranted (because such a belief is not then formed by a normal or alethically reliable process). Moreover, the proposition that some or all of his* beliefs are uncaused is available to S.*

Lemma 1 *If S's belief that p is an ordinary empirical belief, then: S knows that p only if S is in a position to believe with internal justification that it is highly probable that his* belief in p and its grounds are caused, and in such a way that S's belief that p would depend for its justification on the justification for the latter belief.*

Because both the evidence available to us and our inferential capacities are finite, there can be no infinite regresses involving the justification relation between potential beliefs. Moreover, the justification relation is transitive and irreflexive, ruling out any justificatory circles.

Proposition 7 *Let R be a relation whose range is the set of propositions belief in which S is in a position to be internally justified in having, and let R hold between two propositions p and q just in case S is potentially in a position to be in a noetic state in which S's belief that p depended for its internal justification on S's belief that q. Then R is a partial well-ordering (well-founded, transitive and irreflexive).*

Arguably, proposition 6 is too strong, since it may be that the justificatory relationship between two potential beliefs (say, a belief that p and a belief that q) might be indeterminate, in that there could be two stable noetic states available to S, n and n', of such a kind that p depends on q in n, and q depends on p in n'. However, I am confident that the following lemma (Lemma 2) would still follow from a suitably weakened version of proposition 6. Proposition 6 could be reformulated in terms of the dependency relation that holds within each noetic state available to S. Even if S could muster some empirical evidence for the thesis that his* belief that p and its grounds are caused, those empirical beliefs would themselves require further beliefs about their causal history in order to secure their immunity from defeat. Eventually, S's empirical resources must be exhausted, culminating in beliefs whose immunity from defeat is intrinsic (i.e., either self-verifying or strongly a priori justified beliefs).

Thus, since an ordinary empirical belief always depends on the potential justification of belief in the causation of that belief, and since the justification relation on such beliefs and potential beliefs is well-founded and asymmetric, it follows that empirical knowledge must rest ultimately on a belief in the scope of causation that is intrinsically immune to defeat involving doubts about causation, that is, on a belief that is not itself an ordinary empirical belief.

Lemma 2 *If S's belief that p is an ordinary empirical belief, then: S knows that p only if there is a noetic state n and a proposition q of such a kind that (i) S is in a position to be in n, (ii) in state n, S's belief that p depended for its internal justification on S's belief that it is highly likely that his* belief that q is caused, and (iii) this latter belief would not depend for its internal justification on any ordinary empirical belief of S's.*

However, the range of possible self-verifying beliefs is too limited to provide the relevant sort of beliefs about causation. Hence, ordinary empirical knowledge depends on the potentiality of strongly a priori justified beliefs in the causation of one's knowledge-net.

Proposition 8 *There is no noetic state n and proposition p such that S is in a position to be in state n and, in state n, S would believe that it is highly likely that his* ordinary empirical belief that p and its grounds are caused, and this latter belief would depend for its internal justification on any non-belief (i.e., perceptual or mnemonic state) or any self-verifying belief.*

By process of elimination, since S's belief that his* ordinary belief that p and its grounds are likely to be caused cannot be supported by any of S's ordinary empirical beliefs, any of his self-verifying beliefs, or any of his epistemically relevant non-beliefs, S must be strongly a priori justified in believing that it very likely that this belief and its grounds are caused.

Lemma 3 *If S's belief that p is an ordinary empirical belief, then: S knows that p only if there is a proposition q such that S is potentially in a position to be SAP (strongly a priori) justified in believing that his* ordinary empirical belief that q is caused, and in believing that the epistemic grounds of his* belief that q are also very likely to be caused.*

It is implausible to suppose that one could be SAP justified in believing something about the likely causal history of some ordinary empirical beliefs but not others. SAP justified immunity to undercutting defeat will either extend to the whole of S's knowledge-net or to nothing at all. A SAP justified belief is one whose content is a necessarily true proposition[6] belief in which is constitutive of rationality, in the sense that it is a necessary condition of any ordinary empirical knowledge of the kind possessed by human beings. Such SAP justified beliefs must be suitably general in scope, embracing all possible items of human knowledge.

Proposition 9 *Necessarily, if S's belief that p is an ordinary empirical belief, then S is potentially in a position to be SAP justified in believing that it is highly likely that his* belief that p and its grounds are caused only if S is in a position to be SAP justified in believing that it is highly likely that any of the situations in his* empirical knowledge-net are caused.*

Even if I am wrong about this, the the scope of our a priori knowledge of causation will be essentially unaffected. Suppose that SAP justification is *particularistic*: one can be justified in believing that it is likely that this or that belief (and its grounds) are caused, but never justified in believing the corresponding generalization about all of one's knowledge-net. Since there are no a priori limits to what can be thought of, one's knowledge-net could embrace the whole of the Cosmos, in which case one would be SAP justified in believing that the Cosmos as a whole has a cause.

Lemma 4 *Necessarily, if S's belief that p is an ordinary empirical belief, then S knows that p only if S is in a position to be SAP justified in believing that it is highly likely that any of the situations in his* empirical knowledge-net (i.e., his ordinary empirical beliefs and their epistemic grounds) are caused.*

In order to be justified in believing that it is very likely that any situation of one's knowledge-net is caused, one must be able to apply some principle of general causation to a category that includes nearly all of that knowledge-net.

---

[6] Or, at least, a proposition whose truth is necessitated by the existence of human knowledge.

Definition 4 γ *is a* principle of general causation *iff* γ *takes the form: It is nomologically impossible for a situation of type T to be actual in the absence of a cause.*

For such a principle γ, T is γ's *range of application.*

In order for S to be SAP justified in believing that it is highly likely that each of the situations in his* knowledge-net is caused, there must be some type T such that S is SAP justified that every situation in his* knowledge-net belongs to T, and that the probability that a given event has a cause, conditional on its being an actual member of T, is very high. This conditional probability is high only if S can judge the probability of the disjunction of the following three conditions to be very high:

1. If a possible event e is of type T, then there is a non-negligible prior probability there actually exists a potential cause of e's occurrence.
2. If an event e is of type T, then the law-based probability of e's occurring uncaused must be much lower than the probabilistic expectation of its occurring as the result of a cause.
3. It is nomologically impossible for an event of type T to occur in the absence of a cause.

However, it is clear that there is no type that both self-evidently[7] applies to every situation in S's knowledge-net and that meets either condition 1 or condition 2. S's knowledge-net includes situations of arbitrarily low prior probability, and, therefore, the prior probability of the occurrence of a cause of a situation in that net is also arbitrarily low. Hence, the rational probability of T's meeting condition 1 must be very low. S must be justified in judging, for *each* token-situation in his knowledge-net, that the probability of *its* occurring without a cause is very low, no matter how low the prior probability is of the occurrence of that token or of its potential causes.

For the same reason, no matter how low the law-based probability of the uncaused occurrence of an event e might be (assuming that this probability is greater than zero), the probability of the occurrence of a cause of e could be lower still. Thus, condition 2 also has a vanishingly small probability of truth. It is, a priori, very unlikely that the laws of nature should be jury-rigged in such a way to make condition 2 come out as true, since this would require the probability of a token situation's uncaused occurrence being highly sensitive to the probability of the occurrence of one of its potential causes. Thus, the only way that S could be SAP justified in judging

---

[7] By *self-evident*, I mean that S is justified in believing the proposition on the basis of SAP-justified and self-verifying beliefs alone.

that the probability of the uncaused actuality of *each and every one* of the token situations in his* knowledge-net is low would be by judging the probability of condition 3 to be high.

If I'm wrong about conditions 2, then the right conclusion to reach would be that S is SAP justified in believing that his* knowledge-net falls within the range of some *qualified* principle of general causation:

Definition 5 γ *is a* qualified principle of general causation *iff γ takes the following form: The objective probabilities are of such a kind that, for every possible situation s of type T, the probability of s's occurring uncaused is* vanishingly low *(so low that, no matter how unlikely the caused occurrence of S might be according to a possible noetic state, its uncaused occurrence is much more unlikely).*

Proposition 10 S is potentially in a position to be SAP justified in believing that it is highly likely that any of the situations in his* empirical knowledge-net are caused only if S is SAP justified in believing that it is very likely that there is some type T such that (i) some principle (or qualified principle) of general causation γ holds with T as its range of application, and (ii) it is self-evident to S[8] that nearly all of the situations in his* empirical knowledge-net fall within T.

Since there are a small number of types that could meet both conditions (i) and (ii) of proposition 10, and since if types *T1, T2, ..., Tn* each individually meet the pair of conditions, so does their conjunction (since both nomological necessity and self-evident justification are closed under conjunction), we can shift the relative positions of the probability operator and the quantification over types in proposition 10, resulting in proposition 11:

Proposition 11 S is potentially in a position to be SAP justified in believing that it is highly likely that any of the situations in his* empirical knowledge-net are caused only if S is there is some type T such that S is SAP justified in believing that (i) it is very likely that it is nomologically impossible for situations of type T to be actual in the absence of a cause, and (ii) it is self-evident to S that nearly all of the situations in his* empirical knowledge-net fall within T.

From lemma 4 and proposition 11, the main result follows.

Theorem 2 If S's belief that p is an ordinary empirical belief, then S knows that p only if there is some type T such that S is SAP justified in believing that (i) it is very likely that it is nomologically impossible for situations of

---

[8] That is, S's belief is justified on the basis of a combination of self-verifying and SAP justified beliefs.

type T to be actual in the absence of a cause, and (ii) it is self-evident to S that nearly all of the situations in his* empirical knowledge-net fall within T.

VI.6. Consistency of this requirement with a Reidian, common-sense epistemology

Unlike Descartes, Hume, Kant and other early modern epistemologists, I am not assuming that strongly a priori justified beliefs are indubitable, incorrigible, or associated with any special phenomenal quality (like Descartes' clear and distinct ideas). I have argued for the claim that we are SAP justified in believing a causal principle on Moorean grounds: assuming that we do in fact have empirical knowledge, and arguing on that basis that we must be SAP justified in believing the causal principle. I have not argued that we must actually believe the causal principle in order to have empirical knowledge, merely that we must be in a position to do so with with SAP justification.

My conception of SAP justification is something like this: to be SAP justified in believing that p, the disposition to believe p must somehow be constitutive of rationality itself. That fact that it is so may itself be a kind of a posteriori discovery. Thus, I would reject the assumption that if one is SAP justified in believing that p, one must be SAP justified in believing that one is so justified.

It is surprising, to say the least, to find that there must be some SAP justified beliefs. I myself was surprised by this result: I had defended (in *Realism Regained* (2000)) the thesis that all of our knowledge, even our knowledge of the laws of logic, depended on the right kind of causal connection to the relevant facts. I now see that I was mistaken: if we have any knowledge at all, some of that knowledge must be absolutely immune to undercutting defeaters. An SAP justified belief is such that, even if I came to believe that the belief in question had been planted in my mind by a malicious Cartesian demon, I would still be rationally justified in persisting in my belief. I should, in such a case, merely conclude that the demon had, on this occasion, inadvertently supplied me with genuine knowledge.

VII. EPISTEMOLOGICALLY ACCEPTABLE EXCEPTIONS TO THE UNIVERSALITY OF CAUSATION

VII.1. Criteria for acceptability

Firstly, if one is SAP justified in believing that one's knowledge-net falls within the range of application of some PGC (principle of general causation), then it must be metaphysically necessary that any knowledge-net of any person with humanoid consciousness (one who shares with us the same sort of cognitive make-up, the same sort of self-verifying beliefs about his* own mental state, and a similar conception of his* knowledge-net) falls within that same range.

Secondly, the PGC must be crafted in such a way that it is plausible to suppose that it is *self-evident* that its range of application encompasses our knowledge-nets. Our knowledge of the past and of the extent of the universe is entirely a posteriori, as can be seen through the thought-experiment of a humanoid creature with no memories of the past, no traces or testimony of past events, and no sensory presentations or abductive evidence of spatially remote events.

Thirdly, an epistemologically acceptable PGC must be one whose range of application specifies a set of *intrinsic properties* of situations. It is highly implausible that the nomological possibility of a situation's being caused or uncaused has anything to do with that situation's extrinsic properties, including what sorts of effects it might have. Moreover, it is only the intrinsic character of our belief states (their content and associated phenomenological qualities) that are self-evident to us, and it is only the intrinsic natures of things (conferring causal powers) that can be the object of abductive inference.

Fourthly, the boundaries of the range of application of the PGC must be non-arbitrary and metrically isolated, if belief in the PGC is to be SAP justified. If there are cases that are close to, but not within, the range of application of the PGC, then Timothy Williamson's margin-of-error principle would prevent our being justified in applying the principle at its margins. However, this contradicts Theorem 1, which states that we are SAP justified in our confidence in the PGC.

Fifthly, the range of application of the PGC must be closed under proper parthood. That is, if x is a member of the range of application T, and y is a proper part of x, then y must also be a part of T. That is, if we are not in a position to presume that each of a thing's parts have a cause, then we are not in a position to presume that the whole has a cause, either. It might be thought that there are cases in which a complex situation should be presumed to have a cause, independently of any such presumption about its parts, because the complex situation incorporates many coincidences that demand an explanation in terms of a common cause. However, this overlooks the fact that such an inference to the best (causal) explanation is plausible only when the phenomenon to be explained is already supposed to have a cause. Occam's razor gives us grounds for preferring simpler causes to more complex ones, but it gives us no reason to prefer any cause (even a very simple one) to no cause at all.

Finally, an epistemically acceptable PGC must be sensitive to the fact that human cognition includes an open-ended, highly general form of *abductive reasoning*. In order for a situation to constitute possible abductive evidence for a further conclusion about its causes, only two things are required: (1) the situation must have an intrinsic character that is compatible with its having causes, and (2) the situation must have an intrinsic character of a kind that can figure in possible causal laws, which entails that the character is multiply realizable.

In light of these criteria, the following would seem to be a model of an epistemologically acceptable principle of general causation:

Principle 1 *It is (at least) nomologically necessary that if x is composed of some y's, and for each y among the y's, it is metaphysically possible that there exist a situation that approximately duplicates y and has a cause, then it is highly likely that x itself has a cause.*

The range of Principle 1 is clearly determined by a situation's intrinsic characteristics, and it is closed under parthood. In addition, Principle 1's range of application has non-arbitrary boundaries: anything that is very similar to a member of its range also belongs to the range. Principle 1 also respects the open-endedness of abduction, since any phenomenon that could possibly justify an inference to a best causal explanation would have to have an intrinsic character compatible with its having a cause. Moreover, the range of application of Principle 1 is wide enough to encompass the entire knowledge-net of any humanoid creature, and to do so self-evidently. Principle 1 is at least a paradigm of an epistemically acceptable version of the PGC.

VII.2. Unacceptable candidates

As I argued above (in section 3), any acceptable principle of general causation (PGC) must be restricted in its scopes. Given Theorem 2, we are now in a position to assess various candidate restrictions for their compatibility with securing immunity to defeat for our empirical knowledge. The crucial question becomes: can we be SAP justified in believing that nearly all of our knowledge-net falls within the range of application of the proposed PGC?

Let's consider some of the candidate restrictions from section 3.

1. All non-first situations have causes.

How could I be SAP justified in believing that my current belief-state is a non-first situation? In order to do so, I would have to know that there were situations that preceded my current belief-state in time, but my knowledge of the past consists entirely in ordinary empirical beliefs (including memory and testimony), all of which presuppose (as I have argued) belief in the applicability of the causal principle to my current belief-state. Hence, we cannot have a non-circular justification of immunity to defeat, relying on this version of the PGC.

2. All events that don't occur at a first moment in time have causes.

In the same way, it is impossible for me to be SAP justified in believing that my current belief-state is not occurring at a first moment of time. All of my knowledge about the past, even that there were past moments, is dependent on that ordinary empirical knowledge whose immunity from defeat is at issue. It is certainly metaphysically possible for a person with consciousness like mine to exist in a first moment of time.

Moreover, even if it were possible to be SAP justified in believing that my *beliefs* don't occur at a first moment in time, there would be no way to generalize this belief to all of the situations in my knowledge-net, many of which occur in the remote past.

Finally, this principle fails to have a range of application that refers only to the *intrinsic character* of situations. If any sort of situation could occur at a first moment of time and thus lack a cause, then any sort of situation could occur uncaused. This principle reduces to the trivial assertion that situations have causes, unless they don't.

3. All events with finite temporal duration have causes.

Just as I cannot be SAP justified in believing that my current belief-state is not occurring at a first moment in time, so I cannot be SAP justified in believing that that same state has not persisted for an infinite period of time. I know that my current belief-state has endured only for a finite period of time only because I have ordinary empirical knowledge of events that preceded it in time.

A fortiori, it is impossible for me to be SAP justified that my entire knowledge-net has only a finite temporal duration.

4. All events not including infinite causal regresses have causes.

How do I know that the processes internal to my knowledge-net don't include infinite causal regresses? If time is dense, then infinite causal regresses may be quite common throughout the physical world, as Alex Pruss (1998) argued in 'The Hume–Edwards Principle'. Consider Pruss's example of the flight of a cannonball. If time is dense, then there are infinitely many dynamic states of the cannonball occurring after the firing of the cannon. For example, there are states one second after the firing, one-half second after, one-quarter second after, and so on. Each of these states is causally prior to its successors, and in each case the energy and momentum possessed by the cannonball in that state is sufficient to explain its subsequent trajectory.

Even if it is in fact false that such infinite regresses occur within our knowledge-net (if, for example, it turns out that time is discrete), our knowledge of such a fact could hardly be strongly a priori.

5. All events that are not both extremely simple (have extremely low entropy) and cosmic in scope have causes.

It is not at all obvious that my current belief state isn't simple, and I am not SAP justified in believing that my current state doesn't exhaust the cosmos. My belief that there are many currently existing states outside myself is dependent on my ordinary empirical knowledge.

Much depends on how the notion of *extreme simplicity* is cashed out. If we interpret simplicity in Neoplatonic, Plotinian terms, as a kind of metaphysically absolute simplicity, then this version of the PGC will work epistemologically, but it will also be strong enough to support a theistic conclusion. Alternatively, if we interpret *simplicity* in terms of thermodynamic entropy, then it would be incredible to suppose that I have *any* SAP justified beliefs about the entropy of various states.

Furthermore, this version of the PGC picks out events by virtue of one of their extrinsic features: being cosmic in scale (i.e., the non-existence of contemporaneous disjoint events). Such features couldn't plausibly be relevant to the chances of an event's having a cause. Nor is it plausible that I am SAP justified in believing that my belief state is not cosmic in scale.

6. All situations that could (*de re*) be caused have causes.

There is no way that I could be SAP justified in believing that my current belief-state could (*de re*) have a cause. If we suppose that each thing necessitates *de re* its particular origins, then it would follow that any uncaused state is essentially uncaused. This version of the PGC would then collapse into the trivial principle that whatever has a cause has a cause.

7. All situations that are either ordinary empirical beliefs of mine or that mediate causally between those beliefs and their objects (or between those beliefs and causes of their objects) have causes.

There would, of course, be no problem about my being SAP justified in believing that all the situations in my knowledge-net fall within the scope of application of this principle, since this is a trivial logical truth. However, this is an unacceptable PGC because it does not specify its range of application in terms of the *intrinsic character* of situations. It is surely not justified (not to mention SAP justified) to believe that whether or not a situation is (by virtue of its causal connections with my behaviour) among my beliefs or has one of my beliefs among its effects is in any way relevant to the probability that the situation has a cause. Nor would it be justified to believe that it is a metaphysical necessity that these extrinsic features are correlated with some intrinsic character that nomologically entails having a cause.

One could perhaps argue that human belief-states have the sort of intrinsic character that demands, not only that they probably have causes, but that they are probably caused in a particular way (by a long process of natural selection, for example), a way that implies that it is likely that they are causally connected to their objects. It may be thought, for instance, that the functional unity and complexity of human thought entails the likelihood of such an explanation.

However, as I argued above, this sort of inference to the best (causal) explanation presupposes that some more general PGC applies to the situations in question, taken one at a time: it cannot be used as the ground for a more restricted PGC that applies only to the whole. Inference to the best explanation gives us reason to choose the simpler (ontologically weaker) of two causal explanations of a phenomenon: it does not give us a reason to prefer a causal explanation over the hypothesis that the phenomenon was uncaused. If the hypothesis that a situation was uncaused is a viable one, then Occam's razor would always give us reason to prefer that hypothesis over *any* causal explanation, since the utter absence of any cause is simpler (ontologically leaner) than any hypothesis of a cause could be. Thus, unless the particular situations making up our knowledge-net have some intrinsic character that we are SAP justified in believing to entail a high probability of causation, we are in no position to believe that the knowledge-net as a whole has such a cause.

VII.3. Acceptable candidates and the cosmological argument

What am I justified in believing about my knowledge-net, relying solely on SAP justified and self-verifying beliefs? I know, in a way that is immune to defeat from doubts about causation, how I am being appeared to and what are the contents of my thoughts. However, it is implausible to suppose that I am SAP justified in believing a PGC that is specifically tailored to the present contents of my consciousness. Moreover, even if this were so, my immunity to defeat in such a way would be itself too accidental and unreliable to confer warrant on my beliefs. The relevant knowledge must be knowledge that would be shared by all possible humanoid persons.

What, then, would all possible humanoid persons know in the relevant way about their knowledge-nets? They would know that their belief-states are (i) states or acts of consciousness that are (ii) composite, (iii) heterogeneous, and (iv) consisting of elements that are finitary in content. If there are events that mediate causally between these belief-states and their objects, then these events are *natural*, in the sense of occurring in space and time, and having finitary powers and dispositions. An epistemologically adequate PGC would then have to take something like the following form:

Principle 2 *If x is natural (occurring in space and time, or involving finite powers and dispositions), or x is an act or state of consciousness that is finitary in content, or composed of parts that are finitary in content, then x has a cause.*

If this proposition is inserted (in place of Axiom 8) into the proof of the cosmological argument, we would reach the conclusion that there is an uncaused First Cause with the following characteristics:

1. The First Cause does not occur in space or time.
2. The First Cause has only infinite powers.
3. If the First Cause involves consciousness, then it is a metaphysically simple act of consciousness that is infinitary in content.

I argued in 'A New Look' that a necessarily existent situation would consist of the existence of just such a non-natural, infinitary being. Assuming that the connection between necessity and these three characteristics is itself SAP justified, Axiom 8 of my original argument would also be epistemologically acceptable, since one could be SAP justified in believing that everything in one's knowledge-net was wholly contingent.

Could the First Cause be a non-conscious state? Suppose it were. Could I then be justified in the required way in believing that my current belief-state is not token-identical to the First Cause, or to some part of it? I don't see how I could be, for the sort of reasons that are the stock-in-trade of contemporary physicalists in the philosophy of mind. If, as physicalists argue, I can't be SAP justified in believing that my mental state is not token-identical to some physical state, how could I be SAP justified in believing that my mental state is not (at least in part) token-identical to some non-natural state?

I take it to be evident, however, that no one state could simultaneously have two mental contents of radically different sorts, nor could one mental state, with one sort of content, form part of another with a radically different sort. It would seem, then, that the only way for me to be sure that my belief-state is really disjoint from the First Cause (and so subject to the PGC) would be for the First Cause to be itself a conscious state with such an introspectible content that (i) no part of it could be part of a state of humanoid consciousness, and (ii) it could not itself be token-identical to any aggregate of states, any one of which could be token-identical to a part of a state of humanoid consciousness. It seems, in other words, that we need the following PGC to be SAP justified:

Principle 3 *If x is not a metaphysically simple act of consciousness with infinitely rich content, then x has a cause.*

If I am SAP justified in believing principle 3, then I am certainly SAP justified in believing that all of my knowledge-net falls within its range of application. Even if the world were Malebranchian or Berkeleyan in nature, my empirical knowledge would still be secure. Suppose that God causes each of my perception and belief-states directly. In such a case, my knowledge-net would coincide exactly with my belief-state, since there would be no events that mediated between my beliefs and their objects. In a Malebranchian world, God would be the common cause of my beliefs and their objects, and so God himself would not be part of my knowledge-net. In a Berkeleyan world, God would be the common cause of my beliefs about other spirits and their objects, and God himself would be the object of my beliefs about the physical world. I defined *knowledge-net* to include one's belief-states and those events that mediate causally between those belief states and either (i) their objects or (ii) the common causes of those objects and the belief states. The mere fact that my beliefs were directly caused by God would not by itself constitute a defeater of those beliefs, as Malebranche and Berkeley argued persuasively.

Any possible humanoid person must be SAP justified in believing the same things. Thus, we must consider, not just S's knowledge-net, but any metaphysically possible knowledge-net, The only common denominator to all situations in all possible knowledge-nets is this: each is caused by some other situation. This suggests a further constraint on the range of application T of an epistemically acceptable principle of general causation: if it is metaphysically possible that a situation x has a cause, then x belongs to T, i.e., T is broad enough to include any possible effect. The ranges of Axiom 8 (*being wholly contingent*) or principle 3 (*being a metaphysically simple, infinite act of consciousness*) both meet this constraint. As I argued in *Realism Regained*, it is metaphysically impossible for a necessary situation to be caused. (Even if I'm wrong about this, it is surely plausible that a situation that is *intrinsically* necessary is incapable of being caused.) Moreover, it is plausible that a situation that is metaphysically simple and infinite in intensity is intrinsically necessary and incapable of being caused.

Thus, the ranges of application of Axiom 8 or principle 3 are broad enough to include any situation that is possibly caused. In contrast, the ranges of applications of the principles in Section 7.1 are all far too narrow. Even if one of these principles were to apply to one's actual knowledge-net, the immunity to defeat they provide would be too accidental, too dependent on the contingencies one's actual circumstances, to provide adequate warrant for knowledge.

VIII. OBJECTIONS

VIII.1. Oppy's objection

In his reply to my *Faith and Philosophy* paper, Oppy (1999) suggests a causal principle of the following kind: if x is a situation that could possibly have a wholly contingent cause, then x does have a cause. It's impossible for the Cosmos to have a wholly contingent cause (since it includes all wholly contingent situations as parts), so the Cosmos does not fall within the scope of the causal principle.

Problem: it is only under the description *sum of all wholly contingent situations* that the Cosmos is *necessarily* such as to have no wholly contingent cause. There could well be possible worlds in which the entity that constitutes the Cosmos in the actual world exists and has a wholly contingent cause. So, in fact, Oppy's causal principle would apply to the Cosmos, after all, leading to the conclusion that there is a necessarily existent First Cause in the actual world.

We could modify Oppy's principle to this alternative: every wholly contingent situation, except for any situation that contains a cause of all of the other wholly contingent situations, has a cause. This would be too weak to use in proving the existence of a necessary first cause, since the Cosmos might contain a wholly contingent situation that is a cause of all the other wholly contingent situations.

However, this second principle is not powerful enough to escape global scepticism, since it is implausible to suppose that S is in a position to be SAP justified in believing that his* knowledge-net does not contain a situation that is a cause of all the other wholly contingent situations.

VIII.2. Causation and quantum mechanics

A common objection to any PGC appeals to the apparently indeterministic character of the laws of quantum mechanics (in particular, the indeterministic character of wave collapse). Quantum mechanics could be taken as providing empirical evidence that exceptions to any PGC are in fact widespread throughout the physical world.

However, this objection confuses *being caused* with *being determined*. What quantum mechanics suggests is that indeterministic or probabilistic causation is widespread. When an undetermined quantum result is observed, the result is not uncaused: it was caused by the pre-existing quantum system that had the non-zero objective probability of resolving itself into the observed outcome.

A cause raises the probability of its effect, but not necessarily to a probability over 50%. In general, it is enough if the effect has a finite (greater than infinitesimal) probability, conditional on its cause. Thus, if an electron has equal chances of passing through either of two slits and is subsequently observed passing through the left one, then the electron's prior state (together with the causally relevant features of the context) is the cause of its passing through the left slit, even though there was no causal explanation of why it passed through one *rather than* the other. For this reason, I prefer talking about principles of *general causation* rather than a principle of *sufficient reason*.

Quantum systems are thus quite capable of causing effects, even when the probability of the effect is quite small, so long as the probability of the effect would have been virtually zero in the absence of the cause.

IX. CONCLUSION

I have argued that it is surprisingly difficult to avoid both the Scylla of scepticism and the Charybdis of classical theism. This is, to be sure, the first rather than the last word on the subject. There is a great deal more work to be done on the nature of immunity to defeat, on the nature of the related dependency relation between propositions, and on the possible scope of strongly a priori beliefs. However, it seems clear that some sort of a priori commitment to the generality of causation is required to secure warrant for our ordinary empirical beliefs, even though many of those empirical beliefs are basic (in Plantinga's sense) rather than inferred.

Space does not permit to address here a second possible route to theism, one based on reflecting on what would be required to ground ontologically the truth of any principle of general causation. A being capable of serving as a truthmaker for such a principle would have to be characterized by a kind of negative omnipotence, the capacity to prevent the occurrence of any situation at any point in the causal order. Thus, something that is a priori justified (a PGC) plausibly entails the existence of a godlike being, confirming the main result.

REFERENCES

Adams, Ernest W. *The Logic of Conditionals: An Application of Probability to Deductive Logic* (Dordrecht: D. Reidel, 1975).

—— 'The logic of high probability'. *Journal of Philosophical Logic* 15 (1986): 255–79.

Gellman, Jerome. 'Prospects for a sound stage 3 of cosmological arguments'. *Religious Studies* 36 (2000): 195–201.

Gettier, Edmund. 'Is justified true belief knowledge?' *Analysis* 23 (1963): 121–3.

Koons, Robert C. 'A new look at the cosmological argument.' *American Philosophical Quarterly* 34 (1997): 193–211.

—— *Realism Regained: An Exact Theory of Causation, Teleology and the Mind* (New York: Oxford University Press, 2000).

—— 'Defeasible reasoning, special pleading and the cosmological argument: A reply to Oppy.' *Faith and Philosophy* 18 (2001): 192–203.

Kretzmann, Norman. *The Metaphysics of Theism* (Oxford: Clarendon Press, 1997).

Leonard, Henry S. and Goodman, Nelson. 'The calculus of individuals and its uses.' *Journal of Symbolic Logic* 5 (1940): 45–55.

O'Connor, Timothy. 'Scotus on the existence of a first efficient cause.' *International Journal for the Philosophy of Religion* 33 (1993): 17–32.

—— 'From first efficient cause to god: Scotus on the identification stage of the cosmological argument'. In L. Honnefelder, R. Wood, and M. Dreyer (eds) *John Duns Scotus: Metaphysics and Ethics*, pp. 435–54. (Leiden: E. J. Brill, 1996).

Oppy, Graham. 'Koons' [*sic*] cosmological argument.' *Faith and Philosophy* 16 (1999): 378–89.

Plantinga, Alvin. *Warrant and Proper Function* (New York: Oxford University Press, 1993).

Pollock, John. 'Defeasible reasoning.' *Cognitive Science* 11 (1987):481–518.

Price, Huw. *Time's Arrow and Archimedes' Point: New Directions for the Physics of Time* (New York: Oxford University Press, 1996).

Pruss, Alexander R. 'The Hume-Edwards principle and the cosmological argument.' *International Journal for the Philosophy of Religion* 43 (1998):149–65.

—— *The Principle of Sufficient Reason: A Reassessment* (New York: Cambridge University Press, 2006a).

—— 'Some recent progress on the cosmological argument.' Paper delivered at *The Two Tasks Conference*, June 2006b.

—— and Richard Gale, 'A new cosmological argument.' *Religious Studies* 35 (1999): 461–76.

Reichenbach, Bruce R. *The Cosmological Argument: A Reassessment* (Springfield, IL: Thomas, 1972).

Rowe, William L. *The Cosmological Argument* (Princeton, NJ: Princeton University Press, 1975).

Russell, Bertrand. 'On the notion of cause.' *Proceedings of the Aristotelian Society*, 13(1–26) (1913).

Skyrms, Brian. *Pragmatics and Empiricism* (New Haven, Conn.: Yale University Press, 1984).

Smith, Quentin. 'Simplicity and why the universe exists.' *Philosophy* 71 (1997): 125–32.

Williamson, Timothy. *Knowledge and its Limits* (New York: Oxford University Press, 2000).

6

Theism and the Scope of Contingency

Timothy O'Connor

According to classical theism, contingent beings find the ultimate explanation for their existence in a maximally perfect, necessary being who transcends the natural world and wills its acts in accordance with reasons. I contend that if this thesis is true, it is likely that contingent reality is vastly greater than what current scientific theory or even speculation fancies. After considering the implications of this contention for the extent of divine freedom, I go on to discuss its relevance to the problem of evil as an obstacle to rational theistic belief.

I. HOW MANY UNIVERSES WOULD PERFECTION REALIZE?

In classical philosophical as well as religious theology, God is a personal being perfect in every way: absolutely independent of everything, such that nothing exists apart from God's willing it to be so; unlimited in power and knowledge; perfectly blissful, lacking in nothing needed or desired; morally perfect. If such a being were to create, on what basis would He choose?

Since there is a universe, we know that God did not in fact opt not to create anything at all. But was it really an open possibility that He might have done so? There is a strong case to be made that a perfect being would create something or other, though it is open to Him to create any of a number of contingent orders. Norman Kretzmann

Versions of all or part of this paper were read at the following universities: Oxford, Beijing, Western Washington, Colorado at Boulder, St. Louis, Azusa Pacific, and Trinity College, Dublin. I thank the audiences on these occasions for helpful discussions. In particular, I would like to thank Hud Hudson, Andrew Jorgensen, Brian Leftow, Ted Sider, Richard Swinburne, Michael Tooley, and an anonymous journal referee, all of whom made criticisms or observations that resulted in needed changes.

makes this case within the context of Aquinas' theological system.[1] The
central reason is that there is no plausible account of how an absolutely perfect God might have a *resistible* motivation—one consideration
among other, competing considerations—for creating something rather
than nothing. The most plausible understanding of God's being motivated
to create at all (one which in places Aquinas himself comes very close
to endorsing) is to see it as reflecting the fact that God's very being,
which is goodness, necessarily diffuses itself. Perfect goodness will naturally
communicate itself outwardly; God who is perfect goodness will naturally create, generating a dependent reality that imperfectly reflects that
goodness.[2]

If one rejects this 'Dionysian Principle', however, it is difficult to
envision a coherent scenario in which God eternally chooses not to create.
Presumably, God's positively willing *not* to create requires His having some
reason for not doing so. What kind of reason could that be? (Note that God
could not Himself benefit from that choice.) One might suggest that rather
than positively choosing not to create, God might have simply refrained
from deciding one way or other. This is a familiar circumstance for human
beings, who often have a motivation to uncover more relevant information,
and sometimes stall in the hope that the choice will be 'taken from their
hands'. But there can be no analogous factors in God.

Some Christian thinkers will resist our suggestion at this point by
appealing to the doctrine of the Trinity, on which God the Father
necessarily originates God the Son, and through or with the Son originates
the Holy Spirit. The perfect, inter-penetrating relations of love between
the divine persons would suffice as a response to any natural impetus to
communicatively express God's perfect goodness.[3] The reflection driving
this response is suggestive, enough so that there is some force to an argument
going back at least to Richard of St Victor's twelfth-century *De Trinitate*
that if God exists, something like the Christian doctrine of Trinity is apt to
be true.[4] Nevertheless, it is equally plausible that a natural impetus towards

---

[1] See most recently his Wilde Lectures (1997).

[2] This picture is reflected in the fifth-century Neoplatonist, Pseudo-Dionysius. See *The Divine Names and Mystical Theology*, which influenced later medieval thinkers, including Aquinas, who wrote a commentary on it. For discussion of Aquinas' ambivalence regarding this principle, see Norman Kretzmann (1986).

[3] Aquinas points to the this response in his *Scriptum super libros Sententiarum* (*Commentary on the Sentences*) I, d.2, q.1, a.4, s.c., but he does not repeat it in either of his two later major treatises, the *Summa Contra Gentiles* and the *Summa Theologiae*.

[4] *Three* persons because perfect love requires not only mutual love between two persons of equal worth but also the sharing of the delight in the love received from the one with another. See Chapters 14–20 of Richard of St Victor (1979). For modern discussion, see Richard Swinburne (1994: 190–1).

inward expression of divine goodness would be matched by an impetus to outward sharing of goodness with non-divine creatures. And, in any case, the oddity in God's acting on an entirely resistible motivation to create at all is not alleviated by acceptance of intra-Trinitarian generation and love.

Perhaps it is inevitable, then, that a perfect God would create. But what? Let us assume (as perfect being theologians generally do) that there is an objective, degreed property of intrinsic goodness, such that every possible object is intrinsically good to some degree. We need not assume that this property generates a linear ordering in the sense that every object is comparable to every other, such that for every pair of objects a,b, the value of a is greater than, less than, or equal to the value of b. We assume only that objects are 'partially ordered' in the sense that every object belongs to one or another linear ordering of objects and has less goodness than God Himself. We thus replace the image of a linear 'great chain of being' with that of a branching structure whose branches reconnect only at their limit, which is God. And let us further suppose that whole systems of objects and their total histories—i.e., possible universes—are likewise partially ordered by their intrinsic goodness.

Now, if one or more of these creative options on each of the branches are of maximal overall value, it appears inevitable that God would choose one of them. It would be passing strange that God would opt for less than the best when creating the best involves no cost at all! It is implausible that a perfect being should have idiosyncratic preferences for certain kinds of universes, quite apart from their value.

But, on further reflection, it appears anyways unlikely that there is a finite upper bound on possible universes ordered by their intrinsic goodness, if for no other reason than that there is no finite limit to the number of good things one can have or to the space needed to comfortably house them. For every universe, there is a better, with no finite upper bound on the ranked series. Here, matters are *more* puzzling. It appears that no matter which option God might choose (a universe, whose value is, say, 10^{100} s.g.u., or standard goodness units), He must do so in the knowledge that there are options of arbitrarily greater value. Seems like an odd constraint for a perfect being to have to live with, doesn't it?

William Rowe sees here the makings of a serious dilemma for the theist.[5] The central premise of the argument is that a perfectly good God necessarily would create the best world that He can. As he notes, if we accept this

---

[5] Rowe first set out his argument in (1993). A more recent and thorough treatment is given in Rowe (2004).

thesis, we must either deny that God exists or heroically maintain that there is a best possible world (or equally good set of worlds) and that God has created it (or one of them).

One reply to the argument comes from Robert Adams (1972), who contends that there is no moral obligation to create the best and that a choice of less than the best can be adequately accounted for in terms of divine grace, a disposition to love independent of the value or merit of that which is loved. Rowe counters that perfect goodness is not a function simply of meeting one's obligations: it also reflects the disposition to achieve as much good as one can. God's being both perfectly good in this manner and also gracious in His attitudes towards imperfect creatures are not inconsistent; they merely entail that His creative choice would be motivated by something other than love alone. (And what is a more natural candidate motivation than a desire for the best?)

But what if (as I've already suggested) choosing the best is not an option? Perhaps for every world, there is a better one. If that is so (and Rowe concedes that it well might be), it seems one could hardly fault God for choosing some very good world or other. Rowe, however, demurs, on the basis of the following claim:

If an omniscient being creates a world when there is a better world that it could have created, then it is possible that there exists a being morally better than it. (112)

Clearly, a perfectly good being would reject worlds that are on balance bad. But where would He set the minimum? Rowe thinks it evident that, other things being equal, a being whose minimum standards are higher than another's is a better being. Imagine a good, omniscient, and omnipotent creative being faced with a series of increasingly good possible worlds whose value has no upper bound. Being good, it wants to create something, and something very good. Perhaps it has to resort in the end to some arbitrary procedure for settling upon a particular world, subject to the constraint imposed by its judgement about an acceptable minimum level of goodness, n. Now imagine another being just like the first but for whom the minimum acceptable value in a world is twice n. Rowe believes it is clear that this second being is better, in virtue of its higher standards (95). Some will reply that this result is absurd in the context of options with no upper limit of value, since whatever standard such a being sets, there will be an arbitrarily higher one it might have set. How can one be faulted for failing to achieve the best if doing so is impossible?[6]

---

[6] See Daniel and Frances Howard-Snyder (1994).

However, we need to be careful here, says Rowe. We must distinguish three claims:

(a) failing to do the best one can is a defect only if doing the best one can is possible for one to do;
(b) failing to do better than one did is a defect only if doing better than one did is possible for one to do;
(c) failing to do *better than one did* is a defect only if doing *the best one can* is possible for one to do.

While (a) and (b) are true, Rowe argues that (c) is not. Otherwise, we should have to suppose that a being that opted to create a world that was just *barely* good on balance might be wholly above reproach. However one judges Rowe's fundamental intuition, this buttressing argument is less than compelling. Might not one coherently suppose that goodness entails the creation of a world that is *very* good, on balance, while denying that degree of goodness in general is a function of the degree of goodness one is willing to settle for, given that one is inevitably going to have to settle for something sub-optimal?

One should not be quick to dismiss out of hand Rowe's thesis that facts about the structure of possibility space have direct implications concerning the possibility of an infinitely perfect being. We cannot take it as axiomatic that the notion of an absolutely perfect being is a coherent one. Although some challenges to this notion's coherence are purely internal ones, others concern the very possibility of certain omni-attributes, given seeming facts about the structure of facts over which the attributes range (e.g., there are challenges to omniscience from the structure of knowable facts). And since it is less than evident whether or not there is a best possible world, one who is committed to the possible existence of a perfect being may infer that there is, after all, a best possible world.

What, then, are we to make of the issue Rowe presses? One needn't agree with Rowe that moral *goodness* necessarily tracks one's minimum standard for result acceptability in order to find unsatisfactory, or at least highly peculiar, the picture of God arbitrarily selecting one very good option, at the price of rejecting an infinity of alternatives which are of surpassingly greater value.[7] It suggests an inevitable frustration of what, goodness aside,

---

[7] In a recent lecture, Dean Zimmerman persuasively criticizes Rowe's claim that a omniscient and omnipotent who creates a world less good than one it is capable of creating is less than perfectly good. Zimmerman pointed out that one who accepts this claim and the ensuing argument ought to accept a parallel claim that if an ideal gambler is willing to bet n dollars on a horse x but could have bet more, then it is possible for someone to be more certain that x would win. So in a scenario where there is no finite limit to the sum the gambler could bet, we should conclude, whatever the sum

looks to be a natural aspiration (overall value maximization) of a perfect Creator. And yet the claim that our universe is a prominent component of this world's being the best of all possible worlds seems unduly bold.

So the philosophical theologian will naturally seek a different way of framing the matter, one which may lend itself to a better option. I suggest we start by questioning the common assumption that in deciding what to create, God contemplates *possible worlds*, conceived as *total* ways things might have been, maximal propositions that encompass *all* the facts, including facts about God and his acts of creation. If God were to create a particular universe that unfolded by indeterministic processes, then plausibly His creation decision could not be informed by comprehensive knowledge of which particular world-path would eventually be actualized as a result of His creative activity. God's evaluation of the options might focus accordingly on the degree of goodness of the indeterministic universe *type* that His activity directly ensures, independent of the particulars of how this is realized in its details.

Perhaps we should think of a universe type as a massively branching structure, each complete branch of which represents one possible total way that world might unfold if the type is selected. And then the value of a universe-type might be thought of as some sort of function from the values of the individual branches, weighted to reflect their particular probability. (I will not here consider the issue of how to assign values for universe-types with infinitely many branches, each of which would have probability zero on standard assumptions.) It would be a mistake to assume that in a universe-type that incorporates pervasive indeterministic activity, the values of the specific branches will sharply vary, leaving the value of the determinate universe that results hostage to fortune. Plausibly, the value of a determinate outcome is heavily determined by global features that will be invariant across the branches. Granted, the specific choices of human and other responsible agents is a relevant feature. But it is one among many others, including the very fact of there being agents given some measure of control over their destiny, which is independent of how they choose to exercise that control. A second point to bear in mind is that God might well

the gambler bets, that he was less than maximally certain, yet this seems an unwarranted inference.

Note, however, that we may plausibly modify the principle such that the conclusion of the gambler argument, also plausible, is that a maximally certain ideal gamble will inevitably be frustrated in his aim of value maximization. Likewise, in the scenario Rowe envisions, it is plausible to conclude that a perfect Creator will inevitably be frustrated in His creative ambition. Unlike Rowe's argument, this is not a threat to theism, but it does motivate the theist to consider whether there was, after all, a way around making a less-than-optimal choice. If so, it is plausible that God would take it. In what follows in the text, I suggest just such a way.

plan to orchestrate large-scale outcomes for humans, channelling human choices towards optimal overall results. (Think here of Geach's 'chess Grandmaster' analogy.)[8] Finally, a universe-type is perhaps an incomplete type in one more subtle respect: prior to an individual object's coming to be, there are only facts about its possible qualitative nature, a nature which could be instanced more than once by exactly similar yet distinct constituent objects. God could conceive you, for example, only in qualitative terms prior to your coming to be. Your irreducible particularity—your being the very individual that you are—is not an eternally existing quality, but is instead inseparable from you yourself, and so could not have pre-dated your coming to be. Or so I believe.[9] Nonetheless, for expository simplicity, I shall speak of God's considering this or that 'universe'.

Let a 'single universe' be a concrete totality whose components are causally connected to each other but to nothing else save God. A universe is a relatively causally isolated part of the one actual world. Let us say that a 'super-universe' is a collection of one or more totalities that are mutually disconnected save for their common origin within God's creative choice. Clearly, God's choice isn't between the single universes, but between the super-universes. A perfect being would be capable of creating more than one universe, and should God choose to create only one particular universe, there is a super-universe having it as its sole member.

How might thinking of things this way help with our puzzle of creation by a perfect creator? Here is a first pass at a line of thought that seems to me to have considerable plausibility. We have supposed that no single universe has maximal value (as much as or more than that of any other universe). And it is plausible that God, intending to create, would not wish to settle for a universe than which there are an infinity of better universes, whose increase in value over our universe stretches without limit as we go up the series. What is more, since the value of universes is likely not fully

---

[8] 'God is the supreme Grand Master who has everything under his control. Some of the players are consciously helping his plan, others trying to hinder it; whatever the finite players do, God's plan will be executed; though various lines of God's play will answer to various moves of the finite players. God cannot be surprised or thwarted or cheated or disappointed. God, like some grand master of chess, can carry out his plan even if he has announced it beforehand. "On this square," says the Grand Master, "I will promote my pawn to Queen and deliver checkmate to my adversary": and it is even so. No line of play that finite players may think of can force God to improvise: his knowledge of the game already embraces all possible variants of play, theirs does not' Peter Geach (1977: 58).

[9] Robert Adams (1981) has defended this claim; Alvin Plantinga (1983) replies. Christopher Menzel (1991) tries to show the consistency of the claims that there are only general (qualitative) truths concerning non-actual possibilities and the unrealized future with the claim that God knew (for example) that Prior (the very individual) was to be a philosopher, through a novel analysis of the semantics of statements of the latter sort.

commensurate—there is not a linear ordering of the possibilities, given the wide diversity of types—a perfect Creator would be disposed to create universes from among every significant type. So, God has reason not to settle for creating a super-universe which has only one universe as member. Nor will it help for God to create a two- or three-membered super-universe, or, in fact, an n-membered super-universe, for any finite value n. But it would appear to help if God were to create an infinitely-membered super-universe, provided there is no finite upper limit on the value of its members. For example, God could simply bring about the entire, partially-ordered hierarchy of single universes (that super-universe containing all possible universes). On reflection, this simple option appears unsatisfactory, since presumably there is some goodness threshold τ below which God would not create.[10] More likely, then, is that God would elect to create that super-universe containing every single universe at or above τ. But notice that he could also avoid the unwanted consequence by creating every other universe, or every third universe, or every n-th universe, for all finite values of n. So, at least as far as our puzzle is concerned, God retains an infinity of adequate choices among the super-universes. Any of these choices would have the same aggregate value of infinity.

Against this simple, initial line of argument, there is the following natural objection: Won't super-universes also be ordered in a hierarchy according to value, with the result that there is no best super-universe? In that case, wouldn't a perfect Creator who contemplates all possible super-universes confront the same problem as one who merely confined his attention to single universes?

In reply, notice that as we go up the scale of super-universes (unlike universes), eventually the values become infinite, in such a way that the hierarchy seems to 'flatten out'. The super-universe God creates is one of these equally top-valued members, the choice between them to be decided on grounds *in addition to* objective value. To defend this response, I need to explore the formal properties of the value had by possible universes.

It seems that the value of a single universe is measurable in at least three different ways:

(i) the *intensive* value of each of its basic objects, reflecting both the value of its kind and its degree of perfection as an exemplar of its kind;[11]

(ii) the *extensive, or aggregate,* value of those objects taken collectively;

[10] Perhaps it is a vague threshold, but if the subsequent reasoning in the text is correct, this will be of no significance.

[11] Basic objects in the sense intended here will include both unstructured fundamental particulars, such as electrons might be, as well as composite objects which are true unities.

(iii) the *organic* value of the universe as a whole, and perhaps of its subregions. Aesthetic, moral, and other kinds of objective value all attach to situations or complexes partly in virtue of their relational structure. For example, it has been supposed (by Leibniz and many others) that rich complexity achieved through elegant, simple laws governing simple basic elements is an arrangement of great metaphysical goodness and beauty. Still better and more beautiful, *ceteris peribus*, are nested structures or processes, whereby the manifestation of complexity through underlying simplicity is repeated at stages of resolution (as with fractals or living organisms). However precisely we conceive its determinants, the organic value of a universe seems analogous to the intensive value of a natural object. It will be a function both of the value of its constituents objects and their qualitative states and of the relational structure they embody.

Earlier, I suggested that it is plausible to suppose that simple universes may not have 'maximal' value. It would seem that a universe could have infinite value (of cardinality aleph-null only?) *extensively* simply in virtue of its having infinitely many natural objects, all possessing some finite value. But, plausibly, a finite created object could not have infinite intensive value and a universe, however well-ordered, could not have infinite organic value. The limit case, if attainable at all, could be reflected only by that which is perfect goodness itself—God Himself. If there is an absolutely perfect being, it is one for whom nature and existence are not separable. When such a being creates, it cannot convey one of its essential attributes to its creation, so inevitably any candidate creation will be less than maximally perfect. (I'm assuming that a natural assignment of units will assign aleph-null, or countable infinity, as the maximum for organic unity.)

The total value of a universe appears, then, to be a point in a 3-space. Given that none of a universe's objects may have infinite intensive value, its value in this regard (perhaps measured as the average value of its basic objects) will typically not be infinite. (The exceptional case is where a universe instances an infinite number of basic object types whose value can be ordered without a finite upper bound. Note, however, that universes meeting this condition might necessarily be constrained in organic value.) And, crucially, a universe's organic value will be less than maximal. Even allowing for infinite aggregate value, then, no single universe will be of maximal value—the highest possible value along all three dimensions. Hence, there is a natural impetus for a perfect being to create an infinitely-membered super-universe, whose members are ordered by value without an upper bound.

One might worry that these three measures of value vary inversely, at least once values get high enough, as might be the case when it comes to mean intensive value and organic value. In that case, were these equal inputs to the value of a universe—something I will dispute below—it could be that the product of all three measures has a maximum, so that there really is a best possible simple universe. But while I can't show that this isn't so, it doesn't strike me as plausible. Why should the organic value of a certain arrangement be diminished if each of its elements were themselves realized by multiplicities of arbitrary size?

Now let us return to the value of super-universes. Recall the objection that they also might be ordered in a hierarchy according to value, without a maximal value. At first glance, it seems that if a perfect Creator would be dissatisfied creating a single universe, knowing that there are an abundance of alternatives whose additional value is arbitrarily large, a similar dilemma would arise when considering the range of super-universes. In reply we have said that it may be that there is a maximal aggregate value of super-universes, one shared by all infinitely-membered super-universes meeting certain constraints on the value of each of their members. (There does not seem to be anything analogous to organic value for super-universes, however, given their disconnectedness in all respects save their point of origin.)

But now we must confront a substantial complication: there is no highest transfinite cardinal. (There is the infinity of the natural numbers—countable infinity—a still greater infinity of the real numbers, and greater infinities still, without end.) Thus, a strategy that concedes that God would opt for *unlimited* aggregate goodness requires us either to assume that there is an intrinsic upper limit, inscrutable to us, to the size of super-universes omnipotence may create (a limit measured by a particular infinite cardinal) or to suppose that God may create a proper class of universes, one which simply has no measure at all. The latter option would not have sat well with George Cantor, the great nineteenth-century mathematician who first unveiled the limitless structure of the infinite. A devout Lutheran, Cantor thought that God alone (the 'Absolute Infinite') is beyond the limitless hierarchy of transfinite cardinals.

There is a better response, however. It is doubtful that a perfect being would desire to pursue maximal aggregate value at all. Why should a master artisan, even one of maximal goodness and without limitations, pursue mere duplication, much less unlimited duplication, of similar objects and systems?[12] What clearly will be of concern, it seems to me, is not to

---

[12] For a discussion of puzzles concerning value in infinite contexts where the value in question is assumed (unlike here) to be finitely additive, as with utilitarian theories of moral value, see Peter Vallentyne and Shelly Kagan (1997). For example, one might be inclined to think that two universes having infinite aggregate value may nevertheless be ordered by value (as when one contains a duplicate of the other as a proper part).

place arbitrary limits on the intensive value of whatever natural objects, and organic value of whatever overall systems, He contemplates. We've already seen that, plausibly, neither of these could attain infinite value. (God alone, who is an uncreated independent being and the source of every possibility, is an infinitely valuable individual.) If both these claims are right, then the worry about finding an upper limit on the cardinality of the value of super-universes is circumvented. The natural object of a perfect Creator's consideration will be any infinitely-membered, partially-ordered super-universe for which there is no finite upper bound on the organic value of its members (and perhaps intensive value of its member's constituent objects), all of which exceed threshold τ. However, we may need to add one further condition. Imagine two infinite super-universes, SU_1 and SU_2, the members of which can be ordered similarly, such that the first member of each is of the same organic kind, O_1, and so on for each successive pair of members. Now suppose that the SU_2 universe is always a more valuable instance of the relevant kind than the SU_1 universe. If this is possible, then, plausibly, a perfect Creator would opt for SU_2. But equally plausibly, for reasons similar to before, there will not always be a finite upper bound on the values that can be reached by universes that are instances of some organic kind. If this is right, it seems natural to extend our reasoning by supposing that God will select a super-universe in which there is no upper bound on the values taken by the set of universes of value type O_i, for every value-type O_i.[13]

I have argued that all the possibilities deemed creation-worthy by a perfect Creator would conform to a rich structure. Even so, an infinity of options satisfy these constraints, and there is no reason yet uncovered to suppose that any highly particular sort of universe will be deemed necessary. Hence, for all we've seen, the extent of alternatives open to a perfect Creator may be quite wide indeed.

Some will suppose that a perfect being would naturally opt for a *plenitude*, creating as many valuable things as he can. If this were so, it would seem that the existence of every possible universe (recall that I here am speaking of universe types, as described above) is inevitable. I believe this supposition is on a par with the thought that a perfect being would be concerned with mere aggregate value. And so my reply is similar as well: this assumption is far less plausible than the more limited thesis that perfection would opt to realize every basic *kind* of valuable thing, incommensurate with the other basic

Vallentyne and Kagan defend such an intuition through use of the infinitesimals of non-standard analysis.

[13] Thanks to Ted Sider for helpful commentary on a paper I gave presenting some of this material and to the audience at Azusa Pacific University for discussion on this point.

kinds. (Suppose the theist *does* make the stronger assumption. Rowe would object that doing so is to endorse, in the end, the Leibnizian claim that this is the best, or one of infinitely many equally best, of all possible worlds, and this is incredible. But the theist who endorses plenitude may reply that once we recognize that his thesis implies nothing about the organic goodness of our particular universe, we should regard the judgement of its incredibility as totally unfounded.)

II. PERFECTION AND FREEDOM

I have argued that the theist has reason to believe that it is inevitable both that God create something or other and that He create at least a countable infinity of universes (in the broad sense of causally connected and effectively isolated totalities or systems). Both of these conclusions were rejected by most traditional philosophical theologians on the grounds that they compromise God's perfect freedom. This line of thought assumes that freedom is necessarily proportionate to the range of alternative possibilities open to the agent. I suggest that this belief, while natural enough, results from a hasty generalization from particularities of our own case as finite, conditioned agents.

It is plausible that the core metaphysical feature of freedom is being the *ultimate source*, or originator, of one's choices, and that being able to do otherwise is *for us* closely connected to this feature.[14] For human beings or any created persons who owe their existence to factors outside themselves, the only way their actions could find their ultimate origin in themselves is for such acts not to be wholly determined by their character and circumstances. For, if all my actions were wholly determined, then if we were to trace my causal history back far enough, we would ultimately arrive at external factors that gave rise to me, with my particular genetic dispositions. My motives at the time would not be the ultimate source of my willings, only the most proximate ones. Thus, only by there being less than deterministic connections between external influences and choices—and so my having alternative possibilities open to me in the final analysis—is it possible for me to be an ultimate source of my activity, concerning which I may truly say, 'the buck stops here'.

However, the conditions for freedom in the divine and human cases differ in a way that reflects the difference in ontological status between an absolutely independent Creator and a dependent, causally conditioned

---

[14] See Robert Kane (1996), Ch. 6, for an extended defence of the primacy of ultimate origination to freedom of will.

creature. God's choices reflect His character—and His character alone. He was not *given* a nature, nor does He act in an environment that influences the development of individualizing traits. If His character precludes His undertaking various options that are within the scope of his power, this fact cannot be attributed in the final analysis to something else. (And we may note that most of those theologians who hold that there was a real possibility that God not have created anything or have created something other than an infinite Creation, also suppose that God is perfectly good, an essential, not acquired, attribute. God cannot lie or be in any way immoral in His dealings with His creatures. Unless we take the minority position on which this is a trivial claim, on which whatever God does *definitionally* counts as good, this is a substantive limit on the range of open alternatives.) Therefore, the impossibility of His undertaking such actions is solely and finally attributable to Him.[15] Anselm had it right: although God is certain to act with perfect goodness (and, we have added, with a kind of maximal creative ambition), it is not true that God is good out of an 'inevitable necessity'. Instead, his perfect goodness and freedom are both attributes he has 'in Himself', for all eternity (1998: 327).

III. THE MANY-UNIVERSE-CREATION HYPOTHESIS AND THE PROBLEM OF EVIL

My contention that a perfect Creator would opt for an infinite number of universes, ordered without a finite upper-bound, appears to have some relevance to the problem of evil, which in its various versions raises the question of whether the existence, quantity, and/or distribution of human and animal suffering, or of certain horrific instances of such suffering, render

---

[15] Of course, this allows the possibility that God's reasons might lead him to conclusively favour the creation of one specific array of universes. (We have been bold enough to suppose that God's creative choice will be shaped by certain considerations. We are not so bold as to claim to know *all* such considerations.) So, for all that we have argued, it might be that God's creative choice was both certain to occur and yet free.

This might be at odds with certain official theological positions on God's freedom in creation. As Michael Rota has pointed out to me, for example, the Roman Catholic First Vatican General Council (1870) condemns the position that 'says that God created not by an act of will free from all necessity, but with the same necessity by which He necessarily loves Himself'. However, it seems that one might draw the required distinction by maintaining that God's love of Himself is a different sort of activity than would be His 'necessary' choice in creation, if such it is. Plausibly, this self-love is not an intending (as is a creative choice), but is instead a kind of desire (or joint desire and affirmation).

the existence of God unlikely.[16] To put the point crudely, if the question is, 'why didn't God create a realm much like ours in its having significant positive respects, yet without its seemingly avoidable horrific kinds of evil, or without the quantity and distribution of suffering therein?', the answer made possible by the present perspective is: He did—lots of them!

Objection 1

This suggestion is flagrantly *ad hoc*. You are vastly inflating our ontological commitment in order to avoid a straightforward conclusion from the data that we have.

Reply

This objection might be apt if we were positing that God has created a vast plurality of universes in order to respond to some version or another of the problem of evil. But we have argued that this thesis is independently motivated.

Objection 2

A morally perfect being would desire to prevent unnecessary suffering. No doubt there are valuable universes that contain intense, prolonged suffering, and perhaps for all we know the suffering in our universe often or always leads in the end to goods of various kinds. But consider the choice between a super-universe that contains this sort of suffering, and one of *equal* value that contains no suffering at all. Why would God choose a super-universe with suffering (even suffering that leads to good) when He could have chosen a super-universe of equal value that contains no suffering?

Reply

It is not my purpose here to so much as hint at a full-blown theodicy. But I do wish to point out that the present view has an advantage in replying to this kind of question, which is just a version of a question that is standardly posed to theodicies of all kinds. In common with typical theodicies, I

---

[16] Cf. Donald Turner (2003). (I learned of Turner's article after developing the essential ideas of this chapter.) Turner argues that a perfect being would create *all* possible universes above some cut-off point, defined in terms of intrinsic goodness. One instantiation of each maximally specific type, since (he holds, contrary to the haecceitistic position I voiced earlier) qualitatively indiscernible worlds are identical. He uses this assumption in offering a limited response to the problem of evil from the vantage point of his thesis. Also see the related set of ideas developed in a fascinating way by Hud Hudson (2006). This work appeared too late for me to engage with it directly here, but I hope to do so elsewhere.

suggest that certain moral goods entail the real possibility or outright existence of significant suffering. These include the creaturely goods of heroism, perseverance, and trust.[17] A Christian theist may also plausibly contend that suffering is integrally connected to the great goods of divine incarnation and atonement.[18] The sole point I wish to make here is that, given our multiverse theism, we needn't claim that these suffering-entailing or suffering-risking goods are the *greatest* goods, or such that some possible universes that contain these goods as well as significant suffering are on balance better than any possible universe that lacks them. We have argued that a perfect Creator would desire so to act that

(i) there would not be an arbitrary upper bound to the goodness of the universe(s) that He creates, such that He might have created a universe that was better to an arbitrary degree than any that He did create; and

(ii) every significant kind of goodness capable of creaturely realization would be instantiated somewhere or other in the created order.

If these contentions are correct, then on plausible assumptions, God will in fact have compelling reasons to create a universe in which significant suffering is permitted to occur *even if the goods that require suffering are not the greatest goods, or if the universe in which they occur does not belong to a class of supremely valuable realms.* All that is required is that the suffering-risking universes satisfy a minimum threshold of goodness. Since it is plausible that the one-universe theist is rationally committed to something along the lines of the stronger claim—it is another matter altogether whether the rational theist must suppose himself to be able *to show* that our universe plausibly falls into this special class—the present view has the advantage that it can get by with weaker assumptions in responding to the problem of evil.

REFERENCES

Adams, Robert, 'Must God Create the Best?', *Philosophical Review* 81 (1972): 317–32.

—— 'Actualism and Thisness', *Synthese* 49 (1981): 3–41.

Anselm, *Why God Became Man*, in Brian Davies, and G. R. Evans (eds), *Anselm of Canterbury: The Major Works* (Oxford: Oxford University Press, 1998).

Aquinas, Thomas, *Scriptum super libros Sententiarum* (*Commentary on the Sentences*); *Summa Contra Gentiles; Summa Theologiae.*

Geach, Peter, *Providence and Evil* (Cambridge: Cambridge University Press, 1977).

Hick, John, *Evil and the God of Love*, rev. edn (New York: Harper and Row, 1978).

---

[17] Numerous authors develop this sort of point, e.g., C. S. Lewis (1940), John Hick (1978), and, more recently, Richard Swinburne (1998).

[18] Alvin Plantinga (2004) develops this point.

Howard-Snyder, Daniel and Frances, 'How an Unsurpassable Being Can Create a Surpassable World', *Faith and Philosophy* 11/2 (1994): 260–8.

Hudson, Hud, *The Metaphysics of Hyperspace* (Oxford: Oxford University Press, 2006).

Kane, Robert, *The Significance of Free Will* (New York: Oxford University Press, 1996).

Kretzmann, Norman, 'A General Problem of Creation: Why Would God Create Anything at All?', in Scott MacDonald (ed.), *Being and Goodness* (Ithaca, NY: Cornell University Press, 1986).

—— *The Metaphysics of Theism: Aquinas's Natural Theology in Summa Contra Gentiles I* (Oxford: Clarendon Press, 1997).

Lewis, C. S., *The Problem of Pain* (London: Macmillan, 1940).

Menzel, Christopher, 'Temporal Actualism and Singular Foreknowledge', in J. Tomberlin (ed.), *Philosophical Perspectives, 5: Philosophy of Religion* (Atascadero, CA: Ridgeview, 1991), 475–507.

Plantinga, Alvin, 'On Existentialism', *Philosophical Studies* 44 (1983): 1–20.

—— 'Supralapsarianism, or "O Felix Culpa"', in Peter van Inwagen (ed.), *Christian Faith and the Problem of Evil* (Eeerdmans, 2004), 1–25.

Pseudo-Dionysius, *The Divine Names and Mystical Theology*, John D. Jones (tr.) (Milwaukee: Marquette University Press, 1980).

Richard of St Victor, *De Trinitate* in Grover Zinn (tr. and ed.) *The Twelve Patriarchs, The Mystical Ark, and Book Three of the Trinity* (New York: Paulist Press, 1979).

William Rowe, 'The Problem of Divine Perfection and Freedom', in Eleonore Stump (ed.), *Reasoned Faith* (Ithaca, NY: Cornell University Press, 1993), 223–33.

Rowe, William, *Can God Be Free?* (Oxford: Oxford University Press, 2004).

Swinburne, Richard, *The Christian God* (Oxford: Clarendon Press, 1994).

—— *Providence and the Problem of Evil* (Oxford: Oxford University Press, 1998).

Turner, Donald, 'The Many-Universes Solution To The Problem Of Evil', in Alexander Pruss and Richard Gale (eds), *The Existence of God* (Aldershot: Ashgate Publishing, 2003).

Vallentyne, Peter and Shelly Kagan, 'Infinite Value and Finitely Additive Value Theory', *Journal of Philosophy* 94 (1997): 5–26.

7

On Two Problems of Divine Simplicity

Alexander R. Pruss

I. INTRODUCTION

The doctrine of divine simplicity claims that there is no ontological composition in God of any sort, whether of matter and form, or of essence and accident, or of this attribute and that attribute considered as ontologically distinct. The doctrine is a traditional part of Christianity and Judaism, and can be argued to be a reasonable development of the monotheistic ideal of seeing a single entity at the root of reality. Thus Maimonedes (1956: Part I, Chapter 50) wrote that '[t]hose who believe that God is One, and has many attributes, declare the unity with their lips, and assume plurality in their thoughts', which he said was as bad as the case of Christians with their doctrine of the Trinity. While I disagree that the doctrine of the Trinity would violate the basic ideals of monotheism, Maimonedes may be right that the denial of the doctrine of simplicity would. However it is not my point here to argue for the doctrine of divine simplicity, but to defend it against two major objections.

For, divine simplicity, like the complementary doctrine of the Trinity, does lead to intellectual difficulties. I want to consider two objections in particular, and argue that thinking in terms of an account of divine simplicity that was introduced by Graham Oppy (2003), and later independently developed by Bergmann and Brower (forthcoming)[1] as well as Pruss

I am grateful to the audience for the discussion at my presentation at the Society of Christian Philosophers satellite session at the American Catholic Philosophical Association annual meeting in 2003. I am also grateful to Jeffrey Brower, Jon Kvanvig, Mark Murphy and Erik Wielenberg for discussions of some of these topics.

[1] See also Brower (forthcoming in *Faith and Philosophy*), where he points out similar ideas in Wolterstorff (1991).

(2003), shows that the contradictions thought to inhere in these paradoxes can be avoided. The two problems I shall consider are not the only ones the doctrine faces,[2] but they seem particularly problematic.

The first problem is that it appears incomprehensible how we can meaningfully predicate different attributes of God, such as 'perfect mercy' and 'perfect justice' which will be my stand-ins in for any pair of prima facie distinct attributes. For, according to the doctrine of divine simplicity, when God has attributes A and B, then God's being A is ontologically identical with God's being B. The difficulty is that under such circumstances 'mercy' and 'justice' seem to lose their ordinary language meaning and since our linguistic usage is based on ordinary language, it becomes meaningless to use the terms about God. This is the 'multiple attributes' problem.

The second problem comes from noting that the doctrine of divine simplicity entails that in some relevant sense God has no intrinsic accidental properties. Here, an accidental property of x is simply a property that x could lack. I need to emphasize that my use of the word 'property' is entirely that of ordinary language—I am neither affirming nor denying a Platonism about properties. I do not have a definition of an 'intrinsic property', but we can get a rough and ready understanding of what is meant when we think about paradigm cases such as the lump of coal's containing such-and-such a number of carbon atoms or Fred's being in horrible pain, as contrasted with extrinsic properties such as John's being taller than Fred, Bush's being President, and so on. Now, if God had an intrinsic accidental property A, then A would be a property that in some possible world God lacks. But God plainly has at least one non-accidental property, B, such as being God or being good. We could then ontologically distinguish God's having A from God's having B, because the one occurs in all worlds where God exists and the other does not, contrary to divine simplicity.

The problem now is that, contrary to the above argument, God does seem to have intrinsic accidental properties. Although God has created this world, he could have created another—or none at all. But willing one thing rather than another seems to be an intrinsic property, and if God's willing that this world exist is something he did not have to do, then it seems to follow that God has an accidental intrinsic property. Similarly, God believes that Napoleon lost the Battle of Waterloo. But had Napoleon won, God would not have believed it. Since believing a proposition seems an intrinsic property, it seems to follow that God has an accidental intrinsic property.

I will not solve the two problems in the sense of showing *how* it is that it is possible for God to be merciful and just, capable of having willed different

---

[2] For instance, Bergmann and Brower (forthcoming) discuss, and I believe resolve, the 'category problem', that God then becomes identical with a property.

things and capable of having believed different things while being simple. I think the full solution would require a vision of God's essence. But, in Section II.1, I will give a truthmaker-based account of divine simplicity and throughout the paper shall give some reflections that puncture the notion that the multiple attributes and accidentality problems show a *contradiction* between divine simplicity and various attributes of God.

II. MULTIPLE ATTRIBUTES

II.1. Truthmakers and the general issue

The doctrine of divine simplicity had better not say that mercy and justice in general are one and the same property. For that would make the claim that a friend of ours had exhibited more mercy than justice in some situation self-contradictory. Rather, the claim has to be that *God's* mercy and *God's* justice are the same ontologically.

What makes it be true that Socrates is just? Surely it is something about Socrates, something that we might reasonably denote by 'Socrates' justice', i.e., 'that in virtue of which Socrates is just'. It is, perhaps, a virtue that Socrates has, or maybe an activity he always engages in. Socrates' justice is not the same as Plato's justice, because if they were the same, then the same thing would make it be true that Socrates is just as would make it be true that Plato is just. But if that were so, then it would seem to follow that, necessarily, if Socrates is just, then that in virtue of which Plato is just exists, and hence Plato is just. Socrates' justice, then, is a truthmaker of the claim that Socrates is just, where a truthmaker is that in virtue of which a proposition is true.

On some views about truthmakers,[3] if T is a truthmaker for a proposition p, then anything of which T is a part will also make p true. If such a view of truthmakers is correct, then we should further specify that Socrates' justice is the *minimal* truthmaker of the claim that Socrates is just, where a minimal truthmaker of a claim is one such that no proper part of it is also a truthmaker for that claim. Notice, further, that I am not committing myself to the controversial claim that *every* true proposition must have a truthmaker, or to the false claim that every true proposition must have a *minimal* truthmaker.[4]

---

[3] For instance, see the seminal article of Mulligan, Simons and Smith (1984).

[4] To see that the claim about minimal truthmakers is false, take a possible world that contains infinitely many horses, and consider for the proposition, p, that there are infinitely many horses. Any truthmaker for proposition contains an infinite plurality (or aggregate or mereological sum, depending on one's preferred ontology or vocabulary) of horses. But any infinite proper sub-plurality of horses will do just as well as truthmaker for p.

I am not assuming here that Socrates' justice is a self-standing quasi-substance. Socrates' justice likely is a dependent being:[5] as the medievals would say, its *esse* is *inesse*—Socrates' justice exists precisely by *Socrates'* being just. What I said so far should have been neutral between any forms of nominalism, trope theory or Platonism that have a chance at being right, since even Platonism should admit that, on the one hand, there is the property (or Form) of justice and, on the other hand, there is Socrates' instantiating of that property.

Now consider Bob who is a rock and who is hot. Let us suppose that Bob's heat just is the large amount of kinetic energy of Bob's molecules. Bob is hot precisely because of this kinetic energy: whenever Bob's molecules—identified as such—have a lot of kinetic energy, Bob is hot, and that it is hot just is that its molecules have a lot of kinetic energy. Bob's heat is distinct, then, from the heat of a different rock, Jane, and very different from the heat of the sun, since the movement of Jane's or the sun's molecules is different from the movement of Bob's molecules. There is an ontological basis for predicating heat of Bob: the movement of the molecules constituting Bob. It is this ontological basis for the predication that is 'Bob's heat', and it is this ontological basis that makes it true that Bob is hot. Or so I think. But even if I am wrong that heat can be identified the kinetic energy of Bob's molecules, nonetheless it will likely be true that there is such a thing as Bob's heat,[6] and if there is, it will no doubt be distinct from Jane's or the sun's heat.

The claim that God's being merciful and God's being just are identical is, I take it, the claim that the ontological basis for predicating mercy of God is identical with the ontological basis for predicating justice of God. Or, in the above terminology, it is simply the claim that God's justice is identical with God's mercy, i.e., that the same thing is the minimal truthmaker of the claim that God is just and the claim that God is merciful. And this does not entail that Cato's justice is identical with Mother Teresa's mercy, or even that Mother Teresa's justice is identical with Mother Teresa's mercy.

More generally, we can say that the doctrine of divine simplicity states:

(*) All non-tautological truths solely about God or his parts have God as their minimal truthmaker.

It follows immediately from (*) that God has no proper parts, since if A were a proper part of God, then A rather than God would be the minimal truthmaker of the claim that A exists. Bergmann and Brower (forthcoming)

---

[5] A 'moment' in the terminology of Mulligan, Simons and Smith (1984).
[6] I say 'it will likely be' rather than 'it is certainly' because it might turn out that the concept of heat will have to go the way of phlogiston.

use essentially the same account to solve the category problem. For no untoward claims identifying God with a Platonic entity are made here. The truthmakers of claims like 'x is just' are concreta. God is God's justice, but God's justice is not something Platonic—it is simply the truthmaker of 'God is just'.

II.2. Redundancy

So at least the doctrine of divine attribute simplicity, when properly formulated, does not result in an immediate collapse of the perfections of human beings. But there still might be another argument against God's being merciful being identical with God's being just. For if the two are identical, then it seems that a theologian repeats herself when she says that God is merciful and when she says that God is just. Thus, saying that God is merciful and that God seems to be just like saying redundantly that the Lionheart is brave and that the Lionheart is courageous. Our language may not collapse in general, but it would still collapse in the case of God. Since it is essential to theological language that we make multiple claims, such as that God is perfectly good and that God is all powerful, the claim that all of this language is redundant and we might as well limit ourselves to saying that God is, say, just, without mentioning power or goodness or anything else, is absurd.

To respond, I will construct a case where we have two distinct properties, F and G, both of which are predicated of x and both of which are predicated of y, with x's being F not identical with x's being G, even though y's being F is identical with y's being G. Let F denote the predicate 'is round-or-triangular'; let G be the predicate 'is red-or-triangular'. Suppose x is red and round, while y is neither, but is triangular. Then, x and y both are both F and G. Moreover, x is F in virtue of its roundness while it is G in virtue of its redness, and x's roundness and redness are plainly distinct. On the other hand, however, y is F in virtue of its triangularity and this triangularity is also that in virtue of which it is G. Given the sense which we gave above to the expression 'being F', it follows that y's being F is identical with y's being G, though x's being F is not identical with x's being G nor are F and G the same property.

This example shows two things. First, it gives further support to the previous section's claim that there is nothing incoherent in saying that God's justice is identical with God's mercy while Mother Theresa's justice is not identical with Mother Theresa's mercy. Second, although in this case y's being round-or-triangular is identical with y's being red-or-triangular (and both of these are identical with y's being triangular), it is nonetheless true that something different is said when we say that y is round or triangular from what is said when we say that *y* is red or triangular. Two propositions can have the same truthmaker without being redundant.

This is just an opening gambit: the example is clearly gerrymandered. A less gerrymandered case, and one very close to Aquinas' (1920: I, 13, 5) use of Aristotle's account of focal meaning in the context of theological language, would be the following. Take the predicate 'healthy', one of Aristotle's favourite examples (see, e.g., *Metaphysics* IV), also used by Aquinas. Now, a body's being healthy is identical with a body's functioning well as an organism. However, a food item's, say a boiled egg's, being healthy in the typically relevant sense is not identical with the food item's functioning well as an organism. Rather, the food item's being healthy is identical with the food's promoting the health of humans. Here, Aristotle and Aquinas insist we do not have gerrymandering. 'Healthy' is not being used multivocally, but there is a focal meaning of 'healthy', namely functioning well as an organism, and derivative 'analogous' meanings such as 'promoting an organism's being healthy' (e.g., as applied to food) or 'being indicative of an organism's being healthy' (e.g., as applied to urine). Likewise, Aquinas insists that a predicate like 'wise' is used in the case of God in a focal sense but in a derivative sense in the case of creatures.

Let us now go back to the justice and mercy case. A criterion of adequacy for our understanding what it means to say that God is merciful is that there must be something relevantly alike between God's being merciful, say, and Mother Theresa's being merciful. Moreover, there must be something relevantly similar between God's justice and Mother Theresa's justice. Yet, if language is not to break down, then Mother Theresa's mercy and Mother Theresa's justice cannot be relevantly similar. I will now show how this can happen by telling a science-fiction story where a similar thing holds.

II.3. The strange alien and analogy

Suppose I tell you there is a very strange alien about whom I have told you nothing yet other than that it is very strange and that it *hears*. And suppose I next tell you that it *feels*, tactilely that is and not emotionally. By 'It hears' I just mean 'It has a sense of hearing' and 'It feels' means 'It has a sense of touch'. I might then add: 'I talked to the alien and it heard me. I then touched its seventh appendage from the top, and it felt that.' You no doubt would understand what I have said. However, it is important to note how limited your understanding would be. You would not be entitled to infer that the alien had a tympanic membrane that was made to vibrate by my speech, for instance. You might be able to infer that the alien has an *ear* understood as nothing more than *an organ of hearing*, but it might be radically different from our organs of hearing.

When we use terms like 'hears', 'feels' or 'ear' across very different kinds of creatures, we are speaking *analogically*. What we say is true provided that there is something in that creature respectively and relevantly similar to hearing, feeling or an ear in more familiar cases. Now, sometimes the relevant difference between cases is sufficiently great that an understanding of that in virtue of which members of one group are *F* would not tell us anything about that in virtue of which members of another group are *F*. Thomas Aquinas calls such cases 'equivocal predication'. In such cases, we might as well use different words in the two cases, though there might be a common origin of some sort. For instance, if our only understanding of 'button' came from clothing fasteners, a sentence like 'Click on the CLOSE button on the screen' would probably mean nothing to us. Of course, once we saw the screen, we might see a certain vague physical similarity between the buttons used for fastening clothes and the CLOSE button, but this physical similarity would not be sufficient to explain that in virtue of which the on-screen button counts a button (even those on-screen buttons that are vaguely 'button-shaped' are not buttons in virtue of the shape, but in virtue of clickability).

But there are other cases where the predication is not equivocal but properly analogous, and where we do in fact understand what is being said, though our understanding is limited. Thus, even if we do not know anything about a Daphnia, not even that it is a crustacean, the claim that a Daphnia *eats* seems to have content. One has an understanding of what is said by analogy to familiar cases.

Moreover, while the concepts *univocal, equivocal* and *analogical* in the first instance apply to predicates, they also make sense in the case of properties. Roughly speaking, we can say that a property P is had univocally by x and y provided that x and y have P in the same way. In such a case, x's having P and y's having P are relevantly the same kind of thing. We can say that a property P is had equivocally by x and y provided that there is no relevant similarity between x's having P and y's having P. Disjunctive properties, like the one in Section II.2, provide a paradigm example. However, when there is a relevant similarity between x's having P and y's having P, the similarity being relevant at least in the sense that it is on account of this similarity that x and y both have the shared property P, we can say that we have a case of analogy. Much more needs to be said, but that would be a topic for another paper.

Let us then return to our alien. You still know basically nothing about it yet, other than that it is strange, that it has at least seven appendages and that it hears and feels. Suppose I let you know one more thing: the alien's hearing is the same as its feeling. If you were impressed by the argument that divine simplicity rendered our concepts incomprehensible as applied to God, you would have to say that when I added this additional bit of information, I have undercut your understanding of what I was talking about when I said that the alien heard and felt.

But I submit that the understanding is not undercut by my additional claim. Rather, the claim underscores how little you in fact knew about the alien just by being told that it hears and feels. Not only were you not allowed to infer that it had a tympanic membrane, but you were not entitled to infer that it had *distinct* organs of hearing and touch. It is worse than that: for when we say that the alien's hearing is identical with its feeling, we are not just saying that both are done by the same organ, the way the tongue both tastes and partially articulates sounds. Rather, we are saying that there is but one activity in both cases.

Our understanding of God's mercy and God's justice is rather like your understanding of the alien's hearing and feeling at this point in my description of the alien. There *is* a genuine puzzlement about how the two features can be the same. And this puzzlement in each case is due to the inability to go, look and see how the two features manage to be the same—whether in the case of God or of the alien. But we are not entitled to infer that it just cannot be so. We have a genuine puzzle, but we do not have a proof that the puzzle has no solution. And in the case of the alien, at least, with some imagination we might come up with an understanding of how one and the same organ with one and the same activity responds to tactile pressure and to vibrations of the air. In such a case, it might well be true that the alien's hearing is the same as its feeling, and that its hearing is relevantly like our hearing and that its feeling is relevantly like our feeling, even though *our* hearing is not relevantly like *our* feeling. Moreover, we do not repeat ourselves when we say that the alien hears and when we say it feels.

III. ACCIDENTAL PROPERTIES

III.1. The general problem

Assume the entailment principle that if T is a truthmaker for p, then that T exists entails p. If we did not make this assumption,[7] it would be easy to

---

[7] Those who say that what makes it true that Socrates was sitting is Socrates himself will deny the entailment principle.

defend the coherence of the claim that a simple God has intrinsic accidental properties. For it then might be that in one world the same entity is the truthmaker for the claim that God believes p while in another world the very same entity might be the truthmaker for the claim that God believes not-p. If so, then God could have accidental intrinsic properties while yet himself being the minimal truthmaker for all propositions about him—it would simply be a contingent matter as to which propositions he is a truthmaker for—and we have understood simplicity in terms of truthmakers. The entailment principle, however, is deeply plausible, and so let us see if we can defend divine simplicity against the accidental property objection while assuming the entailment principle.

It seems like the truthmaker account is not only no help now, but sharpens the accidentality problem. Let P be an intrinsic property. Then God is the truthmaker of the claim that God has P, since the claim that God has P would be a claim solely about God. But the existence of the truth-maker entails the truth of the proposition in question. Hence, that God exists entails that God has P, and hence P is an essential property of God. Thus, all of God's intrinsic properties are essential, and hence none are acci dental.

Given our account (*) of divine simplicity, the only solution is to bite the bullet and assert that the proposition that, say, God believes that p has a truthmaker that not only includes God but must also include something contingent and distinct from God[8] if we are to escape the entailment principle argument, and hence God's having a contingent property is never a fact solely about God. The structure of a truthmaker-based response to the accidentality problem is now clear. It must be claimed that any correct attribution to God of an accidental property has as its truthmaker God and something contingent besides God, and hence the property is at least in part extrinsic. This appears to be a coherent claim.

It is worth noting at this point that medievals like Thomas Aquinas would object to the idea of God having any accidents, whereas this account attributes to God 'accidental extrinsic properties'. This, however, may be a purely verbal distinction. To the scholastics, roughly speaking an accident was something inhering in, and not a part of the essence of, the thing of which it was an accident. Thus an accident in the medieval sense might even be an essential property in the contemporary analytic sense in

---

[8] I am not assuming here that divine simplicity entails the necessity of divine existence, and hence some of the formulations are somewhat more complex than they would need to be if we could assume that God exists necessarily. I do think that God exists necessarily, and this may in fact be entailed by divine simplicity, but that is a different issue.

which an essential property is one that an entity has in every world in which it exists (see Gorman 2005). The standard example is the human capacity for laughter. What I call 'accidental extrinsic properties' would not be counted as accidents (or properties for that matter) at all by the medievals.

At this point it is also worth recalling that I am attempting to formulate the present account in a way that is neutral between different accounts of properties. For instance, my story is at least prima facie compatible with an anti-Platonic view on which there are no properties, but we can posit them as a useful way of talking about predicates.

III.2. Divine believings and willings in general

Coherent though the claim that the truthmaker of contingent propositions about God always includes something other than God, it is counterintuitive in the cases at hand. The minimal truthmaker of the proposition that, say, Bob believes that p is Bob's believing that p, and analogously for willing. Now, Bob's *knowing* that p and Bob's *bringing it about* that p would go beyond Bob—they require that p actually hold. But mere *believing* and *willing* do not seem to go beyond Bob. In fact, they seem paradigm instances of intrinsic properties.

However, there is nothing incoherent about supposing that some property might be intrinsic in the case of one entity and non-intrinsic in the case of another. Bob's *being-human-or-near-Jane* is an intrinsic property of Bob if Bob is a man far from Jane. For the minimal truthmaker of the claim that Bob is human or near Jane is then Bob's being human, which is found in Bob. On the other hand, if Rufus is a dog near Jane, then Rufus's *being-human-or-near-Jane* is a non-intrinsic property of Rufus, since the truthmaker of the proposition that Rufus is human or near Jane is now something like the token spatial relation between Rufus and Jane. Here I am assuming that P is an intrinsic (respectively, non-intrinsic) property of x if there is a minimal truthmaker of the claim that x has P and that minimal truthmaker is x or in x (respectively, that minimal truthmaker includes something outside x).[9]

Granted, in this case it was once again a gerrymandered disjunctive property that showed the possibility of a property being intrinsic in one case and non-intrinsic in another. But as in the case of the multiple attributes problem, we can make use of the idea of analogy. When the

---

[9] This is not a necessary condition for being an intrinsic property, since it does not apply to cases where there is no unique minimal truthmaker.

claims that x is F and y is F are analogical, there is nothing that surprising about the idea that being F might be intrinsic to x while being F might be non-intrinsic to y. A substantive but controversial example might be teleological language understood in an Aristotelian way. When we say that one of the functions of a dog is to self-replicate, we are, on Aristotle's view, attributing to the dog an intrinsic property. On the other hand, when we say that one of the functions of a computer virus is to self-replicate, we are attributing a non-intrinsic property, since the truthmaker of this claim about the computer virus includes both the virus and the intentions of the programmer. We are using the word 'function' analogically but not equivocally here.

Saying it is an extrinsic property of God that he has a particular belief or engages in a particular willing has substantial and controversial conclusions. It implies that radical content externalism is true of God's beliefs and acts of will. That fact that p is the content of one of God's beliefs or willings is made true in part by the world. Now some content externalism seems innocent. Thus, suppose that on Earth the common colourless, tasteless, wet substance is H_2O, while on Twin-Earth it is XYZ. It is plausible that my brain and even my mind is in the same intrinsic state when I think about what I call 'water' as when someone like me on Twin-Earth thinks about what he calls 'water'. Nonetheless, I am thinking about H_2O and he about XYZ. Thus, thinking about H_2O is not an intrinsic property of me, and thinking about XYZ is not an intrinsic property of him. These familiar essentialist considerations lead to a moderate content externalism.

But in the case of God's beliefs or willings, this content externalism applies to all contingent propositions, not just the ones that involve natural kinds or *de re* particulars. This is odd, but not obviously self-contradictory. I will now proceed to discuss the cases of divine beliefs and willings, and attempt to make more plausible the externalist doctrine in these two cases. The account of willings shall be more satisfactory than that of beliefs, and I will begin with it.

III.3. Willings

My account of willings is mainly based on O'Connor (1999), and a version of it has also recently been defended by Jeffrey Brower (forthcoming). Start by considering how libertarian free will—which I will just call 'free will'—might work. If Curley freely chooses to take the bribe, then, let us assume, there is some time at which it was causally possible that he not take the bribe. Moreover, there is a time after which this is no longer causally possible—the choice has been made. Let t_0 be the earliest time with the property that after t_0 it is no longer causally possible that Curley not take the bribe. There *is* such a time. Before this time, Curley's rejection of the bribe is causally open and after this time it is causally closed.

Moreover, I will assume that this time t_0 is associated with Curley's decision to take the bribe. The decision happens at t_0. This is an assumption that might not hold, for it might be that t_0 is a time prior to the decision to take the bribe, a time at which Curley makes some other earlier libertarian-free decision, for example a decision to do whatever it takes to get ahead financially, which causally necessitates that he eventually make a causally determined decision to take the bribe. In that case, if we are to count the bribe-taking as free, it must inherit its freedom from the freedom of that earlier decision.[10] But if we are to avoid a vicious regress, we will come to some decision with the property that the decision is made precisely at a time t_0 such that after that time some deed is causally determined as far as Curley is concerned and before it it was not. This might not in fact be the decision to accept the bribe, but for simplicity I will assume it is.

Thus, at t_0 there is a branching. Before t_0 it was possible for Curley still to reject the bribe and after t_0 this was no longer possible. There are now two models of free will. On the first model, one accepted by Nuel Belnap (email communication) among others, at t_0 the branching has not *yet* happened: it is *still* causally possible for Curley to reject the bribe. It is only at $t_0 + \delta$ (for every $\delta > 0$) that this is no longer possible. The time t_0 is the *last* time at which matters are still open. On the second model, at t_0 the branching has already happened: t_0 is the first time at which matters are no longer open. Since I am only trying to make plausible the *possibility* of divine willings having a radical content externalism, I will stick to the first model, since it seems at least to be a possible model.

Thus, Curley is deciding at t_0, but it is not yet true at t_0 that he *has* decided. Let S be Curley's state at t_0, i.e., the conjunction of all of Curley's purely intrinsic properties at t_0 (or, if we wish, the conjunction of all purely intrinsic properties occurrent up to and including time t_0). This state S occurs both in the actual world where Curley takes the bribe and in a possible world where he refuses it. Fix such a possible world where he refuses it and call it 'the alternate world'. Now, at any moment of time t_1 after the decision time t_0, the actual and the alternate worlds have already diverged. Curley has already done something: something he

---

[10] This kind of derivative freedom is important in Kane (1996). It is likely also necessary for resolving the problem of how the blessed in heaven can be significantly free even though unable to sin.

is morally responsible for. Perhaps his hand has not yet reached out for the money; maybe his enraged voice has not begun to refuse the bribe. He is at t_1 in a state such that he is set to take or is set to refuse the bribe. (I am simplifying by assuming temporizing is not an option.) A deed has been done before t_1: his will has set into motion a causal chain leading up to the taking or the refusing of the bribe. Now the important thing to note is that the cause of the two different causal chains, the one in the actual world and the one in the alternate world, is the same as concerns intrinsic properties. For the cause is Curley at t_0 in state S. Since this state contains all of Curley's intrinsic properties at t_0, and these are the same in the actual and the alternate world, it follows that we have one and the same person in one and the same intrinsic state being in one world responsible for setting into motion one causal chain and in another, another.

But this seems to severely undercut the objection to divine simplicity based on the contingency of what God chooses. For we now see that one and the same person in one the same state could be in a position to initiate either of two incompatible causal chains. Moreover, note that Curley's actual deciding was at t_0. During the deciding itself there was no difference in his intrinsic properties between the actual and the alternate worlds. The difference only appeared extrinsically to the decision, though as a result of the decision.

Of course the analogy is imperfect. After time t_0, Curley does have different intrinsic properties between the actual and the alternate worlds. But at this point he does not have different intrinsic properties qua chooser, but qua one who had chosen: for at any time after t_0 the choice has already been made. Moreover, the difference in these intrinsic properties appears mainly due to the fact that we humans execute our actions through the use of our bodily and mental components, which are put in different states depending on the choice and through which we interact with the physical world. This need not apply in the case of a being that has an *efficacious* will, one that directly affects external reality, without any internal mediating states.

To see a model of this, suppose that Cartesian dualism holds of Curley (I do not think it actually holds of humans, but the notion of its holding appears perfectly coherent). Then it is at least conceivable that the way Curley's decision worked was that at t_0 his immaterial will did something which affected the state that his physical body was in at every time after t_0. Now, imagine that God smote Curley in the actual and alternate worlds by annihilating his soul at all times after t_0, while leaving the body intact. Then, perhaps, the body would still have been affected by the choice that the will had made at t_0. Moreover, at *no* time would Curley be in a different intrinsic state between the actual and alternate worlds, since by what we said before, he would not be in a different intrinsic state up to and including t_0, and after t_0 he would not be in *any* intrinsic state since he would not exist—only his body would.

Thus, at least if the libertarian story on which at the decision time t_0 the branching has not yet happened is coherent, there is no obvious intrinsic contingency implied in God by the fact that he could have willed otherwise. The content of what he willed is constituted at least in part by what was in fact brought about.

III.4. An objection

Let me now consider a remark that I have heard attributed to Brian Leftow: that God creates creatures explains the existence of the creatures, and hence the existence of creatures cannot be a part of the truthmaker of the claim that God creates creatures. Now, if this remark is correct, it is a serious objection to the account of the preceding section. For on that account the claim that God willed to create, say, horses is in part constituted by the existence of horses, and hence the existence of the horses is a part of the truthmaker of the claim that God willed to create horses.

This objection depends on the principle that the truthmaker of the explanandum cannot be a part of the truthmaker of the explanans. But that principle is false. That Jones wrote a book about cats explains why that book about cats exists. Yet a part of the truthmaker of the claim that Jones wrote a book about cats is that very book which he wrote. The explanation of a proposition is a proposition that removes the mystery about why the explanandum holds. The mystery about why there is a book about cats is dispelled by the claim that Jones wrote a book about cats, even though that book is a part of truthmaker of the explanans. One might, of course, alternately claim that what explains why there is a book about cats is that Jones *willed to* write a book about cats or that Jones *tried to* write a book about cats. And these are, indeed, fine explanations as well. But so is the explanation in terms of Jones *actually* having written the book.

III.5. Divine beliefs

God is essentially omniscient. Given a proposition p such that (a) it is possible that both p is true and God exists and (b) it is possible that both p is false and God exists (if God exists necessarily, then any contingent proposition will satisfy (a) and (b)), God believes the proposition if and only if the proposition holds. Hence, if p holds, it is an accidental property of God that he believes p, and if p fails to hold, then it is an accidental property of God that he does not believe p. If God has no intrinsic accidental properties, the content externalism implied by this seems radical.

Here the best I can do is offer an analogy to a theory of mind that is almost surely false of humans, but that at least prima facie seems coherent, and so perhaps an analogue for God is coherent. Take a naïve form of Descartes' theory on which my mind's eye contemplates phenomena (feels, touches, etc.) as it were appearing on a screen in front of my mind's eye, and where my mind's eye is wholly distinct from the phenomena it contemplates. It is the difference in the phenomena that individuates the state of feeling hot and the state of feeling cold. One state involves my mind's eye standing in a relation of contemplation to *a feeling of heat* and the other involves its standing in that relation to *a feeling of cold*. But now observe that the difference between these two states seems to be *extrinsic* to my mind's eye: it consists in a difference between the feels, and the feels are not a part of the mind's eye. The mind's eye is not intrinsically modified by the things it sees. Maybe, then, God is related to the world the way such a Cartesian mind's eye is to its phenomena.

There is an alternate solution, a version of which was recently defended by Jeffrey Brower (forthcoming in Flint and Rea), and this is Thomas Aquinas' identification of God's knowing and believing. In the previous section I have argued that one can make sense of divine willings given divine simplicity. Suppose we simply say that God's knowing that p just *is* God's willing it that p, at least for positive propositions p.[11] After all, by virtue of intentionally producing a state of affairs an agent has 'intentional knowledge' of that state of affairs. It is essential that the willings here be productive acts of will, not just desires. The disadvantage of this account is that, as Brower notes, it requires compatibilism. For suppose that Jones mows the lawn. Then God's knowing that Jones does this depends on God's willing that Jones do it, and hence Jones is determined by God to mow the lawn. Only if such determination is compatible with free will can we then say that Jones *freely* mows the lawn.

Brower argues that his account is required by the doctrine of aseity which says that God is entirely independent of everything other than himself.

---

[11] This qualification is needed if one does not want to say that God brings about evils. Negative claims would then need to be handled differently. For instance, God might know about the non-existence of Long John Silver's leg not by willing that Silver lack a leg, but by willing some minor or major good incompatible with Silver's having that leg, say the skin's being closed up around the stump. Since I am not defending Aquinas' account of divine knowledge, I will not develop this further.

For unless God produces the objects of his knowledge, he is dependent on them, even if his knowing the objects is an extrinsic property. In other words, Brower believes that the doctrine of aseity rules out the possibility of God's having any accidental properties, extrinsic or intrinsic, unless God has brought about that feature of the world in virtue of which the properties hold.

This, however, is an unnaturally strong account of aseity. The doctrine of aseity says that God is entirely independent of anything other than himself. Dependence in respect of an extrinsic property is not real dependence, just as change in respect of an extrinsic property is not real change but Cambridge change. Extending aseity to extrinsic properties makes aseity entail complete sovereignty, the claim that every proposition p is entailed by what God wills in the productive sense of 'wills'. For if some proposition p were not entailed by what God wills, then God would be dependent in respect of the extrinsic property *being such that p*.

But such an extension of aseity appears excessive, even if Aquinas and some other medievals would accept it. Aseity is more naturally thought of as a denial of God's having any *real* dependence on anything other than himself, and the further claim that every contingent proposition has its truth value determined by what God wills seems a separate claim, one that can be rejected by someone who denies that God has a real dependence on anything other than himself. A Platonist who believes that some mathematical entity (say, the empty set) is intrinsically independent of everything else surely asserts aseity of that entity even if she does not claim that all other entities depend on it. It might be that aseity in the weaker sense implies aseity in the stronger sense through some clever argument—but such an argument would need to be defended.

Aseity, then, is better seen as a claim about God being independent of everything else, not about every fact being determined by God. The defender of an account of divine knowledge that allows for libertarian free will on the part of creatures can accept divine aseity restricted to intrinsic properties and can also accept the weaker additional claim that everything other than God is *dependent* on God. For one can say that Jones' mowing the lawn is dependent on God without saying it is determined by God.

III.6. Final remarks on beliefs and willings

The attentive reader may note at this point that while I have been defending the idea that God's believing or willing that p includes as its truthmaker something outside of God, I have said nothing about what that 'something' is. A natural proposal, though not the only possible one, is that the 'something' is nothing other than a truthmaker of p itself. If so, then it becomes clearer why it is that p holds if and only if God believes that p, as well as why p holds if and only if God wills that p. Moreover, this proposal gives us a different, probably non-Thomistic, reason to accept Aquinas' claim that God's knowing something and God's causing it are identical. For, if this proposal is correct, there is a single truthmaker for the claim that God knows that p and for the claim that God wills that p, namely God plus a truthmaker of p.[12]

IV. CONCLUSIONS

If we understand divine simplicity as the claim that the minimal truthmaker of any claim solely about God and his parts is God himself, then it appears we can make coherent sense of the idea that divine attributes all collapse without endangering language. They collapse not in the language-endangering sense that one is *saying* the same thing by claiming that God is merciful as by claiming that God is just, but in the sense that the very same thing makes both claims true. Understanding how this works in practice almost surely requires a robust theory of analogical predication.

Likewise, once we recognize that a property might be intrinsic in the case of one entity and non-intrinsic in the case of another, we see that there is no immediate contradiction in a simple God having accidental properties such as *willing that p* or *believing that p*, as long as these are not intrinsic properties in the case of God. Medievals like Aquinas would deny that God has accidental properties at all, but at least some of the disagreement here may be merely verbal. For these medievals certainly agree that there are contingent propositions about God, such as that God created horses, and the disagreement may simply consist in the fact that they might resist calling the non-intrinsic properties in question 'properties'.

Nonetheless the idea that that God wills or believes that p are not claims solely about God are hard sayings, especially since the defender of simplicity does not want to opt for a pantheistic account. I tried to assuage some of the hardness of the claim about willings by noting that a plausible account of libertarian free will would allow for cases in finite agents where willing that p is at least partially constituted by events outside of the agent. The case of believings is harder, but a hint at an answer might be found in

---

[12] If negative propositions lack truthmakers, things are more difficult. It may, for instance, be that the claim that God believes not-p where p is a positive proposition is made true, then, by God's perfection together with God's believing q, where q is some positive proposition incompatible with p.

content externalism and Cartesian theaters. This all, however, has to be understood in the way of offering analogies, since there is nothing exactly like God's radical simplicity in the world. For, as Aquinas tells us, 'goodness, which in God is simple and uniform, in creatures is manifold and divided and hence the whole universe together participates the divine goodness more perfectly, and represents it better than any single creature whatever' (Aquinas, 1920: I.47. 1).

REFERENCES

Aquinas, Thomas. *Summa Theologica*, trans. Fathers of the English Dominican Province, 2nd edn. (1920). Online edition on <www. newadvent.org>.
—— *Disputed Questions on Truth*, vol. 1, trans. R. W. Mulligan SJ (Chicago: Regnery, 1952).
Bergmann, M. and J. Brower, 'A Theistic Argument Against Platonism (and in Support of Truthmakers and Divine Simplicity)', forthcoming in *Oxford Studies in Metaphysics* (Oxford: Oxford University Press).
Brower, J. 'Simplicy and Aseity', forthcoming in T. P. Flint and M. C. Rea (eds), *Oxford Handbook of Philosophical Theology* (Oxford: Oxford University Press).
—— 'Making Sense of Divine Simplicity', forthcoming in *Faith and Philosophy*.
Gorman, M. 'The Essential and the Accidental', in *Ratio* 18 (2005): 276–89.
Kane, R. *The Significance of Free Will* (Oxford: Oxford University Press, 1996).
Maimonides, Moses. *The Guide for the Perplexed*, trans. M. Friedländer, 2nd edn. (Mineola, NY: Dover Publications, 1956).
Mulligan, K., P. Simons, and B. Smith, 'Truth-Makers', in *Philosophy and Phenomenological Research* 44 (1984): 287–321.
O'Connor, T. 'Simplicity and Creation', in *Faith and Philosophy* 16 (1999): 405–12.
Oppy, G. 'The Devilish Complexity of Divine Simplicity', in *Philo* 6 (2003): 10–22.
Pruss, A. R. 'On Three Problems of Divine Simplicity', presented at the Society of Christian Philosophers satellite session at the American Catholic Philosophical Association annual meeting, October, 2003.
Wolterstorff, N. 'Divine Simplicity', in J. E. Tomberlin (ed.), *Philosophical Perspectives* 5, *Philosophy of Religion* (Atascadero, CA: Ridgeview, 1991), 531–52.

8

Defending Divine Freedom

Thomas D. Senor

INTRODUCTION

In a series of articles and most recently in his book *Can God Be Free?*, William Rowe has argued that the traditional theistic view of the nature of God is fundamentally incoherent. In particular, Rowe believes that:

  (i) God is essentially omnipotent,
 (ii) God is essentially omniscient,
(iii) God is essentially perfectly good, and
(iv) God creates freely

constitute an inconsistent tetrad. Furthermore, Rowe argues, the theist should not be prepared to give up (iv) because if God's creative acts are not free, then God is not praiseworthy and it is not the case that God is properly thanked for his goodness towards his creatures. In this paper, I'll examine Rowe's argument for this inconsistency. While there is little doubt that there is a prima facie problem here for the classical theist, Rowe's argument can be shown to be unsuccessful, or so I will argue. In the next section of this paper, I will expound Rowe's position. Having done that, I will explain the three ways I think the argument is vulnerable. The three sections after that will be dedicated to giving each objection its voice.

I. ROWE'S ARGUMENT

Rowe begins his discussion by considering the correspondence between Gottried Leibniz and Samuel Clarke in which, among other things, the two

Thanks to Eric Funkhouser and Barry Ward for helpful conversations.

eminent philosophers discuss the nature of divine freedom and its relation to creation. In what turns out to be a crucial component of his overall argument, Rowe writes the following:

> Following Leibniz, we can imagine God considering a variety of worlds he might create. One might be a world in which there are no conscious creatures at all, a world composed solely of dead matter. Another might be a world composed (at some stage in its history) of living, conscious creatures whose lives are meaningful, morally good, and happy. Assume, as seems evident, that the second world is the better world ... If God were limited to these two worlds, he would face three choices: creating the inferior world, creating the superior world, creating no world at all. For God to decide to create no world over creating a world that is, all things considered, a very good world, would be for God to do less than the best that he can do. If so, it seems that God's perfect goodness would *require* him to create the very good world. But if God's perfect goodness requires him to create the very good world, rather than creating the inferior world, or not creating a world at all, what are we to make of that part of the idea of God that declares that he created the world *freely*? To say that God *freely* created the good world seems to imply that he was free not to do so, that he could have created the inferior world, or refrained from creating either world. But if his perfect goodness *requires* him to create the good world, how is it possible that he was free to create the inferior world or not to create any world? This is a simple way of picturing the problem of divine perfection and divine freedom.[1]

A few pages later, Rowe states his Leibnizian argument somewhat more formally:

[ARG 1]:

1. If God exists and is omnipotent, perfectly wise and perfectly good, then he chooses to create the best of all possible worlds.
2. God exists and is omnipotent, perfectly wise and good.

Therefore,

3. God chooses to create the best of all possible worlds.[2]

In order to get a good handle on Rowe's overall argument, two points need to be made.

First, as the argument stands, the conclusion is not a threat to divine freedom. For it says only that God *will* choose the best world, not that God *must* choose the best world (or that, necessarily, God will choose the best world). Although in the text it is clear that Rowe understands the premises to be not merely true but necessarily true, the fact that this isn't explicit in

---

[1] Rowe (2004: 12–13).   [2] Rowe (2004: 16).

the premises as they appear in the argument is problematic. So let's make their modal status explicit as follows:

[ARG 2]:

1. Necessarily, if God exists and is omnipotent, perfectly wise and perfectly good, then he chooses to create the best of all possible worlds.
2. Necessarily, God exists and is omnipotent, perfectly wise and good.

Therefore,

3. Necessarily, God chooses to create the best of all possible worlds.

Although this version of the argument does give us a conclusion that is plausibly inconsistent with divine creative freedom, its weakness is that it works only against the theist who accepts God's necessary existence and essential omnipotence, wisdom, and goodness. However, none of these assumptions are central to the main thread of Rowe's argument. Here's a version in the spirit of the Leibniz/Rowe argument that does not depend on the modally strengthened theistic claims:

[ARG 3]:

1. Necessarily, if God exists and God exemplifies omnipotence, perfect wisdom, and perfect goodness in a stable manner, then God chooses to create the best creatable world in every world accessible to God.
2. God exists and God exemplifies omnipotence, perfectly wisdom, and perfect goodness in a stable manner.
3. Therefore, God chooses to create the best creatable world in every world accessible to God.
4. If S does X in every world accessible to S, then S doesn't do X freely.
5. Therefore, God doesn't freely bring about the best creatable world.

The argument depends on the idea of a being's having a property in a stable manner. Property P is *stable* for a being B at a world W iff (a) B exemplifies P at all times in W[3] and (b) there is nothing B can do to make it the case that B ceases to exemplify P in W. Put somewhat differently, if a person has a property in a stable way, there are no worlds accessible to her in which she doesn't have it. Exemplifying a property in a stable way is, for all practical purposes, as limiting as having that property essentially. For example, suppose that in world W, Ray has the stable (but accidental)

---

[3] In order to make property stability friendly to atemporalists, the first condition can be recast as : (i) B exemplifies P in W and there is no time when B fails to exemplify P in W.

property of being blind. Then not only does Ray not see—Ray *can't* see in W, even though there are other worlds in which Ray has 20/20 vision.

The second point that should be made about Rowe's Leibnizian argument is that it presupposes that there is a best of all possible worlds.[4] But it is by no means obvious that such an assumption is right. For it's epistemically possible that rather than there being a single best world, there is an infinite hierarchy of better worlds so that for any world, there is a world better. In such a case, one might suppose, God's hands are not tied by his perfect goodness. We will go into more detail about this in a subsequent section, but for now the point needs to be made that Rowe's broader argument doesn't depend on this controversial assumption. For Rowe contends that if there is no best world, then there is another serious problem lurking: God might be free but God wouldn't be perfectly good. For, if there is no best world, then for any world that God creates there is a better world that God could have created. And if God creates a world when there is a better world that God could have created instead, then God could have done better than he did. But if God could have been better than he did, then he is not perfectly good.

Here, then, is Rowe's broader argument (although this particular presentation is mine):

[ARG 4]:

1. Either there is a best world or there is an infinite hierarchy of better worlds
2. If there is a best world, then the Creator is not free with respect to either creating at all or creating the world he creates.
3. If there is an infinite hierarchy of better worlds, then the Creator is not perfectly good.

C1. Therefore, either the Creator is not free or he is not perfectly good.

4. The Creator is God only if the Creator is a perfectly good being.

C2. Therefore, either God doesn't exist or the Creator is not perfectly free.

This argument is valid. In the sections that follow, we shall have a look at each of the premises of ARG 4. We will begin with the fourth premise and work backward.

---

[4] For those familiar with what Alvin Plantinga (1974: Ch. 9) calls 'Leibniz's Lapse', the above argument doesn't crucially depend on the claim that God is able to bring about the best possible world. For Rowe's purposes, it is enough that there is a best feasible world, i.e., a best world that God is able to actualize. Having made this point, I will now generally ignore it and speak as though if there is best possible world, God can bring it about.

II. PREMISE FOUR—'THE CREATOR IS GOD ONLY IF THE CREATOR IS PERFECTLY GOOD'

We will spend considerably more time on the first three steps of the argument than we will on this fourth premise. Although Rowe doesn't state the premise in quite this way, the text makes it clear that he is committed to it as stated in 4.[5] What he has in mind is plain and common in the circles in which analytic philosophers of religion run. In as much as the concept of God is the concept of a being with all perfections, and perfect goodness is a perfection, then if there is no perfectly good being, then there is no God, i.e., God doesn't exist. However, there is something very artificial about all this. For my money, there are two good, related options for deciding the content of 'God' and neither entails that if there is no perfectly good being, then there is no God. First, we might treat 'God' as a proper name, and then if the theist is a Kripkean direct reference-theorist about names (as I think she should be), she'll think that the term has reference but no sense. And the reference will be secured by an initial baptism that dates back to the ancient Hebrews, and a successful causal chain that links up that (those) baptismal acts with our current use.

Alternatively, the theist might think of 'God' as a kind term. It is presumably something like this that Rowe has in mind when he says if there is no perfectly good being then God doesn't exist: nothing is of the divine kind if nothing is perfectly good. Now I think the most natural way of making sense of the way standard theists (as opposed to philosophers of religion) understand 'God' when they aren't using the term as a name is again along Kripkean lines: God is a supernatural kind with the intensional content of the term 'God' being like 'the personal creator who revealed himself to the Hebrew people',[6] and with the extension being fixed (again) in a Kripkean, causal manner.[7]

As I said, though, I think 'God' is generally used as a name by worshippers in churches, synagogues, and mosques. Of course, it is true that theists make lots of other claims about the essence or nature of this being, but none of these assertions is such that 'God' fails to refer if one or more aren't true.

---

[5] For example, Rowe (2004: 89) writes: '[I]f the actual world is not the best world that an omnipotent omniscient being could create, God does not exist.'

[6] As I have the intension stated, it does contain some descriptive content so this isn't a pure Kripkean theory. I take it that if the Hebrew prophets were suffering from hallucinations, the causes of which were the roots of a type of plant they had consumed, we should think that the theistic God doesn't exist, not that it is a hallucinogen.

[7] For more on these issues, see Senor (1992).

To deny this is akin to thinking that when a child at age four conceives of her parents as all-knowing and morally perfect, and then at age seven has those illusions dashed, she should conclude that Mom and Dad don't exist. But that, of course, is silly. Learning of her parents' fallibility does not make her an orphan. Now, of course, Rowe doesn't think that if his argument is successful, he's shown that there is no Creator of Heaven and Earth, but only that there is no 'God'. So in a sense, my point is, as they say, 'merely semantic'. However, when philosophers conclude that there is no God because they take themselves to have shown that no being could have one or more of the properties historically attributed to God, they are gaining a rhetorical advantage they have not earned in the argument they've provided.

III. PREMISE THREE—IF THERE IS AN INFINITE HIERARCHY OF BETTER WORLDS, THEN GOD IS NOT PERFECTLY GOOD

One might be tempted to respond to Rowe's Leibnizian argument by claiming that there is no reason to think that there is a best world. For all we know, there might be an infinite hierarchy of very good worlds. If so, God would presumably have the freedom to create from among the infinite set of very good worlds. If God decides that it is better to create than not to create, and God recognizes that there is a hierarchy of infinitely many very good worlds, then God will freely chose from among those possible creations. Hence God's creative freedom is secured by an infinite hierarchy of very good worlds.

Not so fast, thinks Rowe. If the Creator were to create a very good world in such a circumstance, then the Creator is not God. Why not? Because a perfectly good being will always do the best that it is able to do. However, in the above circumstance, no matter how good a world the Creator produces, he will not have done his best since there will be infinitely many better worlds that he could have created but chose not to. Rowe's precise statement of his crucial principle is this (Rowe calls it 'Principle B'):

If an omniscient being creates a world when there is a better world it could have created, then it would be possible for there to be a being morally better than it.[8]

Such a being would not be perfectly good because it isn't possible for there to be a being better than a perfectly good being. Therefore, if there is an

---

[8] Rowe (2004: 89).

infinite hierarchy of good worlds and the Creator chooses to create one of them, the Creator is not God (who by definition is perfectly good).

Daniel and Frances Howard-Snyder have argued against Principle B by telling a story comparing two creators who find themselves having to choose among the infinitely many good worlds.[9] Jove and Juno both decide that since among the very good worlds, every world is such that there are infinitely many very good worlds better than it, the only reasonable way to choose a particular world to create is to first create a randomizing device that will choose among the very good worlds. Suppose, the Howard-Snyders suggest, we begin with the minimally good very good world and assign to it the first positive integer and assign the second positive integer to the second minimally good very good world and continue this way, thus making a one-to-one correspondence between very good worlds and positive integers. Jove uses the randomizing machine to choose the world to create, and it spits out the number 777; Jove then creates that world. Juno's randomizer spits out 999 and Juno creates that world. Now the Howard-Snyders argue that Jove and Juno are morally equivalent since they have followed precisely the same method for creating a world. The only difference between the two concerns the results of the randomizing machine. But if that is correct, then Principle B is false, since it would have us conclude straightaway that Jove is not perfectly good.

Rowe agrees that Jove and Juno are morally equivalent, but he thinks that neither one is morally perfect. Rowe contrasts Jove and Juno with another god used in another example by the Howard-Snyders (although the example is amended by Rowe). Thor also creates with the help of a randomizer, but Thor's standard of minimal goodness in a world he might create is higher than that of Jove and Juno. Worlds 1–800 are deemed by Thor as not good enough to create given the infinity of better worlds. So Thor's randomizing device has world 801 as the least good world and the machine selects world 888 for creation. Rowe argues that even though the world that Thor creates is inferior to that created by Juno, Thor is morally superior to both Jove and Juno because Thor has a higher standard of world acceptability; that is, some of the worlds deemed good enough to create by Jove and Juno are deemed not good enough by Thor. Hence, Rowe insists, Thor is better.

Better, but not morally perfect because Thor doesn't create the best world he's capable of (he could have brought about any one of the worlds in the infinite hierarchy). Therefore, the bottom line is that Rowe thinks because Principle B is correct, if there is an infinite hierarchy of good worlds, then the Creator isn't perfectly good so God doesn't exist.

---

[9] Howard-Snyder (1994, 1996).

There is a tempting reply to Rowe's use of Principle B that can be found (or is at least suggested) in the writings of several prominent philosophers.[10] The objection is roughly that if, necessarily, there is no way to avoid creating a world than which there is a (creatable) better, then God's creating a world than which there is a better doesn't count against God's moral perfection.

There is a weaker and a stronger way to understand this claim. The weaker reading is that, in the circumstances described, God would not be *culpable* for creating a surpassable world—that is, God doesn't do anything for which he is to blame. Here's the principle that could be appealed to in support of this claim:

P1: If, S necessarily does X, then S is not to blame for doing X.

Although Rowe will grant the truth of P1 and its application to the case in question, the objection understood this way isn't sufficiently strong as a response to Rowe's argument. For, while never being culpable for an action is a necessary condition for perfect goodness, it surely isn't sufficient; that is, perfect goodness is more than perfect blamelessness. Suppose Adolf's essential moral character is such that committing murder on a massive scale is something he does at every world at which he has the chance. In such a case, Adolf is not to *blame* for his murderous ways. So Rowe can accept P1 and insist that it poses no problem for him: he isn't claiming that in the present 'no best world' scenario God is *blameworthy* for creating a world that is surpassable, but only that God is not morally perfect if God does so.

The stronger reading of this objection is not subject to this response but it also is not so clearly right. According to the strong reading, creating a world that is not as good a world as the being might have created does not count against *perfect goodness* when there is simply no way to avoid it. Here's the general principle:

P2: If S necessarily does X, then S's doing X does not count against S's moral perfection.

Even apart from the considerations that drive us here, there is reason for doubting P2. Think back to Adolf. Although he can't be blamed for an essential defect in his character, Adolf's having that essential defect guarantees that he will never be completely good at any given world. For having a murderous character rules out the possibility of moral perfection.

---

[10] Objections along these lines can be found in Hasker (forthcoming); Wainwright (1999); Morris (1993); and Kretzman (1990).

That P2 is a fair understanding of the reasoning behind at least some of those objecting in this manner can be seen clearly in this quotation from William Wainwright (as quoted by Rowe):

But ... a type of complaint which is always in place is never in place. A complaint is only legitimate when the person whose conduct is criticized could have acted in such a way that he or she would not be exposed to a complaint of that type.[11]

Yet we see in the case of Adolf that we should agree with the above sentiment only when it is culpability that is at issue. That a person couldn't possibility have avoided a bad course of action can show that the person is not perfectly good even if she isn't blameworthy for performing it. So what if we amend the principle slightly to avoid cases like that of Adolf. To wit,

P3: If in a given circumstance C, it is logically impossible for any person who finds herself in C to avoid taking a certain course of action A, then doing A does not count against A's perfect goodness.

The problem with P3 is that without some helpful, further description of C, it is clearly false. For instance, suppose I have promised to return your bicycle this afternoon, but having desperately wanted to buy a couple new games for my Xbox 360, I hawked it where upon it was immediately mistakenly destroyed in a trash-compacting accident. Now no one in my circumstances would be able to avoid taking the course of action of failing to give you back your bike after promising to return it. However, surely my being in this position counts against my being perfectly good.

Suppose we were able to find a principle, call it 'P4', in the spirit of P3 but that was apparently unassailable. Would that settle the matter against Rowe? Rowe doesn't think so. For suppose P4 is true—i.e., that since God's creating a world that is surpassable is necessary or unavoidable for anyone, having created a surpassable world is not a sign of God's moral imperfection. (Again, because doing what no one could possibly avoid can count against one's moral perfection.) Nevertheless, suppose there is an infinite hierarchy of worlds and that, as things go, God creates very good world W1 when he could have created even-better world W2 (or even-better-than-that world W3, etc.). Then God has done something that is not necessary (create W1) and such that he could have done better (create world W2 or a better world than that). And this much seems undeniable. But if it is right, then given Principle B (i.e., If an omniscient being creates a world when there is a better world it could have created, then it would be possible for there to be a being morally better than it), we get the conclusion that God is not morally perfect (and hence is not God). In other words, Rowe wins.

---

[11] Rowe (2004: 118); taken from Wainwright (1999: 92).

It must be granted that Principle B has significant initial plausibility. However, as Rowe himself points out,[12] the plausibility of a principle must be judged (at least in part) by the plausibility of that with which it is inconsistent. And if it is more plausible that the infinite hierarchy of worlds thesis is consistent with the possibility of a perfectly good, omnipotent being than it is that Principle B is true, then we have some reason to doubt the truth of the latter.

One point that Edward Wierenga (2002) makes rather quickly but that I think deserves a more thorough hearing is the difference infinity makes. Whereas Principle B might be very plausible *given the existence of a best world (or worlds)*, when the possibility of an infinite hierarchy of good worlds is introduced, its plausibility drops dramatically.[13] That this should be the case isn't too surprising: the logic of infinite series is rather different than that of finite series. To see this illustrated rather dramatically, let's briefly consider an exchange between William Lane Craig and Paul Draper on the Kalam argument for God's existence.[14] Craig has argued that there cannot be an actually infinite set of real objects because such sets bring with them absurd consequences. Craig discusses Hilbert's Hotel and other well-known implications of actual infinities. For example, if you add a blue book to a set of infinitely many red books, you end up with a set with the 'same number of members' (i.e., infinitely many) that you had before you added the blue book. Furthermore, if instead of adding a single blue book, you were to add infinitely many blue books to the set of infinitely many red books, you'd still end up with a set of infinitely many members even though that is precisely 'the number' of books you had in the first place.

In his response, Draper claims that Craig's position amounts to noting that the following triad of propositions is inconsistent, and to resolving the inconsistency by rejecting the third. The propositions in question are:

S1: A set has more members than that contained by any of its proper subsets.

S2: If the members of two sets can be placed in a one-to-one correspondence, then neither set has more members than the other.

S3: There are actually infinite sets.

Each of these propositions is initially plausible. But when one sees that the truth of S3 implies that either S1 or S2 is false, one realizes that one of these initially credible propositions will have to go. If we accept S3, then we'll have to dump S1 and S2. Now the key to seeing how to reasonably

---

[12] Rowe (2004: 120–1).   [13] Wierenga (2002).
[14] Craig (2003) and Draper (2003).

do this is to see that S1 and S2 are unquestionably true *when applied to finite sets.* So we needn't deny either if we were to so limit their domains of application to the finite. When we apply S1 and S2 to infinite sets, however, we should immediately sense that something is amiss because there isn't a natural, rational or real number that is 'the number of members' of an infinite set; rather the set contains infinitely many members. So if 'more' means 'a greater number' then S1 is clearly false for infinite sets. However, as Draper points out, there is surely a straight-forward intuitive sense in which, for example, the set of *all* positive integers 'has more members' than the set of *even* positive integers; every member of the latter set is also a member of the former set, but the former set has members that are not in the latter set. Now if 'has more members' can be understood as 'has every member and then some', then we have a way of making sense of S1, and we can see that S1 is true even of infinite sets. However, on this understanding of 'has more members', S2 will turn out to be false. For the set of all positive integers can put into a one-to-one correspondence with the set of all even positive integers even though the former clearly 'has more members' in this second sense of the phrase.

What is the point of this aside into the Kalam argument and actual infinities? I believe this provides us with a good illustration what's wrong with Rowe's steadfast conviction that Principle B is true. Principles S1 and S2 are not only prima facie plausible but are obviously true if we confine their domain to finite sets. However, if we assume the existence of actually infinite sets, then they cannot both be true. My claim is that something similar is going on regarding Principle B. Suppose that there is an omniscient Creator and a single best, creatable world. Now if in this circumstance, the Creator fails to produce the best creatable world, then he could have done better (i.e., made a better world) than he has in fact done. What could account for this? Well, contrary to the claims of Robert Adams and William Wainwright, it can't be that the perfectly good Creator valued something other than goodness/perfection in a world. For what makes a world the *best world* is its overall value and not simply its *moral* goodness or general perfection; if there is a single best world, it will be a world which exemplifies whatever other goods an omniscient, perfectly good being values. Given that the single best world is creatable by the Creator, it would seem that the only explanation for its not being produced is a defect in the will of the Creator. He lacks the volition to do his best. But if the Creator lacks the volition to do his best, then he could have been better (as Principle B says). Hence the Creator is not perfectly good in this scenario.

Consider now the situation in which there is no best world but an infinite hierarchy of very good worlds. If the Creator, recognizing his predicament, decides to use the Howard-Snyders' randomizing machine and thereby produces a very good, but surpassable world, shall we say that he's done his best? This is admittedly a hard question to answer unequivocally, and that is because in these circumstances there is no such thing as *doing one's best*. On the one hand, we might grant, this method for choosing a world to create is, in principle, as good as can be had in the (necessary) circumstances; on the other hand, no matter what world the machine randomly selects, the Creator could have brought about a better world. Yet unlike the situation in which there is a best world that the Creator nevertheless does not bring about, the problem here isn't with his volition or nature. For he is aware of his situation and so knows that it is logically impossible for him to produce an unsurpassably good creation. And it is logically impossible for him to do his best not because of an imperfect will or a flaw in his essence, but because of the external, necessary circumstances. In this case, it is impossible for him to produce an unsurpassably good creation because it is impossible for *anyone in these necessary circumstances*— including the being than which none greater is possible—to do it. Note that this is a different point than that which Wainwright et. al. are making: they claim that if doing X is not possible for a particular person, then that person's failure to do X doesn't rule out her being perfectly good. But the Adolf example shows this is mistaken. The principle I am appealing to is this: if doing X is logically impossible even for a person with a nature as morally perfect as is logically possible, then that person's failure to do X doesn't rule out her being perfectly good. If there is an infinite hierarchy of increasingly good worlds, then the creative product of a morally perfect (i.e., a perfectly good) Creator will be surpassable. Thus, while Principle B is true if there is a best world (or worlds), if there is an infinity of increasingly good worlds, then this prima facie principle turns out to be false.

IV. PREMISE TWO—IF THERE IS A BEST WORLD, THEN GOD IS NOT FREE WITH RESPECT TO EITHER CREATING AT ALL OR CREATING THE WORLD GOD CREATES

We've already looked at the major component of the justification for the premise; it is the Liebniz-inspired argument I have outlined three versions of above. Let's focus on the second version, viz., ARG 2.

1. Necessarily, if God exists and is omnipotent, perfectly wise and perfectly good, then he chooses to create the best of all possible worlds.
2. Necessarily, God exists and is omnipotent, perfectly wise and good.

Therefore,

3. Necessarily, God chooses to create the best of all possible worlds.

Note that the conclusion of this argument doesn't explicitly say that God is not free with respect to bringing about the best of all possible worlds. To get that conclusion explicitly we need an additional premise:

4. If God necessarily chooses to create the best of all possible worlds, then God doesn't freely choose to create the best of all possible worlds.

The justification for this premise is given by Rowe in the following passage:

Thus far we have supposed with Leibniz that among possible worlds there is one that is best. And we have argued that given God's absolute perfection, he would of necessity create the best world. If the reasoning for this conclusion is correct, then in the matter of creating among possible worlds, God cannot be free.[15]

The point, then, is this: if God's creating the best world is necessary, then God is not able to refrain from creating the best world (since there is no world at which God doesn't create the best world). But if one can't refrain from a given action, then one isn't free with respect to that action. Therefore, God isn't free with respect to creating the best world.

One might think that while it might be somewhat disappointing if it turned out that God isn't free with respect to creating, the theist could give up divine freedom with respect to creation without sacrificing anything terribly significant. Rowe, however, disagrees. He thinks that if God is not free with respect to creation, then God isn't free generally. And, if God isn't free, then God is not to be thanked for the good things God does, nor is God worthy of praise since both thanks and praise require the agent's ability to refrain from the relevant actions.[16] Surely, we must agree with Rowe that if the necessity of God's creating the best world entails that God is neither to be thanked nor praised, then the necessity of God's creating the best world would entail some substantial changes in the way the theist sees God.

There are, then, three questions that need addressing with regard to the expanded ARG 2: (i) Does God's essential nature, together with the assumption that there is a single best creatable world entail that God will bring about that world?; (ii) If the answer to (i) is 'yes', does that imply that God doesn't freely bring about that world?; and (iii) If that answer to both (i) and (ii) is 'yes', does that imply that God is not to be thanked or praised for his beneficial actions?

---

[15] Rowe (2004: 74).

[16] On Rowe (2004: 2), Rowe claims that if God is not free, then 'it can be argued' that God is not praiseworthy, nor worthy of our thanks and gratitude.

IV.A. Does God's nature entail that God will create the best if there is a best?

Although Robert Adams and William Wainwright are officially on record with a negative answer to this question,[17] I'm inclined to agree with Rowe here. Given that we understand the 'best' world as the world that has the greatest overall combination of value, then it seems to me that if God is essentially perfectly good, then God will want to bring about the best overall state of affairs that he can. Now perhaps the best overall world is not the world with the happiest or most beautiful and or supremely gifted inhabitants; perhaps the best overall world is a world in which there is ample room for grace and unmerited love (as Adams and Wainwright think). But on the assumption that some creatable world contains uniquely the best overall combination of value, then God's perfect goodness would seem to insure that God would have the will to bring that world about. In any event, for the purpose of this paper, I don't intend to deny this.

IV.B. If, necessarily, God brings about the best creatable world, does that imply that God isn't free?

Rowe is upfront about his incompatibilist sensibility: the fact that God cannot refrain from creating the best world guarantees that God is not free with respect to creating that world. However, despite Rowe's careful reasoning, I find that if I am not keeping his argument firmly in mind, I can lose my grip on just how it is that God lacks the requisite freedom.

In an effort to look at the issue from another angle, let's think about what the theist says about how divine acts are produced.[18] Being omniscient, God knows in any given situation what the best thing is for God to do.[19] Being perfectly good, God will want to do the action that is best. Furthermore, God's omnipotence surely requires that God will have the ability to bring about the best that God can do in a given situation. Suppose, then, in circumstance C, doing X is the best thing that God can do. Then God will know that doing X is the best available action, and God will want to perform it. Since God will have no competing desires (say from inclination or simple self-interest) to thwart God's desire to do the best thing, and since

[17] Adams (1972) and Wainwright (1996).
[18] Points similar to some of those I am making in the discussion that follows can be found in Wierenga (2002).
[19] Strictly 'the best' here is the best that the being is able to do at the time.

God is perfectly rational, God will form the volition to do X. And since nothing external can stop God from doing what God intends, God will do X. So we've deduced that God will do X from the assumption that God is omniscient, perfectly good, omnipotent, and rational. Now so far our only conclusion is simply that God will do X, and from that proposition no immediate inferences can be drawn about God's freedom.

As we have seen above, the problem is that a stronger conclusion can be argued for. For, if it is the case that given God's essential attributes, there is no world at which God fails to bring about the best creation that he can, then it is *necessary* that God bring about the best world he can.[20] Furthermore, even if God exhibits these properties in only a stable manner, then there will be no worlds accessible to God at which God refrains from doing God's best. And from that conclusion, together with the libertarian assumption that freedom requires the ability to refrain in precisely the same circumstances, a conclusion about God's lack of freedom apparently does follow.

While recognizing the strength of the intuition that lead philosophers to claim that freely doing A requires the ability to refrain from doing A in the very circumstances of the action, I can also feel the pull of thinking of God's actions as free even though God fails the 'can refrain' condition. Perhaps a little reflection on the reasons for the 'can refrain' condition will help us understand why God's failing that condition might not be so problematic.

There are, I think, three kinds of cases that strongly motivate the 'can refrain' condition. They are: (a) the problem of past causally sufficient conditions for the action that not only pre-date the volition to perform the action but pre-date the existence of the actor; (b) concerns about manipulation by other agents; and (c) worries about internal compulsions (e.g., addiction/psychological disorder cases).

Regarding (a): if events that occur billions of years before I was born, together with laws of nature that were also in place billions of years before I was born, conspire to set in motion a sequence of events that are causally sufficient for my performing A, the claim that I am nevertheless doing A freely seems far fetched. Why? Because I did not exist when the matter of my doing A was settled. Notice, however, that in the case of God's doing X, there are no conditions or events spatially or temporally prior to God which determine God's actions. Yes, God couldn't refrain from X-ing in circumstance C but there is no set of past series of events and causal laws that is responsible for this.

---

[20] Keep in mind that we are assuming in this section of the paper that there is a best world and that there is not an infinite series of increasingly good worlds.

Regarding (b): This discussion can be very quick. If my performing a certain action is the result of my being manipulated by a nefarious neurosurgeon, devious hypnotist, or controlling creator, then the ultimate cause of my actions is the intentional state the agent who has programmed me. My actions aren't free because another agent is the source of them. Needless to say, this freedom-compromising condition isn't relevant to the volitions and actions of the omnipotent Source of Being.

Regarding (c): Since God is perfectly rational and his volitions and actions are produced by his recognition of the best course of action and his desire to do the best, there can be no worry that God's actions are the result of analogues of human cognitive malfunction brought on either by addiction or psychological disorder. Notice too that the claim that God always does the best because it is the best isn't to be understood as God's having some kind of non-rational, knee-jerk response to the goodness of the action in question. Rather, God's reason for having the volition God has, and for performing the action God does, is God's recognition of the reasons for performing the action in question, God's knowing and appreciating all the reasons for refraining from that action, and God's seeing that the reasons for performing the action are weightier than the reasons for refraining. It's God's understanding of the reasons that leads God to act as God does.

So three primary motivations that lead libertarians to insist that our freedom requires the ability to refrain are simply out of place where God is concerned. That is to say, God's volitions and actions will pass those three tests even though God lacks the ability to refrain from doing what God sees as the best thing to do.

While a libertarian will typically insist that freedom requires the ability to refrain, she will not offer that as a complete analysis of free action. In fact, I can see no reason for a libertarian to not agree with the compatibilist that what we might call 'effective choice' is a necessary condition for free action. One has effective choice regarding an action A if and only if one can do A *if one so wills* and refrain from doing A *if one wills*.[21] A free action would seem to require that my action be able to reflect my volitions. Yet libertarians believe that it's not enough that a person be able to do A if

---

[21] This phrasing comes from Jonathan Edwards (among others). See Edwards (1957). Unrelated to Edwards, a referee commenting on an earlier version of this paper has noted that this condition needs the addition of the requirement that it be possible that either one will A or that one will that one not do A. For without that condition, one has effective choice over actions one can neither will to do nor will to refrain from doing, and that is (to say the least) implausible. I agree with the reader but make the point only in a footnote in order to keep in focus the condition in the text. Of course, in the case at hand, this addition is not a problem: there is no question about it being possible for God to have the relevant will.

she wills and refrain from doing A if that's what she wills. For, if her will is determined by events outside her control, then her action won't be free even if she would be able to act on a different will if she had one.

So, even if God's creating the best world is necessary (or at least unavoidable) given God's nature, the theist can still claim that God's creative act satisfies the following conditions:

(i) God has effective choice over his creative decision (i.e., compatibilist freedom);

(ii) Neither the volition to create nor the creative act is strictly the result of an antecedent causal condition that predates God's existence;

(iii) God's creative action is not the result of a non-rational internal force.

Notice that regarding human agents in a deterministic world, the best that could be said is that conditions (i) and (iii) would hold. That is, the three conditions could not be satisfied by an agent in a deterministic world; so a more general account of the nature of freedom along the lines of (i)–(iii) would be libertarian. However, the addict who can't resist the temptation to take drugs and persons with psychological compulsions are not free with respect to volitions/actions produced by their addictions/compulsions, since those actions are the result of non-rational, internal forces. The same goes for various unfortunate (although fictitious) individuals whose volitions and actions are the result of nefarious neurosurgeons or hypnotists.

The upshot of all of this is that given that God's creative act satisfies the above three conditions, why should God's inability to refrain require us to deny that God's act is free? For what does the 'inability to refrain' come to here other than the inability to act against what he has the best reason to do? Can we really say God would only be free in this context if God were to be able to act against what God sees as the clearly best thing to do, the thing that he has every reason to do and no good reason not to do? That is, that divine freedom would entail the possibility of divine irrationality?

IV.C. If God is not free, is God not appropriately thanked or praised?

Even if what I've suggested above is wrong and its being necessary that God performs an action entails that God is not free with respect to that action, I don't think it follows that God is not to be thanked or praised. In particular, I think that the idea that God's praiseworthiness depends on God's having the freedom to refrain from the good God does is plausible only if one has a needlessly narrow view of what praiseworthiness comes to.

I'm perfectly willing to grant that *moral* praiseworthiness for an action A requires that the agent who performs the action was not caused to do the action by events independent of her character and motivations. As we have seen in the last part of this section, however, this condition of praiseworthiness can be satisfied by God even if God necessarily does the best (and they are not satisfied by anyone whose actions are determined by the past and laws of nature).

Now it might be argued that there is another condition of moral praiseworthiness that God can't satisfy: that an agent who is praiseworthy might have done things that are wrong or at least not the best the agent could do. Given what I said above, I think there is cause to be dubious of this condition. But let's waive such scruples and suppose that this condition is right. If it is, then God is not *morally* praiseworthy. But it hardly follows from this that God is not praiseworthy in some other sense. And I believe that it is another sense of praiseworthiness that is paramount in the theist tradition.

When theists claim that God is to be praised, they often distinguish this from saying that God is to be thanked. Why? Because God is to be praised for *who God is*; God is to be thanked for what *God has done*. Now God's praiseworthiness is surely not just a function of our helplessness before God, of God's ability to do with us as God will. If God were a finite, although very powerful, tyrant, God would be able to dispose of us according to his pleasure but God would not be thereby praiseworthy. What makes God praiseworthy includes his awesome power—the fact that not only is there no being as powerful as God but that there could not be a being as powerful since God is the source of all power. While sheer power might make a being literally awesome, it wouldn't make it praiseworthy. What makes God praiseworthy is God's power together with God's nature as fair, merciful, and loving—God's embodying all that is valuable. God's nature as both the source of all that is and as a benevolent Creator is what makes God worthy of our praise. This sense of praiseworthiness does depend on God's naturally treating us a certain way, but it does not depend on God's *freely* treating us that way—at least not if such freedom requires the ability to refrain from treating us as God does. Even if God isn't strictly speaking a *moral agent* because God isn't strictly speaking a fitting subject of moral praise because God isn't free regarding the good things God does, God is nevertheless metaphysically praiseworthy if he is the ground of all being and power and yet treats such finite, flawed beings as ourselves with love, kindness, and mercy. I submit that when theists offer their praise to God in worship, they are not intending to praise God as a moral agent but as the loving, benevolent source of all being and power. Offering praise to the hero who saves the small child's life at great peril to her own well-being, and offering praise to God for being the loving Creator of the Heavens and Earth is not to offer the same thing to different individuals. The human hero has done something for which she is praiseworthy; God is praiseworthy in virtue of being Who God is.

So much for praiseworthiness. What about thankfulness? Should we think that if God does not have the power to refrain from the blessings God bestows on us, then God is not to be thanked? I think the answer to this is 'clearly not'. Suppose that you have a benevolent aunt who frequently sends you gifts. Suppose you knew that this woman did what she did was because of her upbringing and very strong religious convictions. Indeed, suppose you knew that given your relative need and her relative plenty, her relationship to you, and her belief in the importance of giving (particularly to family) she was not really able to resist giving you generous gifts. Would your understanding of her situation release you of a duty to thank her for her kindness toward you? Of course not. We owe our beneficiaries a debt of thanks when, motivated by a concern for our well being, they bestow benefits upon us. In fact, it might be that the condition that the gift is given out of a 'concern for our well being' is overly restrictive. If I have a self-serving uncle who gives me a gift primarily because it will provide him with a significant tax write off, I still have a duty to thank him provided that he was able to see that the gift would benefit me. His action needn't be praiseworthy; it must only be an undeserved benefit to me.

I conclude, then, that it is not evident that God's inability to refrain from creating makes God unfree; still less is it evident that God's lack of creative freedom (if God indeed does lack such freedom) is inconsistent with God's praiseworthiness or the appropriateness of our offering thanks for his tender mercies.

V. PREMISE ONE—EITHER THERE IS A BEST WORLD OR THERE IS AN INFINITE HIERARCHY OF BETTER WORLDS

In fairness to Rowe, let me begin by noting that he never asserts premise one. In fact, Rowe mentions briefly a third option and credits Thomas Morris with suggesting a fourth. However, Rowe spends almost no time elaborating either of these other two possibilities, or on exploring their implications for his argument. The first he dispenses with in a footnote and the second gets no discussion at all after being mentioned. In this section, we'll look at what can be said for each of these possibilities and what impact they have on Rowe's conclusion.

V.A. The best worlds: a tie

In addition to the two options mentioned in the first premise, there is the possibility that there is no uniquely best world because there is more than one world with precisely the same, unsurpassed level of goodness. That is, there might be a tie at the top. Recognizing that this is an epistemic possibility, we should ask two questions: how plausible is the claim that there is a tie for best world that, if it were true, would help the theist out of Rowe's problem?

One reason for thinking there might be a tie is discussed by Rowe when he considers Aquinas' view that there is an infinite hierarchy of good worlds.[22] One might think, Rowe says, that such a series is impossible since each world will contain God, who is infinitely good and absolutely perfect. So every world (or at least every world with God) will be infinitely good. So there is a massive tie—every world with God is precisely as good as every other: each is infinitely good.

Rowe's reply to this line of reasoning depends on making a distinction between quantitative and qualitative goodness, and then claiming that, while every world with God will contain an infinite *quantity* of goodness, worlds might yet differ with respect to the *quality* of goodness. I haven't the space here to get into the details, but I will say that I find Rowe's reply very unconvincing. For, however compelling is the claim that any world with God contains an infinite (and so equal) *quantity* of goodness will be matched equally, I would think, by the claim that any world with God contains an infinite (and so equal) *quality* of goodness. Rowe denies this and thinks it plausible that worlds with a greater diversity of kinds of beings will contain a greater quality of goodness than worlds with fewer kinds of beings, even if all worlds also contain God. Therefore, Rowe thinks, the claim that all worlds are equally good because all contain the infinite goodness of God can be reasonably resisted.

Whether I'm correct that there is just as much reason to think that the presence of God guarantees a tie in quality of goodness as it does a tie in quantity of goodness, or Rowe is correct in thinking that greater ontological diversity can account for an increase in quality is, in the end, not of great importance. For there is, I believe, a better response to the argument we are now considering for the Tie at the Top thesis. Although there is no doubt that in adding up the total goodness of a world that includes God, God's goodness must be part of the equation, there is no reason to include God's goodness when comparing the worlds that God can bring about since

---

[22] This discussion begins near the bottom in Rowe (2004: 39) and runs through the top half of page 44.

every world God can bring about is, obviously, a world that includes God. So there is simply no reason to include (and good reason to exclude) God's goodness when evaluating and comparing worlds.

Another way to make this point is to say that the relevant unit of comparison is 'possible creations' rather than 'possible worlds'.[23] Leibniz's claim that God would bring about the best possible world can (and probably should) be recast as the claim that God would produce the best possible creation. Since theism insists on the transcendence of God, and on God's being distinct from creation, there is here no concern that all possible creations will be infinitely good because they each contain God; no possible *creation* includes the Creator as a part. And with the God out of the picture (so to speak), there is no worry (at least as far as I can tell) that all creations will contain the same quantity and quality of goodness. Because the phrase 'best possible world' is so entrenched in the discussion of the issues we are concerned with here, I will not avoid using it in the remainder of this paper. But it should be understood that, e.g., the claim 'God will bring about the best possible world' is shorthand for 'God will bring about the best creation he is capable of bringing about (i.e., the best *feasible* creation)'.

So we are back where we started at the beginning of this section: can we rule out the apparent epistemic possibility that there is no single best world because there is more than one world with unsurpassed goodness. Even if it is not true that every world is tied for the 'best world' title, why should we assume that either a single world is best or else every world is surpassable? Is there any reason to rule out the possibility that there are two or more unsurpassable worlds?

One might think that, while it can't be entirely ruled out, the claim that there is a tie for the 'best world' designation is pretty implausible. I take it that Rowe thinks this and that is why he only briefly mentions this possibility and in the end discusses it only in a footnote. However, I want to defend the tie possibility as being every bit as plausible as the best world hypothesis. In fact, I want to say something stronger: if both the infinite hierarchy thesis and the fourth possibility (which we will discuss in the next part of this section) are false, then the tie hypothesis is true. That is, the one possibility that seems very, very unlikely is that there is a single best world. Here's why.

What it would take for a world to be the best world is for the amount of value at that world to be greater than that at every other world. The best world isn't the world with the greatest volume or densest mass or the one that lasts longest; the criterion for 'best' world is a function of world value. Now

[23] In keeping with an earlier point, it is actually 'feasible' rather than 'possible' creations that are relevant here.

one would assume that moral value is a major player here, but there is no good reason to think it is the only one. That is, given the plausible assumption of value pluralism (i.e., there is more than one irreducible kind of value), the best world would likely include whatever other kinds of value there might be as well. That is, it would be the world that contained the highest amount and quality of value or values possible. Now, as I understand it, this is the sole criterion on which worlds are judged in the 'best possible world' competition. Any aspect of a world that doesn't make a value difference is irrelevant. But now suppose there is a world W1 that is a prima facie candidate for being the best world: it has an extremely large quantity of extremely high-quality goodness, and very little (if any) evil. In fact, let's stipulate that W1's net goodness is unsurpassed. Let's go one step further. W1 is not only unsurpassed in net goodness, but there is no possible way of combining values in a world that is equal to the way those values are combined in W1. Put slightly differently, any way of combining values other than the way they are combined in W1 will produce lower net value than that found in W1. So we are supposing (for the sake of discussion) that there is a unique best way to combine values to get the ultimately valuable world and that W1 is it.

So far, it looks as though W1 has a good claim to be the best possible world. However, consider world W2: W2 is just like W1 in every way except that W2 contains one more item than W1 contains, and this item makes no value difference in W2. (W2 may contain an extra elementary particle, say, or maybe an extra chair or blade of grass.) Or consider W3, again the value equivalent of W1 and W2, but whose underlying non-normative 'stuff' is a different kind than what is found in W1 and W2. That is, W3 realizes all and only the value properties that W1 and W2 realize, but these properties supervene on a different type of realizing base. If either W2 or W3 is possible, then although the value of W1 will be unsurpassed, and it will represent the best possible instantiation of value properties, it will not be the uniquely best possible world since W2 and W3 are equally as good. It would be helpful if I knew of a proof for the general thesis that for any world W, if W exhibits the specific combination of realized value properties V, there is another world W* that also exhibits V but which differs from W in some non-normative aspect. However, I know of no such argument. Neverthess, the claim that the best combination of value could be had by worlds that differ in trivial, non-normative ways is highly plausible, and we should conclude that it is more likely that there is more than one unsurpassably good world than it is that there is a single, best world.

What is the impact of this on Rowe's argument? One the one hand, it seems potentially significant. For Rowe apparently thinks that the two primary options are those mentioned in the first premise. And were those options to have exhausted the possibilities, Rowe has arguments in place that either God is not free or not perfectly good (i.e., that there is no God). But, if there are multiple best worlds, then God's perfect goodness, wisdom, and power will not guarantee that actuality of any particular world. God's freedom, it would seem, will not be in jeopardy. Although Rowe spends very little time considering the Tie at the Top hypothesis, he doesn't ignore it completely. He makes two points in response. Here's the first:

[I]f there is a best action for God to perform (e.g., creating the best world), God creates the best world of necessity not freely. And just as clearly, if there are alternative best worlds for God to perform, he will of necessity, not freely, create one of them.[24]

On the assumption that a null creation (i.e., a world at which God doesn't create anything) wouldn't be among the alternative best possible creations, Rowe is certainly correct that God's creating that world is necessary (or at least unavoidable). Whether it is therefore not free is not so obvious (as I argued in the last section). And as we'll see in the next part of the next section, it isn't clear that the null world is not as good as other worlds God could make.

The second point Rowe makes about the Tie at the Top hypothesis is found in a footnote. Here's what Rowe says:

Even though there being several creatable worlds than which there are none better appears to leave God free to create any one of these worlds, Swinburne and other proponents of this view are still burdened with having to defend the rather implausible claim that the actual world with all its evil is a world than which it is logically impossible that there should be a better world than it.[25]

It should be noted that, for reasons that have already surfaced, the theist who adopts the Tie at the Top hypothesis is not necessarily saddled with this consequence. A Molinist can follow Plantinga in claiming that it is possible that the best worlds are not feasible worlds because the true counterfactuals of freedom make them such that even an omnipotent being cannot weakly actualize them. So, at most, the Molinist is committed to the claim that the actual world is one of the best feasible worlds.

There is a related concern for the theist if the Tie at the Top hypothesis is correct because the best combination of values can be instantiated in more than one world. God's 'free choice' among the various best worlds would be analogous to the freedom one would have if, needing a box of breakfast cereal, one went to the town's only store to find that there were a great many different boxes of the same size of Cheerios and nothing else. True, one would did not have to buy the box of cereal one bought, but one's freedom is strictly superficial.

Now if the Tie at the Top hypothesis is true not because there is a single best combination of values that can be instantiated in more than one world, but because there is more than one possible combination of values that lead to maximal value in a world, then God's choice among the worlds would be more significant. For example, suppose there are exactly two unsurpassable worlds X and Y, and that both are equal in overall value. X, however, contains slightly more instances of autonomy (which I assume is component of overall value) but fewer instances of altruism (which I assume is also a component of overall value) than Y contains. Now God's choice between X and Y seems more significant than it would be if there is a single combination of value that can be instantiated either in worlds that don't contain precisely the same objects or in worlds with value-supervenience bases that are distinct while the supervenient values are precisely the same. For although X and Y are equally good worlds, the value difference between them is not trivial. God might prefer worlds with greater altruism to worlds with greater autonomy even though God recognizes that the overall value of the worlds is the same. So a tie of this sort does not lead to insignificant choices or to a freedom that is essentially meaningless. It's the difference between having only the choice of which of many exactly similar boxes of Cheerios to buy on the one hand, and having a choice between your two favorite cereals on the other. You might think the two are equally as good, but on a given day have a preference for one. Given your preference, your freedom here is not trivial.

V.B. Incommensurate worlds

Premise one of Rowe's argument is false if two or more worlds are tied for having the greatest value. However, there is another way that this premise could be false: there might be worlds that are simply incommensurate. If that is the case then there is neither a best world nor an infinite hierarchy of good worlds.

How plausible is the thesis that there are incommensurable worlds? That depends, I would think, on whether or not value monism is true. If there is at bottom one type of value, then it would seem that for any worlds A and B, A would be better than, worse than, or equal to B. For example, if Millian utilitarianism is true, then happiness is the only irreducible value. So the value of a world is strictly a function of the net happiness at that world. If that is right, then surely there are no two worlds that are incommensurate.

Value monism, however, is not a very plausible thesis. And, if it is false, if value pluralism is true, then there would seem to be the possibility of incommensurability. That's not to say that very instance of different value would always been incomparable to other instances. For example, if we were to compare the value of the doodle on my page of notes with that of the sacrifice a war hero makes for his country, there would be little doubt that the doodle would lose: the value of the war hero swamps the insignificant value of my doodle. Still, arguably, the value of a great work of art and the value of a morally very good (but not truly heroic) action might well be thought to be incomparable—even if the value of a great work of art loses out to that of a truly heroic action. Although both the great work of art and the morally very good (but not heroic) action are instances of significant value, since their values are of fundamentally different types, it's plausible to think that they cannot be put on the same scale. There is, of course, a sense in which they can be compared since they can both be seen to have significant value. However, from the recognition that each is greatly valuable it does not follow that either is better, worse, or equal to the other.

Given value pluralism, there are a number of fundamental, irreducible, intrinsic values. I assume that any best world candidate will be a world that exemplifies all the sorts of fundamental value that there are. In many cases, both with respect to world segments and even whole worlds, these segments/worlds are commensurate—i.e., the state of affairs of John's constructing a somewhat artistic doodle is less good than that of John's saving the life of a child. But not all cases are like this. Perhaps in situations where the quantitative and qualitative values of values of fundamentally different types reach a certain threshold, there just is no way of comparing the state of affairs on a better than/less than/equal to scale. So there is a whole host of ways that values can be combined to get the overall value of a world. Indeed, given the finititude of human powers of conception, there are likely possible values that we simply don't have the conceptual wherewithal to appreciate. Given a non-trivial number of distinct intrinsic values (including those, if any there are, that either aren't instantiated in our world or that we don't have the capability of recognizing) and all the ways that these values can be instantiated in a world, why shouldn't we think that there will be many possible total combinations that are incommensurate? Indeed, perhaps there are an infinite number of incommensurably good worlds. And even if that seems unlikely, this much can be said: we have no good reason for thinking that there are not any number of very good but incommensurate worlds. If there are even two, then it's neither the case that God's choice between them is forced nor that for any world God creates, God could have made one that was better.

Now, even if all the above were to work, it might be thought that we've still got the general problem of creation: was God free with respect to creating at all? If there are, say, a dozen incommensurate, very good creatable worlds, then won't God necessarily bring about one of those? As far as I can see, the answer to this last question is 'yes'. But that doesn't bring along the conclusion that God necessarily creates unless it is also true that the null creation is not one of the very good incommensurate worlds. But why shouldn't it be? Perhaps a world in which the only existent is a necessary, absolutely perfect being is incommensurate with a very good world that includes such a being but that also includes causally-dependent, contingent, non-perfect entities. Even if this claim doesn't strike one as self-evident or obviously true, what reason do we have for thinking that it is false? And if we think we can *just see* that a world with just God is of less value (is less good) than at least some worlds with God and contingent, created things, what is this confidence based on? I'm not suggesting value scepticism in general. Perhaps what I have in mind could be called something like 'epistemic humility regarding the value of worlds'. While the judgement that a world that includes an overwhelming amount and quality of pain and suffering with relatively few (if any) off-setting goods is inferior to a world in which the same inhabitants have little pain and suffering, much deep happiness, and there are a great number of other goods each had in abundance is unassailable, the more standard worlds each with a wide variety of different goods and 'bads' will be much more difficult to judge. One reason for this, of course, is the vastness of worlds and the puniness of the human mind. We might not be in a position to make reliable judgements even when there are facts of the matter regarding the relative value of worlds. There is, however, a second potential reason for the difficulty we have in judging the comparative goodness of worlds. My proposal is that one reason for our inability to make judgements in many of these cases is that such worlds are in fact incommensurable.

So if there are two or more incommensurate, very good, creatable worlds, and one of those worlds is a world with only God, then God can be free (in the strong, libertarian sense) both with respect to creating at all and with respect to which world to create if God creates. For God's nature, together with God's options for creation will leave open the possibility of God's not creating at all, and they will also be consistent with God's bringing about any of the incommensurable creations. Notice too that if God does have a choice between multiple, incommensurable creations, then God's choice is significant. For there can be substantial value differences in incommensurable worlds. The example of the values of the great work of art and the morally good action serves to illustrate this. If each is valuable (or even very valuable), but because their values are of such different kinds, they

194 *Thomas Senor*

are incommensurate, there is a basis for a preference, even a value-based preference. This is the point we discussed in the last paragraph of Section V. A regarding the possibility of distinct-but-equal combinations of overall value. Only the possibility in this section seems considerably more plausible: its not that there is a tie at the top, but that there are very good worlds whose value is incomparable. In such a case, God has the freedom to choose among these worlds and his choice can be grounded in what he happens to prefer. Now if his preferences are necessary, then we will have a problem parallel to that of the best world scenario. Although there will not be a single best world, if there is a world that is necessarily preferred by God, then God will necessarily create it. But there is no reason to build such preferences into the nature of God. So his creating one of the very-good-incommensurate worlds can be free and yet substantial.

CONCLUSION

William Rowe's argument that God must either not exist or not be free is without a doubt very powerful. It richly deserves the significant attention it has received. However, I believe that there is some reason to doubt each of the argument's premises, and to also be suspicious of Rowe's claims about the consequences of the Creator's being either not free or not perfectly good. Furthermore, I believe that the incommensurate worlds possibility is rather plausible, and if it turns out to be right, then God's creating the world God created, as well as God's having created at all, can be free and significantly so in a way that does not compromise God's perfect goodness.

REFERENCES

Adams, R., 'Must God Create the Best?', in *Philosophical Review* 81 (1972): 317–32.
Craig, W., 'The Kalam Cosmological Argument', in L. Pojman, *Philosophy of Religion: An Anthology* (Belmont, CA, and Memphis, TN: Wadsworth, 2003): 24–9 (originally in W. Craig, *Reasonable Faith* (Memphis, TN: Crossway, 1994).
Draper, P., 'A Critique of the Kalam Cosmological Argument', in L. Pojman, *Philosophy of Religion: An Anthology* (Belmont, CA: Wadsworth, 2003): 42–7.
Edwards, J., *Freedom of the Will* (1754), ed. P. Ramsey (New Haven, CT: Yale University Press: 1957).
Hasker, W., *Providence, Evil, and the Openness of God* (London and New York: Routledge, 2004).
Howard-Snyder, F., and D., 'How An Unsurpassable Being Can Create a Surpassable World', in *Faith and Philosophy* 11 (1994): 260–8.
—— 'The *Real* Problem of No Best World', in *Faith and Philosophy* 13 (1996): 422–5.

Kretzmann, N., 'A General Problem of Creation', in S. MacDonald (ed.), *Being and Goodness* (Ithaca, NY: Cornell University Press, 1990).

Morris, T., 'Perfection and Creation', in E. Stump (ed.), *Reasoned Faith* (Ithaca, NY: Cornell University Press, 1993).

Plantinga, Alvin, *The Nature of Necessity* (Oxford: Clarendon Press, 1974).

Rowe, W., *Can God Be Free?* (Oxford: Oxford University Press, 2004).

Senor, T., 'God, Supernatural Kinds, and the Incarnation', *Religious Studies* 27 (1992): 353–70.

Wainwright, W., 'Jonathan Edwards, William Rowe, and the Necessity of Creation', in J. Jordan and D. Howard-Snyder (eds), *Faith, Reason, and Rationality* (Rowman & Littlefield Publishers, Inc., 1996): 119–33.

—— *Philosophy of Religion*, 2nd edn. (Belmont, CA: Wadsworth, 1999).

Wierenga, E., 'The Freedom of God', *Faith and Philosophy* 19 (2002): 425–36.

9

The Problem of Evil and the Desires of the Heart

Eleonore Stump

I. INTRODUCTION

The problem of evil is raised by the existence of suffering in the world. Can one hold consistently both that the world has such suffering in it and that it is governed by an omniscient, omnipotent, perfectly good God, as the major monotheisms claim? An affirmative answer to this question has often enough taken the form of a theodicy. A theodicy is an attempt to show that these claims are consistent by providing a morally sufficient reason for God to allow suffering. In the history of the discussions of the problem of evil, a great deal of effort has been expended on proposing and defending, or criticizing and attacking, theodicies and the putative morally sufficient reasons which theodicies propose.

Generally, a putative morally sufficient reason for God to allow suffering is centred on a supposed benefit which could not be gotten without the suffering and which outweighs it. And the benefit is most commonly thought of as some intrinsically valuable thing supposed to be essential to general human flourishing, such as the significant use of free will or virtuous character, either for human beings in general or for the sufferer in particular.[1]

For helpful comments on earlier drafts of this paper or on its contents, I am grateful to Jeffrey Brower, Frank Burch Brown, John Foley, John Kavanaugh, Scott MacDonald, Michael Murray, Michael Rea, Theodore Vitali, and anonymous reviewers for this book.

[1] There is a large, contentious philosophical literature on the nature of human flourishing or well-being, and it is not part of my purpose to try to engage that literature here. For my purposes in this paper, I will understand flourishing to consist in just those things necessary in a person's life for that person's life to be admirable and meaningful.

So, for example, in his insightful reflections on the sort of sufferings represented by the afflictions of Job, the impressive tenth-century Jewish thinker Saadiah Gaon says,

Now He that subjects the soul to its trials is none other than the Master of the universe, who is, of course, acquainted with all its doings. This testing of the soul [that is, the suffering of Job] has been compared to the assaying by means of fire of [lumps of metal] that have been referred to as gold or silver. It is thereby that the true nature of their composition is clearly established. For the original gold and silver remain, while the alloys that have been mingled with them are partly burned and partly take flight... The pure, clear souls that have been refined are thereupon exalted and ennobled.[2]

The same approach is common in contemporary times. So, for example, John Hick has proposed a soul-making theodicy, which justifies suffering as building the character of the sufferer and thereby contributing to the flourishing of the sufferer.[3] Or, to take a very different example which nonetheless makes the same point, Richard Swinburne has argued that suffering contributes to the flourishing of sufferers because, among other things, a person's suffering makes him useful to others, and being useful to others is an important constituent of human well-being in general.[4]

Those who have attacked theodicies such as these have tended to focus on the theodicist's claims about the connections between the putative benefit and the suffering. Opponents of theodicy have argued that the proposed benefit could have been obtained without the suffering, for example, or that the suffering is not a morally acceptable means to that (or any other) benefit. But these attacks on theodicy share an assumption with the attempted theodicies themselves. Both the attacks and the attempted theodicies suppose that a person's generic human flourishing would be sufficient to justify God in allowing that person's suffering if only the suffering and the flourishing were connected in the right way. In this paper, I want to call this assumption into question.

I will argue that the sufferings of unwilling innocents cannot be justified only in terms of the intrinsically valuable things which make for general human flourishing (however that flourishing is understood). I will argue that even if such flourishing is connected in the appropriate ways to the suffering in a person's life, intrinsically valuable things essential to flourishing are not by themselves sufficient to constitute a morally sufficient reason for God to allow human suffering. That is because human beings can set their hearts

---

[2] Saadiah Gaon 1948: 246–7.
[3] Hick 1966. For Hick's defence of his solutions against objections, see, for example, Hick 1968a: 539–46, and Hick 1968b: 591–602.
[4] See Swinburne 1998.

on things which are not necessary for such flourishing, and they suffer when they lose or fail to get what they set their hearts on.[5] That suffering also needs to be addressed in consideration of the problem of evil.

II. THE DESIRES OF THE HEART

The suffering to which I want to call attention can be thought of in terms of what the Psalmist calls 'the desires of the heart'.[6] When the Psalmist says, 'Delight yourself in the Lord, and he will give you the desires of your heart',[7] we all have some idea what the Psalmist is promising. We are clear, for example, that some abstract theological good which a person does not care much about does not count as one of the desires of that person's heart. Suffering also arises when a human being fails to get a desire of her heart or has and then loses a desire of her heart.

I do not know how to make the notion of a desire of the heart precise; but, clearly, we do have some intuitive grasp of it, and we commonly use the expression or others related to it in ordinary discourse. We say, for example, that a person is heartsick because he has lost his heart's desire. He is filled with heartache because his heart's desire is kept from him. He loses heart, because something he had put his heart into is taken from him. It would have been different for him if he had wanted it only half-heartedly; but since it was what he had at heart, he is likely to be heartsore a long time over the loss of it, unless, of course, he has a change of heart about it—and so on, and on.

Perhaps we could say that a person's heart's desire is a particular kind of commitment on her part to something—a person or a project—which matters greatly to her but which need not be essential to her flourishing, in the sense that human flourishing for her may be possible without it. So, for example, Coretta Scott King's life arguably exemplifies flourishing,

---

[5] In Adams 1999, Marilyn Adams makes a distinction which is at least related to the distinction I am after here. She says, 'the value of a person's life may be assessed from the inside (in relation to that person's own goals, ideals, and choices) and from the outside (in relation to the aims, tastes, values, and preferences of others) ... My notion is that for a person's life to be a great good to him/her on the whole, the external point of view (even if it is God's) is not sufficient' (p. 145).

[6] The expression 'the desire of the heart' is also ambiguous. It can mean either a particular kind of desire or else the thing which is desired in that way. When we say, 'the desire of his heart was to be a great musician', the expression refers to a desire; when we say, 'In losing her, he lost the desire of his heart,' the expression refers to the thing desired. I will not try to sort out this ambiguity here; I will simply trust to the context to disambiguate the expression.

[7] Ps. 37: 4–5.

on any ordinary measure of human flourishing; and yet her husband's assassination was undoubtedly heartbreaking for her. If there is such a thing as a web of belief, with some beliefs peripheral and others central to a person's set of beliefs, maybe there is also a web of desire. A desire of a person's heart is a desire which is at or near the centre of the web of desire for her. If she loses what she wants when her desire is at or near the centre of the web, then other things which she had wanted begin to lose their ability to attract her because what she had most centrally wanted is gone. The web of desire starts to fall apart when the centre does not hold, we might say. That is why the ordinary good things of life, like food and work, fail to draw a person who has lost the desires of her heart. She is heartbroken, we say, and that is why she has no heart for anything else now.

If things essential to general human flourishing are intrinsically valuable for all human beings, then those things which are the desires of the heart can be thought of as the things which have the value they do for a particular person primarily because she has set her heart on them. Like the value a child has for its parents, the value they have *for her* is derivative from her love of them, not the other way around. A loving father, trying to deal gently with his small daughter's childish tantrums, finally said to her with exasperated adult feeling, 'It isn't reasonable to cry about these things!' Presumably, the father means that the things for which his little daughter was weeping did not have much value on the scale which measures the intrinsic value of good things essential to human flourishing; and, no doubt, he was right in that assessment. But there is another scale by which to measure, too, and that is the scale which measures the value a thing has for a particular person because of the love she has for it. The second scale cannot be reduced to the first. Clearly, we care not just about general human flourishing and the intrinsically valuable things essential to it. We also care about those things which are the desires of our hearts, and we suffer when we are denied our heart's desires. I would say that it is not reasonable to say to a weeping child that it is not reasonable for her to weep about the loss of something she had her heart set on.

Suffering which stems from a loss of the heart's desires is often enough compatible with flourishing.[8] As far as that goes, for any particular historical person picked as an exemplar of a flourishing life, it is certainly arguable that, at some time in her life, that person will have lost or failed to get something on which she had fixed her heart. Think, for

---

[8] Except for conceptions of flourishing which make flourishing identical to the satisfaction of desires, but equating flourishing just with desire satisfaction is problematic enough that it can be left to one side here.

example, not only of Coretta Scott King but also of Sojourner Truth, who was sold away from her parents at the age of nine, or Harriet Tubman, who suffered permanent neurological damage from the beatings she sustained in adolescence. If any human lives manifest flourishing, the lives of these women certainly do. Each of them is an exemplar of a highly admirable, meaningful life. Yet each of these women undoubtedly experienced heartbreak.

In fact, stern-minded thinkers in varying cultures, including some Stoics, Buddhists, and many in the Christian tradition, have been fiercely committed to the position that human flourishing is independent of the vicissitudes of fortune. On their view, human flourishing ought to be understood in a way which makes it compatible even with such things as poverty, disease and disabilities, the death of loved ones, betrayal by intimate friends, estrangements from friends or family, and imprisonment. But it certainly seems as if each of these is sufficient to break the heart of a person who suffers them if the person is not antecedently in the grip of such a stern-minded attitude.

So, for example, in the history of the medieval Christian tradition, for example, human flourishing was commonly taken as a matter of a certain relationship with God, mediated by the indwelling of the Holy Spirit. On this view of flourishing, most of the evils human beings suffer are compatible with flourishing. That is because, as Christian confessional literature makes clear, a human person can feel that she is in such a relationship with God, even when she is afflicted with serious suffering of body or mind.

This sort of position is also common among the reflective in our own culture. In a moving passage reflecting on his long experience of caring for and living with the severely disabled, Jean Vanier says about the disabled and about himself, too,

we can only accept ... [the] pain [in our lives] if we discover our true self beneath all the masks and realize that if we are broken, we are also more beautiful than we ever dared to suspect. When we realize our brokenness, we do not have to fall into depression ... Seeing our own brokenness and beauty allows us to recognize, hidden under the brokenness and self-centeredness of others, their beauty, their value, and their sacredness. This discovery is ... a blessed moment, a moment of grace, and a moment of enlightenment that comes in a meeting with the God of love, who reveals to us that we are beloved and so is everyone else ... We can start to live the pain of loss and accept anguish because a new love and a new consciousness of self are being given to us.[9]

A particularly poignant example of such an attitude is given by John Hull in his memoir about his own blindness. After many pages of documenting

---

[9] Vanier 1998: 158–9.

the great suffering caused him by blindness, Hull summarizes his attitude towards his disability in this powerful passage:

the thought keeps coming back to me ... Could there be a strange way in which blindness is a dark, paradoxical gift? Does it offer a way of life, a purification, an economy? Is it really like a kind of painful purging through a death? ... If blindness is a gift, it is not one that I would wish on anybody ... [But in the midst of the experience of music in church] as the whole place and my mind were filled with that wonderful music, I found myself saying, 'I accept the gift. I accept the gift.' I was filled with a profound sense of worship. I felt that I was in the very presence of God, that the giver of the gift had drawn near to me to inspect his handiwork ... If I hardly dared approach him, he hardly dared approach me .... He had, as it were, thrown his cloak of darkness around me from a distance, but had now drawn near to seek a kind of reassurance from me that everything was all right, that he had not misjudged the situation, that he did not have to stay. 'It's all right,' I was saying to him, 'There's no need to wait. Go on, you can go now; everything's fine.'[10]

Everything *is* fine, in some sense having to do with relationship to God, and so with flourishing, on this understanding of flourishing. I have no wish to undermine the appealing attitude exemplified in this powerful text. And yet something more needs to be said. The problem is that suffering is not confined to things which undermine a person's flourishing and keep him from being *fine,* in this deep sense of 'fine'. What is bad about the evils human beings suffer is not just that they can undermine a person's flourishing, but also that they can keep her from having the desires of her heart, when the desires of her heart are for something which is not essential for general human flourishing. Suffering arises also from the loss of the desires of one's heart; and, in considerations of the problem of evil and proposed theodicies, this suffering needs to be addressed as well. This suffering also needs to be justified.

III. THE STERN-MINDED ATTITUDE

Stated so baldly, this last claim looks less open to question than it really is. We do not ordinarily suppose that a parent's goodness is impugned if the parent refuses to provide for the child anything at all which the child happens to set its heart on. But, as regards the problem of evil, what is at issue is apparently analogous, namely, God's allowing some human being to fail to have the desires of her heart when those desires are focused on something not essential to her flourishing. Why, someone might ask, should

---

[10] Hull 1991: 205–6.

we suppose that a good God must provide whatever goods not necessary for her flourishing a human person has fixed her heart on?

Now it is certainly true that there can be very problematic instances of heart's desires. A person could set his heart on very evil things, for example, or a person might set his heart in random ways on trivial things or on a set of mutually incompossible things. And no doubt, there are other examples as well. In cases such as these, reasonable people are unlikely to suppose that some explanation is needed for why a good God would fail to give a person the desires of his heart. Even if we exclude such cases, however, there remain many instances in which a person sets his heart, in humanly understandable and appropriate ways, on something which is not essential to his flourishing and whose value for him is derivative of his love for it.[11] Surely, in that restricted class of cases, some justification is needed for God's allowing a person to suffer heartbreak.

But even this weaker claim will strike some people as false. Some people will object, for example, that human flourishing is a very great good, sufficient to outweigh suffering. For those who think of human flourishing as a relationship to God, it can seem an infinite good or a good too great to be commensurable with other goods; and this good is possible even when many other goods are lost or denied.[12] If God provides *this* good for a human being, then, an objector might claim, that is or ought to be enough for her. A person who does not find this greatest of all goods good enough, an objector might say, is like a person who wins the lottery but who is nonetheless unhappy because she did not get exactly what she wanted for Christmas.

In the history of Christianity in particular, there have been stern-minded thinkers who would not accept the claim that the suffering caused by any loss of the heart's desires requires justification. In effect, this stern-minded attitude is unwilling to assign a positive value to anything which is not essential to general human flourishing. For this reason, the stern-minded

---

[11] Elsewhere I consider the complication of cases in which an apparently appropriate heart's desire is such that its fulfilment would undermine the flourishing of the person who has it. So, for example, the great English poet John Milton apparently had a heart's desire to be an administrator in the Puritan government of his time; but his government work kept him from writing poetry. All his greatest poetry was written after the fall of the Puritan regime. There are also cases in which a person sets his heart on what he himself takes to be essential to his flourishing, when in fact he is mistaken on this score. Viktor Klemperer supposed that his flourishing was dependent on his writing a great study of eighteenth-century French literature, and he describes his own sense of the blight of his life in consequence of his inability to write a great book in his stunningly excellent diaries, published now to rave reviews. For consideration of complicated cases such as these, see my *Wandering in Darkness: Narrative and the Problem of Suffering* (Oxford, forthcoming).

[12] For a persuasive statement of a case for such a view, see Adams 1998.

approach is, at best, unwilling to accord any value to the desires of the heart and, at worst, eager to extirpate the desires themselves. Such an attitude is persistent in the history of Christian thought from the Patristic period onwards.

In its Patristic form, it can be seen vividly in a story which Cassian tells about a monk named 'Patermutus'. It is worth quoting at length the heartrendingly horrible story which Cassian recounts with so much oblivious admiration:

Patermutus's constant perseverance [in his request to be admitted into the monastery finally] induced [the monks] to receive him along with his little son, who was about eight years old ... . To test [Patermutus] the more, and see if he would be more moved by family affection and the love of his own brood than by the obedience and mortification of Christ, which every monk should prefer to his love, [the monks] deliberately neglected the child, dressed him in rags ... and even subjected [the child] to cuffs and slaps, which ... the father saw some of them inflict on the innocent for no reason, so that [the father] never saw [his son] without [the son's] cheeks being marked by the signs of tears. Although he saw the child being treated like this day after day before his eyes, the father's feelings remained firm and unmoving, for the love of Christ ... The superior of the monastery ... decided to test [the father's] strength of mind still further: one day when he noticed the child weeping, he pretended to be enraged at [the child], and ordered the father to pick up [his son] and throw him in the Nile. The father, as if the command had been given him by our Lord, at once ran and snatched up his son and carried him in his own arms to the river bank to throw him in. The deed would have been done ... had not some of the brethren been stationed in advance to watch the riverbank carefully; as the child was thrown they caught him ... Thus they prevented the command, performed as it was by the father's obedience and devotion, from having any effect.[13]

Cassian plainly prizes Patermutus's actions and attitude; but surely most of us will find it chilling and reprehensible. For my part, I would say that one can only wonder why the monks bothered to catch the child, if the father's willingness to kill the child was so praiseworthy in their eyes. Can it be morally praiseworthy to will an act whose performance is morally prohibited?

An attitude similar to Cassian's but less appalling can still be found more than a millenium later in some texts (but not others) of the work of Teresa of Avila, to take just one example from among a host of thinkers who could have been selected. Writing to her sister nuns, Teresa says,

Oh, how desirable is ... [the] union with God's will! Happy the soul that has reached it. Such a soul will live tranquilly in this life, and in the next as well. Nothing in earthly events afflicts it unless it finds itself in some danger of losing God ... : neither

---

[13] Cassian 1999: 55–6.

sickness, nor poverty, nor death … For this soul sees well that the Lord knows what He is doing better than … [the soul] knows what it is desiring … But alas for us, how few there must be who reach [union with God's will!] … I tell you I am writing this with much pain upon seeing myself so far away [from union with God's will]—and all through my own fault …. Don't think the matter lies in my being so conformed to the will of God that if my father or brother dies I don't feel it, or that if there are trials or sicknesses I suffer them happily.[14]

Not feeling it when one's father dies, not weeping with grief over his death, is, in Teresa's view, a good spiritual condition which she is not yet willing to attribute to herself. Teresa is here echoing a tradition which finds its prime medieval exemplar in Augustine's *Confessions*. Augustine says that, at the death of his mother, by a powerful command of his will, he kept himself from weeping at her funeral, only to disgrace himself in his own eyes later by weeping copiously in private.[15]

In the same text from which I just quoted, Teresa emphasizes the importance of love of neighbour; but it is hard to see how love of neighbour coheres with the stern-minded attitude manifested by Teresa and Augustine in the face of the death (real or imagined) of a beloved parent. As I have argued elsewhere, it is the nature of love to desire the good of the beloved and union with him.[16] But the desire for the good of the beloved is frustrated if the beloved gets sick or dies. Or, if the stern-minded attitude is unwilling to concede that point, then this much is incontrovertible even on the stern-minded attitude: the desire for union with the beloved is frustrated when the beloved dies and so is absent. One way or another, then, the desires of love are frustrated when the beloved dies.

Consequently, there is something bad and lamentable, something worth tears, something whose loss brings affliction with it, about the death of any person whom one loves—one's father, or even one's neighbour, whom one is bound to love too, as Teresa thinks.

Unmoved tranquillity at the death of another person is thus incompatible with love of that person. To the extent to which one loves another person, one cannot be unmoved at his death. And so love of neighbour is in fact incompatible with the stern-minded attitude.

The stance Teresa wishes she might take towards her father's death, as she imagines it, can be usefully contrasted with Bernard of Clairvaux's reaction to the death of his brother. Commenting on his grief at that death, Bernard says to his religious community, 'You, my sons, know how deep my sorrow is, how galling a wound it leaves.'[17] And, addressing himself, he says, 'Flow

---

[14] Teresa of Avila 1979: 98, 99, 100.   [15] *Confessions* IX.12.
[16] Stump 2006.   [17] Cited in Astell 1990: 126.

on, flow on, my tears ... Let my tears gush forth like fountains.'[18] Reflecting on his own failure to repudiate his great sorrow over his brother's death, his failure, that is, to follow Augustine's model, Bernard says,

> It is but human and necessary that we respond to our friends with feeling, that we be happy in their company, disappointed in their absence. Social intercourse, especially between friends, cannot be purposeless: the reluctance to part and the yearning for each other when separated indicate how meaningful their mutual love must be when they are together.[19]

And Bernard is hardly the only figure in the Christian tradition who fails to accept and affirm Cassian's attitude. Aquinas is another.

There are isolated texts which might suggest to some readers that Aquinas himself is an adherent of Cassian's attitude. So, for example, in his commentary on Christ's line that he who loves his life will lose it, Aquinas reveals that he recognizes the concept of the desires of the heart; but, in this same passage, he also seems to suggest that such desires should be stamped out. He says,

> Everyone loves his own soul, but some love it *simpliciter* and some *secundum quid*. To love someone is to will the good for him; and so he who loves his soul wills the good for it. A person who wills for his soul the good *simpliciter* also loves his soul *simpliciter*. But a person who wills some particular good for his soul loves his soul *secundum quid*. The goods for the soul *simpliciter* are those things by which the soul is good, namely, the highest good, which is God. And so he who wills for his soul the divine good, a spiritual good, loves his soul *simpliciter*. But he who wills for his soul earthly goods such as riches and honors, pleasures, and things of that sort, he loves his soul [only] *secundum quid* ... He who loves his soul *secundum quid*, namely with regard to temporal goods, will lose it.[20]

And the implication seems to be that, for Aquinas, the person who does not want to lose his soul should extirpate from himself all desires for any good other than the highest good, which is, as Aquinas says, God.

But it is important to see that what is at issue for Aquinas in this passage is the desire for worldly things, that is for those goods, such as money or fame, which diminish when they are distributed. On Aquinas' scale of values, any good which diminishes when it is distributed is only a small good. When it comes to the desires of the heart for things which are earthly goods but great goods, such as the love of a particular person, Aquinas' attitude differs sharply from Cassian's. So, for example, in explaining why Christ told his disciples that he was going to the father in order to comfort them when they were sad at the prospect of being separated from him, Aquinas says,

---

[18] Cited in Astell 1990: 130.   [19] Cited in Astell 1990: 133.
[20] *Super Evangelium S.Ioannis Lectura*, John 12: 24–5, Lectio IV.7, 1643–1644.

'It is common among friends to be less sad over the absence of a friend when the friend is going to something which exalts him. That is why the Lord gives them this reason [for his leaving] in order to console them.'[21]

Unlike Teresa's repudiation of grief at the prospect of losing her father, Aquinas is here, as in many other places, accepting the appropriateness of a person's grief at the loss of a loved person and validating the need for consolation for such grief.

So Aquinas is not to be ranked among the members of the stern-minded group, any more than Bernard is; and, of course, in other moods, when she is not self-consciously evaluating her own spiritual progress, Teresa herself sounds more like Bernard and Aquinas than like Cassian. As far as that goes, the Psalmist who authored Psalm 37 is not on Cassian's side. The Psalmist claims that God will give the desires of the heart to those who delight in the Lord; so the Psalmist is supposing that, for those who trust in God, God himself honours the desires of the heart. On this subject, then, the Christian tradition is of two minds. Not all its influential figures stand with Cassian; and, even among those who do, many are double-minded about it.

IV. A POSSIBLE CONFUSION

But, someone will surely object, isn't it a part of Christian doctrine that God allows the death of any person who dies? Does anyone die when God wills that that person live? So when a person dies, on Christian theology, isn't it the will of God that that person die? In what sense, then, could Teresa be united with God in will if she grieved over her father's death? How could she be united with God, as she explains she wants to be, if her will is frustrated in what God's will accepts or commands?

The position presupposed by the questions of this putative objector, in my view, rests on too simple an understanding of God's will and union with God's will.

To see why, assume that at death Teresa's father is united with God in heaven. Then the death which unites Teresa's father permanently with God has the opposite effect for Teresa: at least for the time being, it deprives Teresa of her father's presence and so keeps her from union with him, at least for the rest of Teresa's earthly life. For this reason, on the Christian doctrine Teresa accepts, love's desire for union with the beloved cannot be fulfilled in the same way for Teresa as for God. If Teresa's will is united with God's will in desiring union with a beloved person, then Teresa's will

---

[21] *Super Evangelium S.Ioannis Lectura*, John 14: 27–31, Lectio VIII.1, 1966.

must also be frustrated at the very event, her father's dying, which fulfils God's will with respect to this desire.

Something analogous can be said about the other desire of love, for the good of the beloved. If Teresa desires the good of her father, she can only desire what her own mind sees as that good; but her mind's ability to see the good is obviously much smaller than God's. To the extent to which Teresa's will is united with God's will in desiring the good of the beloved, then Teresa will also desire for the beloved person things different from those desired by God, in virtue of Teresa's differing ability to see the good for the beloved person.

It is easy to become confused here because the phrase 'the good' can be used either attributively or referentially.[22] In this context, 'the good of the beloved' can be used either to refer to particular things which are conducive to the beloved's wellbeing; or it can be used opaquely, to refer to anything whatever, under the description *the good of the beloved*. A mother who is baffled by the quarrels among her adult children and clueless about how to bring about a just peace for them may say, despairingly, 'I just want the good for everybody.' She is then using the phrase 'the good' attributively, with no idea of how to use it referentially.

If Teresa were tranquil over any affliction which happens to her father, because she thinks that in this tranquillity her will is united to God's will and that she is therefore willing the good for her father,[23] 'the good' in this thought of hers is being used attributively, to designate *whatever* God thinks is good. But this cannot be the way 'the good' is used in any thought of God's, without relativizing the good entirely to God's will. If we eschew such relativism, then it is not the case that anything God desires is good just because God desires it. And so it is also not true that God desires as the good of a beloved person *whatever* it is that God desires for her. When God desires the good for someone, then, God must desire it by desiring particular things as good for that person. Consequently, to say that God desires the good for a person is to use 'the good' referentially.

For this reason, when, in an effort to will what God wills, Teresa desires *whatever* happens to her father as the good for her father, she thereby actually *fails* to will what God wills. To be united with God in willing the good requires willing for the beloved particular things which are in fact the

---

[22] 'The commander of the armed forces' is used referentially when it refers to the particular person who is the President; it is used attributively when it refers to anyone who holds the office of commander without reference to a particular person who in fact currently holds the office.

[23] It is important to put the point in terms of what *happens* to her father, rather than in terms of any state or condition of her father, since there are certainly things her father might do which cause Teresa a grief she would approve of having.

good for the beloved, and doing so requires recognizing those things which constitute that good.

At the death of Mao Tse-tung, one of the groups competing for power was called 'the Whatever Faction', because the members of that group were committed to maintaining as true, and compulsory for all Chinese to believe, anything Mao said, whatever it was.[24] In trying to desire whatever happens as good because God wills it, a person is as it were trying to be part of a Whatever Faction for God. She is trying to maintain as good anything that happens, whatever it is, on the grounds that it is what God wills. By contrast, in his great lament over the death of his brother, Bernard of Clairvaux is willing to affirm both his passionate grief over the loss of his brother and his acceptance of God's allowing that death. Bernard says, 'Shall I find fault with [God's] judgment because I wince from the pain?';[25] 'I have no wish to repudiate the decrees of God, nor do I question that judgment by which each of us has received his due ... '[26] Bernard grieves over this particular death as a bad thing, even while he accepts that God's allowing this bad thing is a good thing.

Understanding the subtle but important difference in attitude between Teresa and Bernard on this score helps to elucidate the otherwise peculiar part of the book of Job in which God rebukes Job's comforters because they did not say of God the thing which is right, unlike God's servant Job, who did. What the comforters had said was that God is justified in allowing Job's suffering. Job, on the other hand, had complained bitterly that his suffering is unjust and that God should not have allowed it to happen. How is it that, in the story, God affirms Job's position and repudiates that of the comforters? The answer lies in seeing that the comforters took Job's suffering to be good just because, in their view, Job's suffering was willed by God. In effect, then, the comforters were (and wanted to be) part of the Whatever Faction of God. Job, by contrast, was intransigent in his refusal to be partisan in this way. And so, on the apparently paradoxical view of the book of Job, in opposing God, Job is more allied with God's will than are the comforters, who were taking God's part. That is why when in the story God comes to adjudicate, he sides with Job, who had opposed him, and not with the comforters, who were trying to be his partisans.

The apparent paradox here can be resolved by the scholastic distinction between God's antecedent and consequent will. On this distinction,

---

[24] The official formula was 'Whatever policy Chairman Mao decided upon, we shall resolutely defend; whatever directives Chairman Mao issued, we shall steadfastly obey.' See MacFarquhar 1991: 372.

[25] Cited in Astell 1990: 133.   [26] Cited in Astell 1990: 130.

whatever happens in the world happens only because it is in accordance with God's will, but that will is God's *consequent* will. God's consequent will, however, is to be distinguished from his antecedent will; and many of the things which happen in the world are not in accordance with God's *antecedent* will. Roughly put, God's *antecedent* will is what God would have willed if things in the world had been up to God alone. God's *consequent* will is what God in fact wills, given what he knows that his creatures will. God's consequent will is his will for the greatest good available in the circumstances which are generated through creaturely free will.

To try to be in accord with God's will by taking as acceptable, as unworthy of sorrow, everything that happens is to confuse the consequent will of God with the antecedent will. It is to accept as intrinsically good even those things which God wills as good only secundum quid, that is, as the best available in the circumstances. But God does not will as intrinsically good everything he wills; what he wills in his consequent will, what is the best available in the circumstances, might be only the lesser of evils, not the intrinsically good.

And so to accept as good whatever happens on the grounds that it is God's will is the wrong way to try to be united with God's will. One can desire as intrinsically good what one sees for oneself is good in the circumstances, or one can desire[27] as intrinsically good whatever happens, on the grounds that it is God's will. But only the former desire can be in accordance with God's will, given that God's consequent will is not the same as his antecedent will. For the same reasons, only the former desire is conducive to union with God. Although it appears paradoxical, then, the closest a human person may be able to come, in this life, to uniting her will with God's will may include her willing things (say, that a beloved person not die) which are opposed to God's (consequent) will.

It is also important to see in this connection that, in principle, there cannot be any competition between the love of God and the love of other persons. On the contrary, if one does not love one's neighbour, then one does not love God either. That is because to love God is to desire union with him; and union with God requires being united in will with him. But a person who does not love another, his father or brother, for example, cannot be united in will with a God who does love these people. So, in being tranquil and unmoved in the face of the death of a beloved father or mother, a person is not more united with God, or more in harmony with God's will, but less.

---

[27] Or try to accept—a distinction manifested by Teresa's own description of herself.

V. DENYING ONESELF

Something also needs to be said in this connection about the Christian doctrine mandating denial of the self. This much understanding of the two different ways in which one can try to will what God wills shows that there are also two correspondingly different interpretations of that doctrine.

Cassian and others who hold the stern-minded attitude manifest one such understanding. A person who shares Cassian's attitude will attempt to deny his self by, in effect, refusing to let his own mind and his own will exercise their characteristic functions. That is because a person who attempts to see as good whatever happens, on the grounds that whatever happens is willed by God, is trying to suppress, or trying to fail to acquire, his own understanding of the good. And a person who attempts to will as good whatever happens, on the same grounds, is trying to suppress the desires his own will forms, or trying not to acquire the desires his will would have formed if he were not in the grip of the stern-minded attitude. To attempt to deny the self in the stern-minded way is thus to try not to have a self at all. A woman who says sincerely to her father, 'I want only what you want,' and 'whatever you think is good is good in my view, too,' is a woman who is trying to be at one with her father by having no self of her own.

On the other hand, it is possible to let one's own faculties of intellect and will have their normal functioning and still deny oneself. This is a stance with which we are all familiar from our experiences of ordinary, daily life. Consider, for example, a mother with the stomach flu who creeps out of bed to care for her baby who also has the flu. When she leaves her bed to tend the baby, she is preferring to meet the baby's needs rather than her own. That is, she desires to stay in bed, but she also desires that the baby's needs take precedence over her own needs and desires. In her desire about the rank-ordering of desires, she does not cease to desire to stay in bed. She still has that desire; she just acts counter to it. This is to deny the self by first having a self to deny. Unlike the no-self position, this position is compatible with sorrow, and tears, for the things lost in the desires denied.

On reflection, it is clear that, contrary to first appearances, the no-self position is actually incompatible with the Christian injunction of self-denial. That is because one cannot crucify a self one does not have. To crucify one's self is to have desires and to be willing to act counter to them. An adherent to the Whatever Faction of God cannot deny his self, however, because he has constructed his desires in such a way that, whatever he wills, he does not will counter to his own desires. A person who is a partisan of the no-self position has a first-order desire for whatever it may be that is God's will, and he attempts to have no first-order desires which are in conflict with whatever it may be that is God's will. That is why (unlike the real Teresa, who was full of very human emotions) such a person would not weep if her father died. In theory, at any rate, whatever happens to her is in accordance with her first-order will and is therefore not a source of sorrow to her. In virtue of the fact that she has tried to extirpate from herself all desires except the one desire for whatever it may be that is God's will, such a person has no desires which are frustrated by whatever happens, as long as she herself remains committed to willing whatever God wills.[28]

The self-crucifying denier of the self, by contrast, has first-order desires for things his own intellect finds good, so that he is vulnerable to grief in the frustration of those desires. But he prefers his grief and frustration to the violation of God's will. In this sense, he also wills that God's will be done. His second-order desire is that God's desires take precedence over his own. When Christ says, 'not my will but yours be done', he is not expressing the no-self position, because he is admitting that he has desires in conflict with God's desires. On the other hand, in virtue of preferring his pain to the violation of God's will, he is also willing that God's desires take precedence over his. This is the sense, then, in which he is willing that God's will be done.

VI. THE DESIRES OF THE HEART AND THE FLOURISHING OF A PERSON

So, for all these reasons, the stern-minded attitude is to be repudiated. Whatever its antiquity and ancestry, such influential thinkers as Bernard and Aquinas do not accept it. More importantly, it is an unpalatable position, even from the point of view of an ascetically minded Christianity. It underlies the repellent and lamentable mind-set exemplified in Cassian's story, and it is incompatible with the love of one's neighbour and consequently also with love of God. There are things worth desiring other than the intrinsically valuable things necessary for human flourishing, and the desires for these things should not be suppressed or stamped out. On the contrary, as Cassian's story makes plain, the attempt to extirpate any desires of the heart does not lead to human excellence, as Cassian thought it did, but to a

---

[28] The last clause is a necessary caveat because, presumably, even an adherent to the position would be distressed at finding sin in himself (and maybe even at finding sin in others), since sin cannot be considered in accordance with God's will.

kind of inhumanity willing to murder one's own child in the service of a confused and reprehensible attempt at self-denial.

There is an apparent paradox here, however. As I introduced the phrase, the desires of the heart are desires which are central to a person's web of desires but whose objects have the value they do for her because of her desire for them, not because of their connection to general human flourishing. On the face of it, then, losing the objects of such desires or giving up those desires themselves is compatible with general human flourishing for that person. But the rejection of the stern-minded attitude seems to imply that a person's flourishing requires that he have desires of the heart and that he strive to have what he desires. Consequently, it also seems to imply that it is essential to a person's flourishing that he have desires of the heart. But, then, if the desires of the heart are required for his flourishing, it seems that the objects of those desires are as well. And so it seems to follow, paradoxically, that it is essential to human flourishing that a person desire and seek to have things at least some of which are not necessary to human flourishing.

In recent work, Harry Frankfurt has argued that it is useful for a person to have final ends.[29] The central idea of his argument is the thought that a person with no final ends at all will have a life which lacks flourishing. And so final ends *are* useful as a means to an end, namely, human flourishing. The apparently paradoxical claim about the desires of the heart can be understood analogously. Human beings are constructed in such a way that they naturally set their hearts on things in addition to and different from intrinsically valuable things essential to general human flourishing. That is why confining a person's desires just to human flourishing has something inhuman about it. A person's flourishing therefore also requires that he care about and seek to have things besides those that are intrinsically valuable components of or means to human flourishing.[30] On Frankfurt's view, having a desire for something which is not a means to anything else is a means to a person's flourishing. On the view I have argued for here, having a desire for things which are not essential to flourishing and seeking to have those things is also necessary as a means to flourishing.

And so, although no particular thing valued as a desire of the heart is essential to a person's flourishing, human flourishing is not possible in the absence of the desires of the heart.

---

[29] Frankfurt 1998.

[30] In this respect, the desires of the heart are to human flourishing what accidents are to a primary substance. Any particular accident is not necessary to a substance, but it is necessary to a substance that it have accidents. Analogously, no particular desire of the heart is necessary for a person's flourishing, but it is necessary for her flourishing that she have desires of the heart.

VII. CONCLUSION

For all these reasons, we can safely leave the objections of the stern-minded attitude to one side. It therefore remains the case that justification is also needed for suffering stemming from unfulfilled or frustrated desires of the heart. For this reason, theodicies which focus just on one or another variety of general human flourishing as the morally sufficient reason for God's allowing evil are, at best, incomplete. Even if we give a theodicy such as Hick's or Swinburne's everything it wants as regards the relation between suffering and flourishing, however flourishing is understood in their theodicies, there remains the problem of suffering stemming from the loss of the desires of one's heart.

Take the story of Job, for example. For the sake of argument, let it be the case, as Saadiah Gaon appears to hold in his excellent and impressive commentary, that Job's suffering is necessary to his ennobling and purification, morally acceptable as a means to these things, and outweighed by them, in the sense that (on some objective measure) Job's ennobling and purification are a greater good than his suffering is an evil. Even if this were entirely so, and even if it were right that ennobling and purification constituted consummate human flourishing, something more would be needed for theodicy in Job's case. Job might care about his children at least as much as about his own ennobling and purification; and he might be heartbroken at the loss of his children, even with the benefit to him of his ennobling and purification. Something also needs to be said about the moral justification for God's allowing such heartbreak.

Someone might object that if the benefit to Job really is connected to his suffering in the way I have just described, then nothing more is needed for theodicy, because the good given to Job through his suffering defeats the suffering. But this is to accord no value to the desires of Job's heart. It is, in effect, to say with regard to Job a much sterner version of what the loving but exasperated father said to his daughter: It is not reasonable to weep about these things. But, as I have been at pains to show, disregarding or downplaying the desires of the heart is itself unreasonable. Suffering is a function of what we care about, and we care not only about human flourishing; we care also about the things on which we have set our hearts. The suffering stemming from the loss of the heart's desires also needs to be redeemed. The benefit which outweighs the suffering for Job, as Saadiah Gaon sees it, outweighs that suffering only on the scale of values which measures the intrinsic worth of things essential to human flourishing in general. It does not outweigh it on the scale which measures things that have the value they do for a particular person only because he has set his heart on them.

That this is so helps to explain why so many people feel uneasy or disappointed at attempted solutions to the problem of evil which focus on some global good for humanity in general—the significant use of free will, for example—as a morally sufficient reason for God to allow suffering. If a person's own flourishing is not sufficient to justify God in allowing her to be heartbroken, then, a fortiori, some component of or contribution to the flourishing of the human species considered as a whole cannot do so either.

And so the desires of the heart also need to be considered in connection with the problem of evil. For my part, I think it is possible to find a way to develop traditional theodicies to include satisfactory consideration of the problem posed by the desires of the heart;[31] but, clearly, that complicated and challenging task lies outside the scope of this paper.

REFERENCES

Adams, Marilyn, *Horrendous Evils and the Goodness of God* (Ithaca, NY: Cornell University Press, 1999).

Astell, Ann, *The Song of Songs in the Middle Ages* (Ithaca, NY: Cornell University Press, 1990).

Cassian, *The Monastic Institutes,* tr. Jerome Bertram (London: Saint Austin Press, 1999).

Frankfurt, Harry, 'On the Usefulness of Final Ends', *Necessity, Volition, and Love* (Princeton, NJ: Princeton University Press, 1998).

Hick, John, *Evil and the God of Love* (New York: Harper and Row, 1966).

—— 'God, Evil and Mystery', *Religious Studies* 3 (1968a): 539–46.

—— 'The Problem of Evil in the First and Last Things', *Journal of Theological Studies* 19 (1968b): 591–602.

Hull, Jonathan, *Touching the Rock. An Experience of Blindness* (New York: Vintage Books, 1991).

MacFarquhar, Roderick, 'The Succession to Mao and the End of Maoism', in *The Cambridge History of China*, vol.15, *The People's Republic, pt.2: Revolutions within the Chinese Revolution: 1966–1982* (Cambridge: Cambridge University Press, 1991).

Saadiah Gaon, *The Book of Beliefs and Opinions,* tr. Samuel Rosenblatt (New Haven, CT: Yale University Press, 1948).

Stump, Eleonore, 'Love, By All Accounts', Proceedings and Addresses of The American Philosophical Association, Vol. 80, No. 2, November 2006.

[31] I argue for this claim in detail in my *Wandering in Darkness. Narrative and the Problem of Suffering* (Oxford, forthcoming).

—— *Wandering in Darkness: Narrative and the Problem of Suffering* (Oxford: Oxford University Press, forthcoming).

Swinburne, Richard, *Providence and the Problem of Evil* (Oxford: Oxford University Press, 1998).

Teresa of Avila, *The Interior Castle* (Mahwah, NJ: Paulist Press, 1979).

Vanier, Jean, *Becoming Human* (Mahwah, NJ: Paulist Press, 1998).

10

What Does an Omniscient Being Know about the Future?

Peter van Inwagen

I want to consider the question whether the existence of an omniscient being is compatible with human free will. But is this an important question? Well, I believe in free will and I believe in God and omniscience occurs in all the standard lists of the divine attributes, so naturally I find the question *interesting*. But a question one regards as interesting need not be a question one regards as important. Suppose that Sally believes that God is omniscient and that human beings have free will. If someone convinces her that human free will and divine omniscience are incompatible, why should she not proceed to say something like, 'Oh, that's interesting. I see that I must give up at least one of two beliefs I happen to have. If I can find some time to devote to the question which of the two beliefs to give up, I must think about the matter. Until I find the time for such reflection, I'll just give them both up. I'll thereby avoid logical inconsistency, and I'll also avoid making an arbitrary choice about which of them to give up, which is what I'd have to do if I decided to give up only one of them without devoting sufficient thought to the very complex issues they involve.'? If she did say something of that sort, she'd thereby show that she didn't regard the question whether free will and divine omniscience were compatible as important. I would suppose that one will regard the question of the compatibility of two of one's beliefs as *important* only if one is unwilling simply to give them both up.

Am I willing to stop believing that human beings have free will and that God is omniscient? Am I in fact willing to stop believing *either* of these things? Let us first consider God's omniscience. If I decide to stop believing that God is omniscient, I confront a serious prima facie difficulty, a difficulty that can be summed up in the following argument. God is *aliquid quo nihil maius cogitari possit*, something than which nothing greater can be conceived. And if God were ignorant of various things, it would be possible to conceive of something greater than he, to wit a being otherwise like him but *not* ignorant of those things. God must therefore be omniscient. And the premise of this argument, that nothing greater than God is so much as conceivable, is something I believe and not something I am willing to stop believing—for to my mind, this Anselmian idea expresses the *concept* of God, the *meaning* of the word 'God'.

But (you may want to ask me), if you think that argument is right, where's the problem? If God must be omniscient and if his omniscience is demonstrably incompatible with human free will (as we are assuming), then, obviously, if I wish to be consistent I must stop believing in human free will. Unfortunately, if I go so far as to agree that God must be omniscient and that divine omniscience is incompatible with creaturely free will, I thereby create for myself a prima facie difficulty that I cannot evade simply by ceasing to believe in creaturely free will. And this difficulty is no less serious than the difficulty I should confront if I chose to stop believing that God was omniscient. This difficulty, too, can be summed up in an argument. The argument turns on the importance of the free-will defence to an adequate response to the argument from evil. The argument is simplicity itself. The single most important reply to the argument from evil turns on the possible truth of the story called the free-will defence, and that story entails both that God exists and (of course) that at least some creatures have free will. If, therefore, I concede that divine omniscience is incompatible with creaturely free will, I deprive the apologist for theism of the single most important response to the argument from evil.

Most Christian philosophers would, I think, contend that these reflections are beside the point for the simple reason that divine omniscience is *not* incompatible with creaturely free will. In my view, however, this sanguine view cannot be maintained. The following argument for the incompatibility of divine omniscience and creaturely free will (it is modelled on certain well-known arguments for the incompatibility of determinism and free will) seems to me to be irrefutable—*provided* (an important qualification) that God is not 'outside time'.

Suppose I must now make a choice between lying and telling the embarrassing truth. If God is omniscient, he either knew (and hence believed) in the year 1900 that I should lie, or else he knew (and believed) in that year that I should tell the truth. Suppose he knew (and believed) that I was going to lie. It follows that I am about to lie. Can it be that this thing I am about to do, this lie I am about to tell, will be a free act? Only if I am able to do otherwise than lie: only if I am able to tell the truth. *Am* I able to tell the truth? If I am, I have, as one might say, access to a possible future (a possible continuation of the present state of affairs) in which I tell the truth. But every continuation of the present state of things in which I tell the truth has *this* feature: in it, in that future, one of the following two statements is true:

(1) God believed in 1900 that I was going to lie, and this belief was false
(2) God did not believe in 1900 that I was going to lie.

And I have no access to a future in which either proposition is true. Proposition (1) is flatly impossible, as impossible as the proposition that a round square exists, and it is therefore true in no possible future. Proposition (2) is not impossible in that sense, but it is impossible in *this* sense: it is not true in the present state of affairs, and in every possible continuation of the present state of affairs, the same propositions about the 'present past' (the past before the present moment) are true as are true in the present state of affairs.[1] I therefore have no access to any possible continuation of the present state of things in which I tell the truth (since in *no* possible continuation of the present state of things do I tell the truth). I am therefore unable to tell the truth. And, therefore, the lie I am about to tell will not be a free act. A parallel argument shows that if God knew in 1900 that I should tell the truth, my telling the truth would not be a free act. Therefore, I do not have free will with respect to whether I lie or tell the truth. And, of course, this argument can be generalized, the conclusion of the general argument being that divine omniscience is incompatible with human (and, more generally still, creaturely) free will.

I said that this argument seemed to me to be irrefutable provided that God was not outside time. The reason for this qualification is evident: in that case the argument has a false premise—to wit, that God believed *in 1900* that I was going to lie (or, as it may be, was going to tell the truth). Nevertheless, or so it seems to me, it is possible to reconstruct the argument in such a way that the reconstructed argument applies to a non-temporal God—and, nevertheless, retains much of the force of the original argument. And here is the argument.[2]

Suppose I told a lie at 11:46 a.m. Eastern Standard Time, on 23 December 2006. An omniscient but non-temporal God has—given only that, for every time t,

---

[1] One can, of course, enter into subtle arguments about which propositions that are apparently about the past are *really* about the past (is the proposition that it was true in 1900 that human beings would set foot on Mars in the twenty-first century really about the past?), but almost all philosophers would agree that any proposition to the effect that someone (God or anyone else) believed something in some past year is really about the past. (And those philosophers who don't assent to that thesis should. If some philosopher's definition or analysis of 'about the past' has the consequence that the proposition that God believed in 1900 that I was going to lie at a certain moment is not 'about the past', that proposition constitutes a counterexample to that philosopher's definition.)

[2] I apologize for the fact that there is some confusion of tenses in the argument that follows. It is hard to write coherently about the beliefs and acts and abilities of a non-temporal being. I have done the best I could.

any proposition that is about states of affairs subsequent to t, is 'already' true at t or already false at t—the following ability: He is able (acting, of course, extra-temporally) to cause a monument to have come into existence *ex nihilo* in 1900, a great slab of stone on which the following words were inscribed: 'On 21 September 1942, a human being named Peter van Inwagen will be born. On 23 December 2006, at 11:46 a.m. Eastern Time (or Eastern Standard Time, as Eastern Time will then be known), he will have to choose between lying and telling the truth. He will choose to lie.' Suppose God has done this thing he is able to have done. Can it be that my lying—my telling a lie at 11:46 a.m. EST, 23 December 2006—was a free act? That is, was I able, on that occasion, to tell the truth? Well, was there, just before that moment, a possible continuation of the (then) present state of affairs in which I told the truth? Let us consider all the possible continuations of that state of affairs. It is true in every one of them that a monument (inscribed with just the words recorded above) came into existence *ex nihilo* in 1900—and true that its coming to be was caused by God's extra-temporal act of creation. Is it true in any of the possible continuations of the then-present state of affairs that the words inscribed on the monument did not express a true proposition? No, for in that case God would either have been mistaken or have been a deceiver, and both are impossible. My act (my telling the lie), was therefore not a free act, for if it were, I should have had access to a possible continuation of the then-present state of affairs in which no monument (so inscribed) was brought into existence by God in 1900 *or* in which one was but the words inscribed on it did not express a true proposition—and no continuation of that state of affairs that answers to either of these descriptions exists. We may say that the monument in this imaginary case is a 'Freedom-denying Prophetic Object'. The concept of a Freedom-denying Prophetic Object is a very abstract one: a divinely inspired human prophet who has foretold certain actions of human beings would also be a Freedom-denying Prophetic Object. It is no doubt true that very few human actions can be shown to be unfree on the ground that that they were 'foretold' by the statement that they should occur having been somehow being encoded in the structure of a Freedom-denying Prophetic Object—for (no doubt) very few human actions have been so foretold. But this seems irrelevant to the question whether human beings have free will. Suppose God should reveal to us that on a distant, uninhabited planet, he had created, before the existence of the first human being, a vast library that contained minutely detailed biographies (correct in every detail) of all the human beings who would ever live. Would the following be a reasonable reaction to this revelation: 'Ah, then human free will does not exist. But if God had not created that library (and had not done anything relevantly similar), human free will *would* exist.'? Obviously not: although it follows logically from the story of the monument that my lie was not a free act, the fact that my lie was not a free act cannot be supposed to be a *consequence* of the existence of the monument. The case is precisely parallel to this case: if God were to cause there to be a monument in Montana that bore the inscription, 'Tokyo is the capital of Japan', it would follow logically from the features and provenance of monument that Tokyo was the capital of Japan; but the fact that Tokyo was the capital of Japan would no more *depend on* the existence and features of that monument than it would depend on the existence and features of any other object in Montana.[3]

Might it be that this argument, too, has a false premise, namely that all propositions (including propositions 'about the future') have truth-values?—a premise that both Aristotle and some philosophers of our own time have maintained entails the impossibility of free will for reasons that are independent of any theological considerations. Anyone who wishes to embrace the thesis that at least some propositions about events subsequent to *t* are neither true nor false at *t* will have to find some sort of response to the following argument (it can obviously be generalized, for it does not depend on any feature peculiar to propositions about future sea-battles):

The proposition that there will be a sea battle at *t* [where *t* is some moment in the future] is true if and only if there will be a sea battle at *t*

The proposition that there will be a sea battle at *t* is false if and only if it is not the case that there will be a sea battle at *t*

hence,

Either the proposition that there will be a sea battle at *t* is true or the proposition that there will be a sea battle at *t* is false.[4]

This argument—it is formally valid—is a rather hard argument to get round. I should not like to have to try to find something wrong with it. (And, in any case, it is hard to see how someone who believes that God exists outside time and is omniscient can coherently suppose that propositions about events subsequent to *t* are neither true nor false at *t*.)

Whatever other philosophers may think, I find the above arguments for the incompatibility of divine omniscience and human free will convincing. I am therefore faced with a serious problem. Must I concede either that God is not omniscient or that human beings lack free will (and concede, therefore, that the free-will defence is not an acceptable reply to the argument from evil)?

I will respond to this problem by engaging in some permissible tinkering with the concept of omniscience. At any rate, I believe it to be permissible. (I'll later give my reasons for thinking that the tinkering is permissible.) That is to say, I'll revise the standard concept of omniscience in such a way

---

[3] I confess that I am not entirely happy about the final part of this argument—the part that starts with 'It is no doubt true that very few human actions ... ' It lacks the demonstrative rigour of the original argument and the earlier part of the reconstructed argument. It is for this reason that I claim for the reconstructed argument only that 'it retains much of the force of the original argument'.

[4] Cf. pp. 52–4 of my book *An Essay on Free Will* (Oxford: Clarendon Press, 1983).

that the existence of a being who falls under the revised concept is consistent with the existence of human free will, and I'll defend the conclusion that it is possible to regard a being who is omniscient in the revised sense (and is not omniscient in the standard or traditional sense) as *aliquid quo nihil maius cogitari possit.*

In what follows, I am going to suppose that God is everlasting but temporal, that he is not outside time. I make this assumption for two reasons. First, I do not know how to think coherently and in detail about a non-temporal being's knowledge of what is 'from out point of view' the future. (*Vide* my difficulties with tense in my statement of the 'monument' argument.) Secondly, it would seem that the problem of God's knowledge of what is to us the future is particularly acute if this knowledge is *fore*knowledge, if what is from our point of view the future is the future from God's point of view as well.

Now what concept, exactly, is the concept of omniscience—the standard or traditional concept that I confessed I was going to tinker with? One might define 'classical' omniscience like this:

An omniscient being is a being who, for every proposition, either knows that that proposition is true or knows that that proposition is false (and whose beliefs are consistent),[5]

or like this:

An omniscient being is a being who, for every proposition believes either that proposition or its denial, and whose beliefs cannot (this is the 'cannot' of metaphysical impossibility) be mistaken.

These definitions are not equivalent. (Except possibly in this sense: any metaphysically possible being who was omniscient according to one would be omniscient according to the other. Perhaps no metaphysically possible being satisfies either, or perhaps God is the only metaphysically possible being who satisfies either.) The first does not entail the second because knowledge does not entail the impossibility of mistake. (Not, at any rate, if fallible beings like ourselves have any knowledge that is more extensive than 'worst-case Cartesian' knowledge—knowledge of our own existence and of the present content of our own minds and of a few truths along the lines of '$1 + 1 = 2$'.) Does the second definition entail the first? Not obviously, for someone might maintain that a being who believed that *p* and who could not (in the strongest possible sense of 'could not') be mistaken in

---

[5] The point of the parenthetical qualification is this: someone might contend that a being might know (and hence believe) that *p* was true, and, at the same time, believe, inconsistently, that *p* was false.

believing that *p* would not necessarily *know* that *p*—since the impossibility of mistake is not sufficient for knowledge. We might try to address this person's worry by adding something like the following clause to the second definition: 'And that being *knows* that its beliefs have that modal feature'. With that qualification (if it is indeed necessary), I would say, the second definition entails the first.[6]

I'm going to employ the second definition in the arguments that follow, not because it's the stronger of the two, but simply because I find that the way it's worded enables me to state those arguments more simply than I should be able to if I employed the first.[7]

Now consider these two propositions:

(i) X will freely do A at the future moment *t*
(ii) Y, a being whose beliefs cannot be mistaken, now believes that X will do A at *t*.

Either (i) and (ii) are consistent with each other or they are not. If they are consistent, there is no problem of omniscience and freedom. (If (i) and (ii) are consistent, of course, there must be some mistake in the argument I have presented for the conclusion that that free will is inconsistent with divine omniscience.) Suppose then that they are inconsistent. If (i) and (ii) are inconsistent, and if X will freely do A at *t*, it is impossible for an infallible being (so to call a being whose beliefs cannot be mistaken), now to believe that X will do A at *t*. More generally, if free will exists, it is

---

[6] Here is a third possible definition:

An omniscient being is a being who (at any time) knows every truth (and whose beliefs are consistent).

If this is an acceptable definition of omniscience, there is an interesting argument for the compatibility of divine omniscience and free will. Simply assume, with Aristotle, that propositions about the future free acts of creatures are *now* neither true nor false. Then, if Sally must in a moment freely choose between doing X and doing Y, God does not now know that she will do X and does not now know that she will do Y—but it doesn't follow that he's not omniscient, since neither thing is 'there' to be known. Being omniscient, God knows all truths, but the proposition that Sally will do X is not a 'truth' and the proposition that Sally will do Y is not a 'truth'. This argument faces two serious difficulties. First, it depends on the assumption that certain propositions about the future are neither true nor false. If our 'sea battle' argument is correct, however, then every proposition is either true or false, and the third definition and the first are equivalent. Secondly, I think that most proponents of the standard or traditional or classical conception of omniscience will insist that in the imagined situation God is *not* omniscient; they will insist that the doctrine of divine omniscience entails that either God now knows that Sally will do X or now knows that Sally will do Y.

[7] In any case, I doubt whether any theist would want to say anything along the following lines. 'As a theist, I'm committed to the doctrine that God knows everything. But knowledge does not entail the impossibility of mistake. I therefore see no reason to regard myself as committed to the thesis that God's beliefs cannot be mistaken.'

impossible for there to be an omniscient being—an infallible being who for every proposition believes either that proposition or its denial.[8]

The inconsistency of (i) and (ii) might seem, at least to the uninitiated, not only to imply that, if free will exists, an infallible being cannot be omniscient, but also to imply that, if free will exists, an infallible being cannot be omnipotent. For, if (i) and (ii) are incompatible, then it is intrinsically or metaphysically impossible for an infallible being to *find out* prior to *t* what a free agent will do at *t*—and thus such a being cannot be omnipotent, since it is unable to find out (prior to the event) what a free agent will do. But this argument is invalid on both the Cartesian and the Thomist conceptions of omnipotence. A being that is omnipotent in the Cartesian sense is able to do intrinsically impossible things; a being that is omnipotent in the Thomist sense is, as it were, excused from the requirement that it be able to do things that are intrinsically impossible. And this suggests a solution to the problem of free will and divine foreknowledge: why should we not qualify the 'standard' definition of omniscience in a way similar to that in which St Thomas, if you will forgive the anachronism, qualified the Cartesian definition of omnipotence? Why not say that even an omniscient being is unable to know certain things—those things knowledge of which is intrinsically impossible?[9] Or we might say this: an omnipotent being is *also* omniscient if it knows everything it is able to know.[10] Or if, as I prefer, we frame our definition of omniscience in terms of belief and the impossibility of mistake: an omnipotent being is also omniscient if it is infallible *and* it has beliefs on every matter on which it is able to have beliefs.

The way that point had to be worded is rather complicated; perhaps an example will make its point clearer. Suppose that today I made a free choice between lying and telling the truth and that I told the truth. Suppose that that state of affairs is logically inconsistent with the proposition that yesterday an infallible being believed that today I should tell the truth.

---

[8] Does 'If free will exists, it is impossible for there to be an omniscient being' mean 'For any world *w*, if there are free agents in *w*, then no being who exists in *w* is omniscient in any world' or does it mean 'For any world *w*, if there are free agents in *w*, then no being [who exists in *w*] is omniscient in *w*'? The former thesis is the stronger, for it entails the latter and the latter does not entail the former. The answer to this question depends on the precise definition of 'being whose beliefs cannot be mistaken', which figured in the definition of 'omniscient'. Since our interest is in the weaker thesis, I need not resolve this ambiguity. (For a further point related to this ambiguity, see n. 11.)

[9] For a brief statement of (essentially) the same idea, see Richard Swinburne, *Providence and the Problem of Evil* (Oxford: Oxford University Press, 1998), pp. 133–4.

[10] It is, I concede, difficult to evaluate this suggestion, since it is difficult to provide a satisfactory definition of omnipotence. (See, for example, the discussion of omnipotence in my book *The Problem of Evil* (Oxford: Oxford University Press, 2006), pp. 22–6.) The suggestion should be regarded as presupposing a satisfactory definition of omnipotence.

Then any infallible being who existed yesterday must *not* then have believed that today I should tell the truth; and, of course, it can't be the case that yesterday it believed that today I should lie. That is, an infallible being must yesterday have had *no* belief about whether I should today lie or tell the truth. And if that infallible being was also omnipotent, it was unable, despite its omnipotence, then to have had or then to have acquired any belief about what I should freely do today. To ask an infallible being now to have or now to acquire any determinate belief about the future actions of a free agent is to ask it to bring about a metaphysically impossible state of affairs.

How might a formal definition of omniscience that embodied this idea be stated? I would tentatively suggest the following. A being *x* is omniscient (in the restricted sense) if and only if it satisfies the following three conditions at every moment *t*:

x is able at *t* to consider or hold before its mind 'simultaneously'and in complete detail every possible world. (Possible worlds are here understood as Plantinga understands them in *The Nature of Necessity*.)

For every set of possible worlds that contains the actual world and is such that it is possible (for any being) to know at *t* of that set that it contains the actual world, *x* knows at *t* of that set that it contains the actual world. (Here 'the actual world' is a definite description, a non-rigid designator of the world that happens to be actual. We could thus also have said, 'For any set of worlds some member of which is actual and is such that it is possible to know of it at *t* that one of its members is actual, *x* knows of it at *t* that one of its members is actual'.)

x's knowledge is closed under entailment (that is, if *x* knows that *p*, and if the proposition that *p* entails the proposition that *q*, then *x* knows that *q*) and *x* believes only what *x* knows (if *x* believes that *p*, *x* knows that *p*).

Using the same apparatus, we could define classical omniscience as follows: a being is classically omniscient if and only if it is at every time able to consider every possible world 'simultaneously' and in complete detail, and then knows *which* of those worlds is the actual world (or 'for any set of possible worlds some member of which is actual, then knows of that set that one of its members is actual' or 'then knows of one of those worlds that it is actual') and its knowledge is closed under entailment and it believes only what it knows. Note that a being who is omniscient in the classical sense will be omniscient in the restricted sense. A being who is omniscient in the restricted sense will be omniscient in the classical sense if and only if classical omniscience is possible. A being may be omniscient in the restricted sense even if classical omniscience is impossible.

Let us consider an example. Under what conditions would x, an omniscient being in the restricted sense, now know that Alice will lie tomorrow? Under the following conditions (if Alice will lie tomorrow, a classically omniscient being will satisfy these conditions; but it does not follow—logically or formally—from the proposition that some being satisfies them that a classically omniscient being is possible): For some set S of possible worlds that contains the actual world, Alice lies tomorrow in every member of S, and x now knows of S that it contains the actual world. Might there be no such set? Yes, at least given any of various assumptions to the effect that it is impossible to know certain sorts of things. Consider this case, for example. Suppose that in the actual world, Alice will *freely* lie tomorrow (and will not also tell some 'unfree' lie tomorrow); suppose that freedom is incompatible with strict causal determinism; suppose that it is possible for any being to know only those things about the future that are now causally inevitable. Then no being can now know of any set of worlds such that Alice lies in every member of that set that it contains the actual world—for, if it knew that of any such set of worlds, it would now know that Alice was going to lie tomorrow, and would thus know something about the future that was not causally inevitable. From the premise that there is no such set, we may easily deduce the conclusion that no being is classically omniscient; it does not follow that no being is omniscient in the restricted sense. Thus, if Alice will lie tomorrow and x does not know this, it does not follow that x is not omniscient in the restricted sense.

This definition is, as I have said, tentative. Such definitions have a way of turning out to require further work. It will at any rate do to go on with.

But, you may well ask, whether this definition of 'restricted omniscience' ultimately turns out to be satisfactory from the point of view of someone who has my worries about omniscience and freedom or not, who am I go about qualifying or tinkering with the standard definition of omniscience? What justifies me in calling the tinkering I have proposed 'permissible'? I said earlier that one (very good) reason for supposing that God was omniscient (in the standard or traditional or classical sense) was that his being omniscient seemed to be a consequence of the Anselmian thesis that he was the greatest possible being. But note: a proposition of the form 'The greatest possible being would have the property F' will be false if F is an impossible property. (Unless the property 'being the greatest possible being' is itself an impossible property. In what follows, I'll assume that 'being the greatest possible being' *is* a possible property—simply in order to avoid having repeatedly to insert the qualification 'unless the property "being the greatest possible being" is an impossible property' into my text. In any case, I don't suppose that this assumption will be controversial among Christians or among theists generally.) If, therefore, 'knows what the future acts of free agents will be' (or 'has beliefs that cannot be mistaken about what the future acts of free agents will be') is an impossible property, it is not a property of the greatest possible being. And neither will the greatest possible being be omniscient in any sense of omniscience that entails that property, for omniscience in that sense will be an impossible property.[11]

I contend, therefore, that there is no good a priori or philosophical reason to suppose that God is classically omniscient—not if classical omniscience is an impossible property. Might there be some good *theological* reason to suppose that God is classically omniscient?

I will not consider theological reasons for supposing that God is classically omniscient that are binding only on the members of some particular Christian denomination or communion or confession. If the Westminster Confession or the Articles of Religion or the *magisterium* of the Roman Catholic Church require certain Christians to believe that God foreknows the future free acts of human beings, then those Christians are committed to the proposition that there is some sort of error in the argument I have presented for the conclusion that God's foreknowing our future acts is incompatible with our having free will. If there are Christian denominations whose members are required to believe that human freedom and God's knowing every aspect of the future are compatible, then how to deal with the argument is an internal problem (maybe easy, maybe hard, maybe insoluble, but certainly internal) for each of those denominations. I shall ask only whether there are

---

[11] But does classical omniscience in fact entail 'knows what the future acts of free agents will be'? Suppose God were classically omniscient but had not created any free agents. Would he have that property? I think it is reasonable to understand 'would know what the future acts of free agents would be' in a sense ('for every free agent, knows what all the future acts of that agent will be') in which in those circumstances he would have the property 'vacuously'. But then 'knows what the future properties of free agents will be' is not an impossible property even by my lights, since it can be had vacuously if in no other way. And classical omniscience will not be an impossible property (even by my lights) since God (for example) will be—at least nothing I have said rules this out—classically omniscient in worlds in which there are no free agents. I think that these difficulties, minor and technical though they are, are real enough. But I would point out that everyone who believes that God is classically omniscient also believes that he has this property *essentially*—that 'being the greatest possible being' entails being *essentially* classically omniscient. And I would put the point made carelessly in the text more carefully this way: 'And neither will the greatest possible being be essentially omniscient in any sense of omniscience such that "being essentially omniscient" entails the property "possibly knows what the future acts of free agents will be", for essential omniscience in that sense will be an impossible property.'

This problem, of course, arises only in relation to the first definition of classical omniscience. It should be noted that on the second definition, classical omniscience may entail the property 'in every possible world in which there are free agents, has beliefs that cannot be mistaken about what their future acts will be'. (A property that I contend is an impossible property.) Whether it did would depend on how the ambiguity in the phrase 'being whose beliefs cannot be mistaken' [note 8] was resolved.

theological reasons for believing that God foreknows the future free acts of human beings that are reasons *all* Christians have for believing this.

Since the three great first-millennial creeds are silent on this matter, it would seem that any such theological reason must be scriptural. Does it say in the Bible (or can philosophical reflection on something said in the Bible demonstrate) that God knows the future in complete detail, and, in particular, knows what the future free choices of human beings will be? It might be argued that, on the contrary, there are passages in the Bible that imply that this thesis is false, for Scripture sometimes represents God as being sorry about what he has done and sometimes represents him as changing his mind about what he intends to do ('And the Lord was sorry that he had made man upon the earth', Gen. 6: 6; 'And the Lord repented of the evil which he thought to do to his people', Ex. 32: 14). And these things would seem to be possible only for a being who does not know the whole future in every detail. But I don't want to make anything of such passages. Many Christians would insist that, like 'they heard the sound of the Lord God walking in the garden in the cool of the day', they're not to be taken literally (that, in them, anthropomorphic language is used of God, perhaps as a concession to the limitations of human readers). And, even if one takes these passages literally, they imply at most that God does not always know what *his* free actions will be; it might still be that God always knows what the free actions of human beings will be (except insofar as those actions depend on his own actions). Such passages aside, I know of no place in Scripture in which God is represented as ignorant of any aspect of the future. And he is certainly represented as knowing a great deal about the future, including facts about what particular human beings—Pharaoh, Darius, Peter, Judas—are going to do on particular occasions. But it seems to be consistent with what the Bible says to suppose that God knows only those future events that are causally inevitable (for this reason if for no other: because he himself has already decreed that they shall occur). And it seems to be consistent with what the Bible says to suppose that some aspects of the future are not causally inevitable and that God does not know about them. God knew what Pharaoh would do because he had hardened Pharaoh's heart, and thus had made it impossible for Pharaoh to play any role in the Exodus story but the role that God had decreed for him. And perhaps something similar was true in the cases of Peter and Judas (or perhaps God knew that certain features of their 'hearts' made the denial and betrayal of Jesus causally inevitable in the situations in which he had ordained that Peter and Judas should find themselves). If something along these lines is true, and if causal inevitability is incompatible with free will, it is consistent with Scripture to suppose that God knows what human beings will do only in those cases in which they do not have free will, only in respect of those occasions on which they are unable to act otherwise than they do.

But what of those passages in Scripture that seem flatly to imply that human beings do not *have* free will—not at all, not on any occasion? (Rom. 9: 14–24, for example, the passage in which Paul, echoing Jeremiah, compares God to the potter and human beings to the clay, and tells us that some human beings are vessels created for destruction.) Well, I can say only that if such passages imply that human beings perform no free actions, they do not imply that God foreknows the free actions of human beings. If human beings do not have free will, there is no problem of free will and divine foreknowledge (or at most, it is a problem about whether free will *would be* compatible with divine foreknowledge if there *were* such a thing as free will, and that is not a very urgent problem). The question I am considering now is the question whether, *given* that human beings have free will, there is any passage in Scripture that clearly implies that God knows how they will exercise their free will in the future. I can say only that I know of no passage that should convince a reader of Scripture that God does know such things.

Now one final problem, a rather serious one, for the position I have been defending. If one believes that human beings have free will and that God does not know how human beings will act when they act freely, does this not imply that God was not in a position to make the promises that (Christians believe) God has in fact made? The Bible, for example, a record of two (or perhaps three) covenants God has made with human beings, indisputably predicts that *some* human beings will be saved (and, in fact, a rather large number of them, even if it is small in comparison with the total number of human beings). But if human beings have free will, and if—as Christians who believe in free will want to maintain—any human being can freely refuse God's offer of salvation, there must be (given that free will is incompatible with strict causal inevitability; but this is a thesis that anyone who believes that God cannot foreknow the future free acts of human beings must accept, for God certainly knows everything about the future that is now causally inevitable) a non-zero probability that the present state of things will evolve into a state in which *no one* is saved (or only one person, or only two persons ...). For if an event is causally possible, given the present state of things, there is now a non-zero probability that it will occur. But if such a non-zero probability exists, how can God be in a position to promise that *many* human beings will be saved?

Professor Geach, in an attempt to defuse this problem,[12] has used the following analogy. God is, in relation to us, like a great chess master

---

[12] P. T. Geach, *Providence and Evil* (Cambridge: Cambridge University Press, 1977), p. 58.

playing a match with a beginner. The master, perhaps, does not know what particular moves the beginner will choose to make, but the master knows that he will win *whatever* moves the beginner makes, and is thus in a position to promise to win. But it's not at all clear that an appeal to this analogy does defuse the problem. Suppose that Alice is a great chess master and that she and Bertram, a rank beginner, are playing chess. It seems impossible to deny that there *is* a non-zero probability that Bertram beat her. For suppose that Bertram has decided to choose his moves at random, perhaps by tossing a coin according to some system that codes each possible move as a sequence of heads and tails. (Such a policy can hardly be expected to improve the play of even the rankest amateur.) Now suppose that it's possible to outplay Alice. Suppose, that is, that Alice is not a perfect player, that her play is not guaranteed to consist entirely of optimal moves.[13] It

[13] In every position in which a chess player can find himself, there is a non-empty set of optimal moves he can make—in the sense that no possible move is superior to any of the moves in that set. Define a perfect player as a player who will make some optimal move in every situation. It can be shown that a perfect player will always defeat a player who is not perfect—who makes even one non-optimal move. If Alice is a perfect player (since the number of possible combinations of pieces on a chess board is finite, a perfect player need not be an infinite being), it is difficult to say whether there is any chance that Bertram will defeat her, for even if his coin tosses always yield optimal moves, it is not known what would happen if two perfect players played each other. What is known is this—and even this is known only relative to a suitable definition of 'the game ends in a draw', a point I will not go into. Define a perfect game as a game between two perfect players. The following disjunction has been proved:

Either

    In every perfect game, the player who moves first wins

or

    In every perfect game, the player who moves second wins

or

    Every perfect game ends in a draw.

(Since the three disjuncts are incompatible, only one of them is true, but it is not known which. Many chess players are convinced on 'empirical' grounds that the second disjunct is false.) This very result, however, shows that it was 'fair' for us to assume that Alice, the great chess master, was not a perfect player—and thus that there was a non-zero probability that Bertram would defeat her. It obviously follows from the disjunction (and the fact that a perfect player never loses to a non-perfect player) that no perfect player has ever lost both a game in which he moved first and a game in which he moved second. But all human chess masters have lost both games in which they moved first and games in which they moved second. (If anyone protests that God, if he played chess, *would* be a perfect player, I must point out that Geach's analogy is only an analogy and cannot be pressed too far. If we think of God as playing a game with a perverse humanity, a game that God will 'win' if a certain number of human beings are saved, we have no reason to suppose that in that game, like chess, a perfect player must always defeat a non-perfect player. And, of course, we have no reason to suppose that there isn't a non-zero probability that perverse humanity will always make the 'move' that is optimal with respect to ensuring God's 'defeat'.)

follows that there is a non-zero probability that Bertram *will* outplay Alice and win the game—since there is a non-zero probability that all his moves will be optimal (and a non-zero—in fact very high—probability that Alice will make some non-optimal moves). Of course, the probability of Alice's losing is so small that no one would blame her for promising to win the match even she had conceded that there was a minuscule probability that she might lose. And nothing in our argument shows that the probability of some set of human beings of the requisite size being saved isn't of the same order as (or vastly lower than) the probability of Bertram's beating Alice. But must a morally perfect being like God not be held to a higher standard than a human chess master? Could a morally perfect being *promise* that an event *x* would happen if that being knew that the probability that *x* would not happen was very small but not 0—that it was, say, 0.0000000000013? I'm not entirely happy about this, but it seems to me that I am going to have answer 'Yes' if, as I do, I accept the following five propositions:

God does not foreknow the free acts of human beings;

God knows everything about the future that is causally determined (*sc.* by the laws of nature and the present state of things);

If it is causally undetermined whether an agent will do *x* or *y*, there is a non-zero probability that the agent will do *x* and a non-zero probability that the agent will do *y*;

Each human being is able freely to reject God's offer of salvation;

God has promised that some human beings will be saved.

11

Omnisubjectivity

Linda Zagzebski

ABSTRACT

In this paper I describe and begin a defence of the possibility of a divine attribute I call omnisubjectivity. Omnisubjectivity is, roughly, the property of consciously grasping with perfect accuracy and completeness the first-person perspective of every conscious being. I argue that omnisubjectivity is entailed by omniscience or, at any rate, by cognitive perfection. If God is omnisubjective, that would solve two puzzles of omniscience: (1) an omniscient being ought to be able to tell the difference between the different qualia of conscious beings, and (2) an omniscient being ought to be able to tell the difference between the first-person and third-person perspectives on the same state of affairs. Using the model of human empathy, I argue that it is possible for a being to assume the first-person perspective of another being without assuming identity with the other being or forgetting who he is. I end by briefly identifying some interesting metaphysical, moral, and theological consequences of omnisubjectivity.

I. INTRODUCTION

If God is omniscient, he must know every aspect of his creation, including the conscious states of his creatures. But what does it take for one person to know a state of consciousness of another? In one way it seems trivial, and in another way it seems impossible. Surely I can know that Mary feels frustrated or sees the colour of the paint sample, but how can anybody but

I wish to thank members of the audience of the University of Texas at San Antonio Philosophy Symposium Feb. 2007, and the 2007 Baylor Philosophy of Religion Conference, as well as two anonymous referees.

Mary grasp exactly what her feeling of frustration feels like or see the colour exactly the way she sees it? An even harder problem arises for knowing what is expressed by indexicals like 'now', 'here', and 'I'. For example, if Mary knows <I spilled the sugar in the supermarket>, she is the only one in the universe who can know *that*, or so it would seem.

I take for granted that if we could really 'get' what it is like to feel what another feels, see what she sees, and know what she knows from her own viewpoint, we would have a deeper and better kind of knowledge of her than if we merely know that she sees grey, feels frustrated, and knows she made a mess in the market. The depth of the grasp of some objects of knowledge admits of degrees, and the deeper the grasp, the better the knowledge. In fact, it is not crucial for my point that the deeper kind of grasp be a form of knowledge. Perhaps it is understanding. In any case, it is an epistemic state, and it is epistemically better to have it than not to have it. If an omniscient being has perfect epistemic states, an omniscient being should have it. An omniscient being would have to have the deepest grasp of every object of knowledge, including the conscious states of every creature. The issue I want to address here is whether this is possible and what the state of grasping or knowing or understanding the consciousness of another being would be like.

I will argue that omniscience entails a property I call omnisubjectivity. I will explain this property in more detail as the paper progresses, but briefly, it is the property of consciously grasping with perfect accuracy and completeness the first-person perspective of every conscious being. I say that omniscience entails omnisubjectivity, but since I wish to avoid disputes over the definition of omniscience, my thesis can be read instead as the thesis that cognitive perfection entails omnisubjectivity. But, in what follows, I will continue to use the term 'omniscient' since that is the traditional term for the perfection of the divine intellect. I will use the model of human empathy to argue that omnisubjectivity explains how an omniscient being is able to distinguish between first-person and third-person knowledge of the same fact, and it explains how an omniscient being is able to know what it is like for conscious creatures to have their distinctive sensations and emotions, moods, and attitudes. I will then argue that omnisubjectivity has interesting theological, moral, and metaphysical implications.

II. OMNISCIENCE, QUALIA AND KNOWLEDGE *DE SE*

II.1. What it is like to see colour?

Let us begin with Frank Jackson's story in 'What Mary Didn't Know' (1986). Mary has been confined to a black-and-white room her entire life.

She is educated through black-and-white books and television and comes to know everything there is to know about the physical world by these means. There is no physical fact Mary does not know. But Mary does not know all there is to know because when she leaves the room and begins to see in colour, she learns something she did not know before. In common philosophical parlance, she finds out *what it is like* to see red, blue, and other colours. Since physicalism entails the thesis that if you know every physical fact, you know everything there is to know, Jackson concludes that physicalism is false.

I want to use this story for a different purpose. Although I assume that physicalism is false, I do not endorse Jackson's argument for it. In particular, I do not assume that when Mary leaves her black-and-white room and begins to see in colour, she comes to *know* something she did not know previously. Whether or not Mary knows something she did not know before, she is in a different conscious state. Her qualia after leaving the room are different than before. A cognitively perfect being ought to be able to distinguish them, and a cognitively perfect creator ought to be able to distinguish one part of his creation from another. If any two items of his creation are distinct, God ought to be able to tell them apart and he ought to be able to know what the difference consists in. In the case of Mary, if the difference in her conscious states is not reducible to a difference in physical facts about Mary and the world around her, but is a difference in what it is like to see in colour vs. what it is like to see in black and white, then God can tell the difference in Mary's mental states only if he can tell the difference between what it is like to see colour and what it is like to see black and white. Further, since what it is like for Mary to see colour may differ somewhat from what it is like for other persons to see colour, God does not really understand the difference between Mary's mental states unless he knows what it is like for *Mary* to see in black and white before she leaves the room and what it is like for Mary to see in colour after she leaves the room. But since no one can know what it is like to be in a conscious state without adopting that conscious state themselves, at least in imagination, God must be able to adopt Mary's mental states, at least in imagination.

But it is not obvious that this is possible. The particular conscious space each of us inhabits may not be shareable, and it may be necessarily such that it is non-shareable. Perhaps every human conscious state under normal conditions is accompanied by an awareness of self. So Mary's awareness of red might include awareness of herself, Mary, seeing red. Necessarily, no other person can be in that state since necessarily no other person is Mary. There may be other ways in which conscious states might be necessarily non-shareable. If they are necessarily non-shareable and if the only way to accurately grasp what a conscious state is like is to have it, then necessarily, no conscious being can accurately grasp what the conscious state of another conscious being is like. Necessarily, no being but Mary can accurately grasp what her conscious states are like, and so not even God can accurately grasp what Mary's state of seeing red is like. Further, if the grasp of what Mary's conscious states are like is a necessary condition for the ability to tell the difference between them, then no being but Mary can tell the difference between them. Nor can any being tell the difference between the state Mary is in when she sees red and the state Sam is in when he sees red if their states are necessarily non-shareable. But an omniscient being ought to grasp what every part of his creation is like, and he ought to be able to tell the difference between one part of his creation and another.

It will be objected that it is no violation of omniscience to be unable to do what it is impossible to do. For example, those who deny infallible foreknowledge typically claim that the future is unknowable in an infallible way. Hence, the lack of infallible foreknowledge is no violation of divine omniscience. Similarly, it can be argued, if the conscious states of other beings are unknowable in the way they know those states themselves, then it is no violation of omniscience if God fails to have such knowledge.

It seems to me perfectly true that it is no violation of omniscience to be unable to do the impossible, but just as defenders of infallible foreknowledge maintain that there is a very strong prima facie case that omniscience (more accurately, essential omniscience) includes infallible foreknowledge, similarly I want to maintain that there is a very strong prima facie case that omniscience entails the ability to perfectly grasp the conscious states of every conscious being and to be able to distinguish among them. If the ability I describe in this paper is impossible, then it is not entailed by omniscience and God doesn't have it. But I will argue that it is not impossible, at least, its possibility should not be ruled out.

II.2. Knowledge *de se*

Perhaps the clearest class of cases of a potential problem for knowing the consciousness of another being is the knowledge of propositions expressed by sentences containing the indexical 'I'. Some philosophers maintain that these propositions are not equivalent to propositions expressed by sentences without the respective indexicals. So, according to an argument that comes from John Perry (1979), if sugar is coming out of a hole in a sack in my supermarket cart and I come to know the proposition expressed by

(1) I made a mess in the market and everybody is staring at me,

what I know is not identical to the proposition I and other people know when they know what is expressed by

(2) Linda Zagzebski made a mess in the market and all the bystanders are staring at her.

One reason to think that (1) and (2) do not express the same proposition is that when I stop myself short, pick up my sugar sack, and start to clean up, my behaviour can be explained by my knowledge of (1), but not by my knowledge of (2) unless the latter is supplemented by my knowledge that I am Linda Zagzebski, which, of course, reintroduces the indexical 'I'. Furthermore, to adopt a point made by Arthur Prior, my embarrassment at being the object of the stares of my fellow shoppers can be explained by my knowledge of (1), but not by my knowledge of (2) unless, again, my knowledge of (2) is supplemented by my knowledge that I am Linda Zagzebski.[1] Somebody else could be embarrassed at my mishap. Perhaps my spouse is embarrassed, and I will return to the case of being embarrassed on my behalf, but it does look like only *I* can be embarrassed at being the agent of this mess.

Similar considerations suggest that the proposition expressed by (1) also differs from what is expressed *de re* by

(3) She (e.g., that woman in the mirror) is making a mess and people are staring at her,

also discussed by Perry. Clearly, other people can know (3) when they do not know (1), and even I can know (3) without knowing (1) since it might come as a shock to me to discover (1) when I already know (3). For example, I might see myself in a mirror trailing sugar without realizing that I am looking at myself, only to suddenly recognize that I am the person in the mirror.

Some writers conclude that only one person can know what I know when I know (1) and that is I. Others disagree.[2] Perry proposes that when I know (1) and somebody else knows (3), the object of our respective epistemic states is the same. We do know the same thing. However, we are in different belief states. Others can be in the belief state I am in when I know (1), and they are in that state when they believe that *they* are making a mess. What is unique to me is the combination of the two:

Anyone can believe of John Perry that he is making a mess. And anyone can be in the belief state classified by the sentence 'I am making a mess.' By only I can have that belief by being in that state. (Perry 1979: 19).

---

[1] Patrick Grim (1985) refers to Prior in making this point.
[2] Grim (1985) argues for the incompatibility of *de se* knowledge and omniscience. In response, Stephan Torre (2006) distinguishes two senses in which someone else can know what I know when I have *de se* knowledge, arguing that omniscience is compatible with one of them.

I wish to remain neutral on the issue of the nature of the difference between knowing (1) and knowing (2) or (3) for the same reason I am neutral on the issue of the nature of the difference between Mary's mental state before and after she leaves the black-and-white room. Perhaps the proposition expressed by (1) differs from the proposition expressed by (3), and so a person who knows (1) does not know the same thing as a person who knows (3), but perhaps, as Perry suggests, the propositions do not differ; it is only the belief states in the two cases that differ. Or perhaps the difference is not one of belief states but is something else. In any case, it is clear that there is *some* difference between what is going on when I know (1) and what is going on when somebody knows (3). If there is a real difference, an omniscient being must know that difference. It is not enough that an omniscient being knows *that* there is a difference. He must understand what the difference consists in. But if physicalism is false, the difference does not amount to a difference in physical states, so it is not enough that an omniscient being know the difference between the physical states of somebody who knows (1) and somebody who knows (3). In order to tell the difference between the state of a subject who first knows *de re* that she is making a mess and then comes to know *de se* <I am making a mess>, an omniscient being must be able to assume her first-person point of view. This is a challenge to omniscience whether or not the subject *knows* anything different in the two cases.

To recapitulate, I do not assume that when Mary leaves her black-and-white room and begins to see in colour, she comes to know something she did not know previously. Nor do I assume that I know something different when I know (1) than what is known by a person who knows (3). But as long as there is a difference between Mary's mental states before and after she leaves the room, and there is a difference between my mental state when I know (1) and somebody's mental state when they know (3), an omniscient God must be able to tell the difference between the two states. And this point can be generalized. If any two qualia differ, God must be able to tell the difference between them. If the first-person perspective on some state of affairs differs from the third-person perspective on the same state of affairs, he must be able to distinguish them. The only way to distinguish qualia is to have them, and the only way to distinguish first- and third-person perspectives is to adopt those perspectives.

Human beings understand each other's conscious states and the differences between them by reconstructing the states in our imagination. The more complete and accurate the reconstruction, the better the knowledge of the consciousness of another. But since we rely on relevant similarities between ourselves and others to imagine what their sensations and emotions are like, it is very easy to reconstruct their states inaccurately. Imagining first-person knowledge that someone made a mess is one of the easier ones and that is why it is a good example for a philosophy paper. It only takes a couple of sentences to give us the idea. But grasping the state of mind of a person who not only knows she made a mess, but is embarrassed and self-conscious about it, is harder, and it is harder still to imagine the details of her perspective, including the way she notices and interprets the looks of the bystanders and how she reacts to that, the emotions she has had in the past that are triggered by the incident, the things it reminds her of, and so on. Some of these things she can tell us, but it is notoriously difficult for B to explain her feeling to A in a way that permits A to grasp what it is like. Typically, the way A grasps B's feeling is by imaginatively projecting himself into B's situation as he believes B sees it, and imagining how he would feel in that situation. B's description of her feeling and her outward behaviour also contribute to A's imaginative simulation of B's feeling, but there are obviously many ways in which this process can go awry.

Even if A is able to imaginatively simulate B's feeling accurately, his epistemic state does not count as *knowledge* of B's feeling unless A satisfies the problematic third condition for knowledge. A would need to have evidence that his imaginative reconstruction is accurate, or he would have to reconstruct B's feeling in an intellectually virtuous or reliable or properly functioning way. At a minimum, A does not know B's feeling or belief or any other conscious state without both having an accurate representation of that state in his own imagination, and doing so in a way that is non-accidental.

On the classical view of God, God's knowledge is direct, unmediated by concepts, percepts, the structure of language, logical inference, or any of the other cognitive aids we use in order to know the world around us. And it surely cannot be mediated by imagining what it would be like for *him* to be in our place. I don't think we have a perfect model of direct awareness of another's conscious state, but the closest model in our experience is empathy. In the state of empathy there is a transference of emotion from one person to another, and empathy is the primary way we come to know the emotions of others. It seems to me that the structure of empathy can be generalized to the transference of psychic states other than emotions. Beliefs, hopes, wishes, desires and moods can also be transferred in a way analogous to the transference of emotion in empathy. In the next section I will look at empathy more closely since I propose that God's knowledge of our conscious lives is something like the perfection of empathy.

III. EMPATHY

III.1. Human empathy

Accounts of the structure of empathy generally agree on its central feature:

(i) Empathy is a way of acquiring an emotion like that of another person.

Most writers maintain that the emotion one acquires need not be identical to the target emotion, but presumably it should be close. I will return to this issue below. Empathy is not just any transfer of emotion, however. Justin D'Arms (2000) says that empathy is responding 'to the perceived feelings of another with vicarious emotional reactions of one's own, and empathy is the capacity for, or the occurrence of, such a vicarious experience'. That suggests that it is not enough that one pick up the emotion of another, but that one must acquire the emotion in the process of perceiving or coming to believe that the other has it. So emotional contagion, or the spread of an emotion through a crowd, is not empathy. Fear, anger, joy, and despondency can be picked up from others without conscious attention to the emotional states of the person or persons from whom one gets the emotion. In contrast, when A empathizes with B, A focuses attention on B and B's emotion, and is aware of the similarity between B's emotion and her own.

Furthermore, when empathizing, A must see the fact that B has the emotion A acquires as a reason for her to have the emotion. Suppose A watches a television report on a suicide bombing and sees a member of a victim's family interviewed in a state of distress. A's perception of B's distress might lead her to feel distress at the bombing herself, but she is not empathizing with B unless she perceives B's distress as a reason for her own distress, not simply the cause of it. So a second feature of empathy is this:

(ii) A thinks that the fact that B has a given emotion is a reason for her to have the same emotion.

Why would A think that she has a reason to have the same emotion as someone else? There are at least two obvious reasons. A might care for B or even love him. Sharing B's emotions is a way of being close to B, of sharing emotional space with him. Alternatively, A might want to understand B whether or not A feels any affection or even sympathy with B. Empathy is a way of making the emotional states of others intelligible to us. Understanding their emotions is often important if we want to understand their actions, and we can have many reasons for wanting to do that. So it is possible to empathize not only with the victims of a suicide attack, but with the culprit. This suggests that the emotion I feel when I empathize with another is not one I feel 'in my own right', so to speak, but is something I feel on behalf of another, or in her place. But my reasons for having an emotion like hers are my own.

When I have an emotion in the place of another, I take on her emotion in the way she does. I assume her perspective in such a way that the emotion makes sense to me in the way it makes sense to her. So empathy has a third feature:

(iii) When A empathizes with B, A takes on the perspective of B.

As Robert M. Gordon (1995) expresses the point, empathy involves an 'imaginative shift in the reference of indexicals' where the imaginer 'recenters his egocentric map' (p. 172).

This brings out the difference between imagining yourself in someone else's situation and imagining being that person in that situation. Julinna Oxley (2006) gives the example of empathizing with a friend whose mother died. In Oxley's example, her friend has had a difficult relationship with her mother whereas Oxley has a good relationship with her own mother. When Oxley empathizes with her friend's feeling at the death of the friend's mother, Oxley imagines how her friend feels, given her difficult relationship, not how she would feel if her own mother died. Oxley imaginatively adopts the same feeling as her friend for her friend's reasons. Perhaps Oxley's friend feels grief mixed with anger and guilt. When Oxley acquires that emotion (or set of emotions), she projects herself onto her friend's situation with her friend's history of difficult experiences with her mother.

Notice that Oxley must adopt her friend's perspective in order to acquire the particular sort of grief her friend feels for her friend's reason, but since Oxley is empathizing, she acquires her friend's perspective out of a concern for her friend and a desire to understand her. Oxley therefore has a dual perspective. There is a level of consciousness at which she imagines being her friend, and at that level she adopts her friend's emotion, but there is another level of consciousness underlying that, one that motivates her to adopt the perspective and emotion of her friend. At this level she is motivated by the emotions and desires of friendship. This suggests a further feature of empathy:

(iv) When A empathizes with B, A is motivated from A's own perspective to assume the perspective of B.

The idea that the empathizing person has a dual perspective is endorsed by Oxley and by Alvin Goldman (1993). Goldman says that paradigmatic cases of empathy are those that 'consist first of taking the perspective of another person, that is, imaginatively assuming one or more of the other person's mental states' which 'are then operated upon (automatically) by psychological processes, which generate further states that (in favourable cases) are similar to, or homologous to, the target person's states'. (p. 351). The empathizer 'is aware of his or her vicarious affects and emotions as representatives of the emotions or affects of the target agent' (ibid.).

The fact that A has a dual perspective when empathizing with B means that A's emotion is not identical to B's, or as Goldman says, it may begin as an imitation of B's emotion, but A's own beliefs and emotions operate on it immediately, resulting in an emotion that Goldman calls 'homologous' and Oxley calls 'congruent' with B's emotion. In the example of Oxley's empathy with her friend's feeling at the loss of her mother, Oxley simulates her friend's complex combination of grief and anger, but she is always aware that she is simulating, or feeling as if she were in the place of another. But Oxley cannot feel *as if* she were in the place of her friend unless she continues to be aware that she is not in the place of her friend. Empathetic grief or anger is never exactly the same as the grief or anger with which one empathizes because the empathizer is aware of her emotion as a copy, whereas the target emotion is not a copy of anything. Oxley's friend's emotion of grief has the loss of her mother as its intentional object. Since Oxley's empathetic grief is a copy or simulation of that emotion, and Oxley is aware of it as a simulation, Oxley does not grieve *at* her friend's mother's death. When A empathizes with B's anger at C, A is not angry at C. When A empathizes with B's jealousy of C, A is not jealous of C. When A empathizes with B's grief over the death of C, A does not grieve over the death of C. It is possible, of course, for A to grieve over C's death also, but I am suggesting that the empathizer does not adopt the intentional object of the target emotion as her own intentional object. The empathizer A aims to represent the emotion of B, so she has a representation of B's emotion from B's point of view with B's intentional object, but A does not adopt the intentional object of B's emotion. So another feature of empathy is this:

(v) An empathetic emotion is consciously representational. The empathizer does not adopt the intentional object of the emotion she represents as her own intentional object.

To summarize, when A empathizes with B, A becomes conscious of an emotion of B and sees the fact that B has that emotion as a reason for her to acquire the same emotion. She acquires a similar emotion by taking on B's perspective, but she is simultaneously aware that her emotion is a simulation of the other's emotion and she does not adopt the intentional object of B's emotion as her own.

Since the point of empathy is to copy another person's emotion, to represent it accurately, it seems to follow that the more accurate the copy, the better the empathy, and that includes accurately copying the strength of the target emotion. In human beings, having an empathetic emotion that is equal in strength to its target emotion can be a disadvantage. All of the problems of excessively strong emotions can be transferred to the empathetic emotion, and the empathizing person may have no deeper insight into a situation than the person with whom she empathizes if she feels just as strongly about it. Nonetheless, I think we can say that the empathizing person does not fully grasp the emotion of another if she does not accurately copy its strength as well as its quality. While it does not serve all the purposes of empathy to copy it exactly, copying it exactly is *epistemically* superior to copying it weakly or inexactly.

Earlier I mentioned the possibility that each person's conscious states are necessarily such that they are possessed by that person and no other. That would be the case if each person's conscious state is accompanied by an awareness of the self. On this view, when I feel frustrated, I am simultaneously aware that it is I who is frustrated. When Oxley's friend feels grief, she is aware that *she* is the one feeling the grief. The dual perspective account of empathy I have endorsed is compatible with this position. The empathizer's copy of the target emotion is not an exact copy in that she is aware of her emotion *as a copy* of another person's emotion, whereas the target emotion is not a copy. In this case the copy would include a copy of the awareness of a different 'I'. Oxley's empathetic grief would include thinking of herself as her friend thinks of herself when the friend feels grief. Oxley probably cannot do that very well, but I do not see any reason why she cannot do it to some degree.

III.2. Divine empathy

If it is possible to adopt the perspective of another in order to represent that person's emotion, it ought to be possible to adopt their perspective in order to represent any of their conscious states, and to do so in a way that parallels the structure of empathy. When we empathize we represent someone else's emotions. What I will call *total empathy* is the state of representing all of another person's conscious states, including their beliefs, sensations, moods, desires, and choices, as well as their emotions.

If perfect empathy includes a complete and accurate representation of another person's emotions, perfect total empathy includes a complete and accurate representation of all of another person's conscious states. If A has *perfect total empathy* with B, then whenever B is in a conscious state C, A is conscious that B is in C and takes that fact to be a reason to acquire C herself. A acquires a state that is an accurate copy of C both in quality and in strength, and A is aware that her conscious state is a copy of C.

I propose that an omniscient being must have perfect total empathy with you and with all conscious beings. This is the property I call omnisubjectivity. An omnisubjective being would know what it is like to be you, as well as what it is like to be your dog, the bats in the cave, the birds, the fish, the reptiles, and each human being yet to be born. An omnisubjective being would know everything you know or understand from living your life.

It seems to me that it is possible that there is an omnisubjective being, at least, I know of no reason to think it is impossible. And I also see no reason to think that the same being could not be both omniscient and omnisubjective. I will not address the issue of whether omnisubjectivity is compatible with the other traditional divine attributes, but I want now to argue that if an omniscient being is omnisubjective, that would solve the puzzles for omniscience posed in Section II.

The first puzzle was how an omniscient being can tell the difference between Mary's conscious states before and after she leaves the black and white room, as well as the difference, if any, between what Mary sees when she sees red, and what Sam sees when he sees the same patch of red. If an omniscient being has perfect total empathy with Mary, he represents her conscious experience of seeing first in black and white, and then in colour, with perfect accuracy. Since an accurate representation of Mary's black-and-white qualia differs from an accurate representation of her colour qualia, he can tell the difference between Mary's qualia. If he also accurately represents Sam's colour qualia, he can tell the difference between Sam's way of seeing red and Mary's way of seeing red, if there is such a difference. If there is no difference, he can tell that also.

When an omnisubjective being acquires a representation of Mary's conscious state of seeing red, he sees red as if he sees through Mary's eyes, but since he is aware of that state as a copy of Mary's state, there is no problem that he would be led to make judgements of the world from his own perspective based on conscious states that are copies of Mary's perspective. But if he has total empathy with Mary, he will also acquire a perfect conscious representation of any such judgements Mary makes, and again, he is aware that he is acquiring a copy of a judgement, so he has a dual perspective. In the same way, when Mary leaves the room and is surprised to see that objects are coloured, the omnisubjective being will acquire a perfect conscious representation of that surprise. And if Mary chooses to touch a red object to find out if objects in the coloured world feel the same as objects in the black-and-white world, the omnisubjective being will acquire a conscious representation of Mary's choosing to touch.

Now I would like to offer a conjecture about an interesting difference between empathizing with sensations and emotions, on the one hand, and empathizing with judgements and choices, on the other. A person cannot empathize with an emotion or a sensation without feeling the emotion or sensation because a copy of an emotion is an emotion, and a copy of a sensation is a sensation.[3] But a copy of a judgement is not a judgement and a copy of a choice is not a choice. Of course, we can tell the difference between sensing red ourselves and empathizing with someone else's sensation of red, just as we can tell the difference between our own emotion of surprise and empathizing with someone else's emotion of surprise. We can tell the difference if I am right that in empathy we are always aware that our conscious states are copies of someone else's conscious states. But to empathize with surprise is to feel surprise, and to empathize with the sensation of colour is to have coloured qualia. In contrast, to empathize with a judgement is not to make a judgement, even a half-hearted one. One might, in fact, judge not p while empathizing with a person who judges p. And to empathize with a choice is not to make a choice.

I suggest that when God empathizes with a human being's emotion of fear, anger, hatred, or jealousy, God consciously represents each of those emotions from the human's point of view, but since having a copy of an emotion with an intentional object does not include adopting that intentional object as one's own, omnisubjectivity does not have the unwanted consequence that God fears, hates, or is angry at the things we fear, hate, or are angry at. God does not love what we love in the state of empathy either, although, of course, he may love those things from his own point of view. I am assuming that no conscious state is intrinsically evil in the absence of its directness towards a certain intentional object, so if God lacks the intentional object, his conscious representation of the state is not evil. My suggestion, then, is that God does 'get' what it's like to feel anger, lust, vengeance, and perverse pleasure, but God's copies of those states are not directed at anything and God is aware of the copies as copies.

This leads to the second puzzle, which was how an omniscient being is able to distinguish between first-person and third-person knowledge of the same fact. I suggested that even if a person who knows of me

(3) She made a mess,

knows the same thing I know when I know

(1) I made a mess,

there is a difference in our conscious states. An omniscient being should be able to tell the difference between them. If an omniscient being is also

---

[3] It might be too strong to say that a copy of a sensation *is* a sensation since the meaning of 'sensation' may include having a certain external cause, but a copy of a sensation is something very much like a sensation.

omnisubjective, he consciously represents both my first-person judgement (1) and someone's third-person judgement (3). If the states are different, his conscious representations of the states also differ and he can distinguish them. And if I am also right that he does not actually judge either (1) or (3) when he copies the respective judgements, there is no problem that an omnisubjective being judges that *he* made a mess when he empathizes with my judgement (1), nor does he judge that I made a mess when he empathizes with someone's judgement (3). Of course, he may make the judgement if the judgement is true, but that does not follow from being omnisubjective.

Suppose instead that Patrick Grim is right and the proposition expressed by (1) differs from the proposition expressed by (3), and only I can know (1). This is a problem for omniscience if omniscience entails knowing the truth value of all propositions. But if the only difference between knowing (3) and knowing (1) is the point of view, it is reasonable to think that a being who knows (3) and who also perfectly empathizes with me when I know (1) knows everything I know when I know (1). This solution will not satisfy anyone who insists that an omniscient being must know the very same proposition I know and that the proposition expressed by (1) differs from that expressed by (3), but I think that this account succeeds in preserving cognitive perfection even if it does not succeed in preserving one traditional account of omniscience. On the view of this paper God knows exactly what is going on at every moment, and in addition, God knows what each conscious state directed at what is going on is like, including first-person states. It seems to me that this account makes God's knowledge more perfect than it is on the standard account of omniscience even if Grim is right that God doesn't know propositions like (1).

Is God omnisubjective? The psalmist writes:

> Lord, you search me and you know me
> you know my resting and my rising,
> you discern my purpose from afar.
> You mark when I walk or lie down,
> all my ways lie open to you.
>
> Before ever a word is on my tongue
> you know it, O lord, through and through.
> Behind and before you besiege me,
> your hand ever laid upon me.
>
> (Psalm 139)

Some lines in this poem might suggest the image of God following me around like a shadow, marking my movements, his hand ever upon me. But when the psalmist says, 'All my ways lie open to you', 'Before ever a word is on my tongue, you know it', that suggests that God is much more intimately bound to me than a shadow. God perceives my mind and heart, discerning my thoughts and purposes. If God is in my mind as an observer of my thoughts and feelings, that is not omnisubjectivity. The relationship I am proposing is even more intimate than that. God knows me the way I know myself, knowing my thoughts, feelings, and purposes from my own perspective. This is the most intimate relationship possible. The problem is that it might be *too* intimate to be possible. But in this paper I have tried to begin building a case for the view that it is not impossible and, in fact, is required of an omniscient being.

Omniscience is standardly interpreted as the property of knowing the truth value of all propositions. If I am right, a being can satisfy that definition without knowing all there is to know. A divine being who knows all there is to know ought to be able to distinguish between distinct items in his creation, in particular, the mental states of his creatures. And such a being ought to know at least as much as what you know, as well as know what it is like to know it the way you know it. If God is omnisubjective, God knows you as well as you know yourself. God could not only write your biography, God could write your autobiography.

IV. IMPLICATIONS OF OMNISUBJECTIVITY

I would like to conclude by briefly describing some interesting theological, ethical, and metaphysical implications of omnisubjectivity. For one thing, omnisubjectivity has radical consequences for the way God hears prayers. An omnisubjective deity would not be like a very close listener, but, rather, God would know your prayers the way you know them, when you first have the desire, then possibly struggle for the words, and perhaps use the wrong words. Omnisubjectivity would also be an important concomitant of providence. I will not claim that providence requires omnisubjectivity, but a being who has total empathetic identification with your subjective viewpoint has a much deeper grasp of what is good for you than one who does not.

Omnisubjectivity also has implications for the moral point of view. Theists usually believe that morality derives in some important way from the divine viewpoint, but that is usually interpreted as a third-person point of view. That can be problematic since some ethicists think that the first-person viewpoint is ineliminable. If God is omnisubjective, the divine viewpoint would not be limited to a third-person viewpoint. It would include first-person viewpoints, in fact, it would include *every* first-person viewpoint. The grounding of morality in the divine perspective would therefore be consistent with a view of morality according to which one's personal viewpoint is ineliminable. Furthermore, since an omnisubjective being's perspective is not limited to a view from nowhere, it combines the advantages of subjective and objective points of view. Thomas Nagel has argued that that is the perspective that would be needed to solve our most entrenched philosophical problems, and it is our inability to assume both perspectives simultaneously that explains why we cannot solve them. If we combined Nagel's point with the argument of this paper, we would conclude that we cannot solve entrenched philosophical problems because we are not God.

Finally, I think that omnisubjectivity could be used to explain the unique metaphysical status of the actual world within the realm of possible worlds. I have always found it puzzling that the only thing distinguishing the actual world from other possible worlds is that the former has the crucial but mysterious property of actuality, a property unlike any descriptive property. I would like to offer the conjecture that a merely possible but non-actual being has no subjectivity. There is no such thing as what it is like to be a conscious being who will never exist. There is nothing that is what the world looks like to such a being. A merely possible conscious being can have general properties such as liking chocolate, but there is no such thing as what this particular piece of chocolate would taste like to that being. My conjecture, then, is that the subjectivity of the beings in the actual world is something that no other possible world has. Omnisubjectivity explains (in part) what an omniscient being knows when he knows that this world is actual. I am not suggesting that this position on possible worlds is entailed by the account I have given in this paper, but I mention it because I think it is one of many interesting lines of research that could be pursued with the idea of omnisubjectivity for those with an interest in the problem.

Few of us dare to speculate on what the mind of God is like, and my proposal in this paper is intended merely to introduce a possible divine attribute for discussion. Omnisubjectivity is a property that is distinctively personal, yet incomprehensibly immense. I think that omnisubjectivity makes more sense as a model of how a cognitively perfect and benevolent being knows his creatures than the model of the deity reading off all the propositions about the world in his mental encyclopedia.

REFERENCES

D'Arms, Justin, 2000. 'Empathy and Evaluative Inquiry', *Chicago-Kent Law Review* 74: 4.

Goldman, Alvin, 1993. 'Ethics and Cognitive Science', *Ethics* 103: 2 (Jan), 337–60.

Gordon. Robert M., 1995. 'Sympathy, Simulation, and the Impartial Spectator', *Ethics* 105: 4 (July), 727–42.

Grim. Patrick, 1985. 'Against Omniscience: The Case from Essential Indexicals', *Nous* 19, 151–80.

Jackson, Frank, 1986. 'What Mary Didn't Know', *Journal of Philosophy* LXXXIII, 5, 291–5.

Oxley, Julinna, 2006. *Empathy and Contractual Theories of Ethics*, PhD Dissertation, Tulane University, Ch. 1.

Perry. John, 1979. 'The Problem of the Essential Indexical', *Nous* 3–21.

Torre, Stephan, 2006. '*De Se* Knowledge and the Possibility of an Omniscient Being', *Faith and Philosophy* 23:2 (April), 191–200.

Index